My friends

Christ Methodist Ch

| | DUE DATE | | |
|---|---|---|---|
| | | | |
| | | | |
| | | | |
| | | | |
| | | | |
| | | | |
| | | | |
| | | | |
| | | | |
| | | | |
| | | | |
| | | | |
| | | | |
| | | | |
| | | | |
| | | | |
| | | | |
| | | | Printed in USA |

# JEFF STEINBERG

## *Masterpiece*

### IN PROGRESS

. . . . . . . . . . . . . . . . . . . . . . . . . . . . . . . . . . . . .

## with James C. Hefley

## New Leaf Press

**Library of Congress Catalog Number: 86-50369**
**ISBN: 0-89221-183-0**

*Dedicated to*

*My Mom and Dad, who gave me life,*
*and, in their own way,*
*made me determined to become.*

# CONTENTS

# FOREWORD

This is the story of a giant.

Oh, I know that Jeff Steinberg is only 4 feet 6 inches tall, but I'm not talking about feet and inches. I've known some really big men in my time, including Roosevelt Grier, Mr. T, Merlin Olsen, Wilt Chamberlin, Kareem Abdul Jabbar. These are big guys, sure—but I'm talking about big *men,* so big on the inside that the external is really inconsequential.

I first met this giant when we appeared together at a Christian music festival in Sacramento, outdoors on a hot late summer afternoon. I flew in just in time for my part of an all-day rally, and as I was driven to the fairgrounds, I was told I would be following a singer named Jeff Steinberg. My host didn't tell me much about Jeff, but thought I would enjoy hearing him sing, and especially what he had to say.

We drove up behind the stage area, out of sight of the audience, and as I got out of the car I heard a very pleasing voice, sort of a cross between B. J. Thomas and Neil Diamond, singing to some lovely music. Intrigued, I made my way backstage and into the wings—and was astonished at what I saw.

Out there on a huge stage stood this diminutive fellow, whose voice seemed bigger than his whole body! And he had the audience enthralled.

Afterward, we got to know each other somewhat, and I became an admirer instantly. I heard something of the incredible odds he had survived, his early days in and out of hospitals and surgery and homes. I heard about his baptism and bar mitzvah, and he told me about some of the uphill struggle in his effort to become a singer and Christian activist. I learned about his wife and his perfectly normal son, and how Jeff had assisted in the birth process. At that point, I was fighting back tears—not of sympathy, but of pride and shared joy.

I knew I was talking to a "mensch," the Jewish term for real man.

Since that day, Jeff and I have shared the platform many a time, the Easter Seal telethon for six years running, and fully expect to be involved in other worthwhile things down the road as far as either of us can see.

In the Bible, Jesus said, "A man's life consists not in the abundance of the things he possesses," and I'm sure now, through my friendship with Jeff, that Jesus included in that such things as arms and legs. After all, Jesus himself taught that arms, legs, and eyes were expendable if they in any way impede our spiritual development (Matthew 5:27-30).

Well, Jeff was denied by the circumstances of his birth things we take for granted, like two arms and legs. So Jeff had to grow inside, spiritually and emotionally and mentally.

He's like a flower growing through concrete; you've seen them haven't you? Those apparently delicate little weeds that find the cracks in impenetrable barriers, even *create* those cracks, and work their way irresistibly into the sunlight?

That's Jeff to me—a rough, tough weed, one that occasionally flowers into something beautiful, fighting and clawing and willing and praying his way through impenetrable barriers, and against all odds. He has rough edges, sure. Shake hands with that hook one time, and you'll get the idea that he's a force to reckon with. But then see the smile behind the hook, and get more of the picture—meet a man who has learned that his life doesn't consist of whatever things he possesses—or doesn't possess. His life consists of who he *is* and *who* he is growing to *be*.

I enjoy knowing this gentle giant. Meet Jeff Steinberg!

*Pat Boone*
Beverly Hills, California

· · · · · · · · · ·
# PREFACE

"Why?"

I think that must be the word most used in English, next to Mom, Dad, yes, and no.

We all want to know, "Why." Why war, why pain, why poverty. And why me?

I must have asked myself that at least a million times. I still do.

Allow me to introduce myself. I am a Jew of Orthodox descent on both sides of my family. My father, Irving Steinberg, born in Sandomierz, Poland, was the only son of Morris and Molly Steinberg. The Steinbergs immigrated in 1933 with their son and four daughters to New York City where they faithfully practiced their religion.

My mother, Ruthe Vedatsky, was born in Philadelphia. Her parents, Harry and Anna Vedatsky, came to America from Lithuania. Mom has one brother, Uncle Morty, a bachelor, who moved to Los Angeles many years ago.

Persecution was no stranger to my ancestors. Many

Steinberg relatives, left behind in Poland, later died in Nazi concentration camps. In Lithuania, Grandmom Vedatsky's parents, brothers and sisters were made to dig their own grave by the Nazis and were then buried alive. Both she and my Uncle Morty, who was born in Lithuania, have painful memories of Jewish suffering in the dread pogroms that drove hundreds of thousands of Jews from Eastern Europe to seek freedom in America.

My Steinberg grandparents, Zayde and Bubbeh ("grandfather" and "grandmother" in Yiddish), were overjoyed when their son entered The Yeshiva in New York City, now a respected university. But ultimately, he was forced to drop out to support his parents. The story goes in the family, that he was passing by the apartment of a friend on the Lower East Side of New York when he heard a clear alto voice coming through a lower window. He took just one look at the beautiful, petite, young singer with short brown hair, and leaped through the window to introduce himself to Ruthe Vedatsky who was visiting from Philadelphia.

My father, a mere 5 feet 6 inches tall, 135 pounds, and already balding, was not exactly a "Casanova." I understand that while in Military Service (the U.S. Army Air Corps) he proposed to the entrancing Lithuanian girl by letter, stating that if she didn't marry him he would haunt her for the rest of her life. Of course, it took time and quite a few trips to Philadelphia, but he did marry her. I can't say that I blame Dad for his determination to marry Mom, for even today she is a very beautiful woman.

Zayde and Bubbeh Steinberg were bitterly disappointed at discovering that Mom had given up trying to keep a kosher home. "It was too much trouble to keep up two kitchens," she said. They hardly ever came to visit, and on one of their visits, they ate only dairy products, as if they didn't trust her, so Mom mixed her dishes together.

There were other, far more wrenching disappointments yet to come for Irving and Ruthe Steinberg. With such a beautiful daughter, Linda (and later came two more, Sheryl and Harriet), how can it be that she and Dad could have given birth to such a horribly deformed child, so totally unlike any other known relative on both sides? How could such an ugliness have happened to them? What purpose could there possibly have been behind such a tragedy in the Steinberg family?

I believe I'm beginning to understand some of the whys. I share with you my story.

*"My mother groan'd, my father wept:*
*Into the dangerous world I leapt . . ."*

**WILLIAM BLAKE,** *Infant Sorrow*

# CHAPTER ONE
· · · · · · · · · · ·

# THAT TERRIBLE THING

I was "that terrible thing" that happened to Irving and Ruthe Steinberg on a sultry Saturday, August 18, 1951, at Jewish Hospital in northeast Philadelphia, Pennsylvania.

My Grandmom, Anna Vedatsky, was the first to see me and she wanted to scream. A head and torso, but no arms, and thin, bent legs that curled inward.

She called my father at the postal substation on 30th Street where he sorted mail. She knew that he was not allowed to receive calls. However, this was a medical emergency and she simply had to speak to him.

"Irving, come quickly! . . . Oy, mein God . . . It's terrible! Get to the hospital fast. Something terrible has happened!"

"Ruthe, is she all right?" he wanted to know.

"Ruthe is fine. It's the baby. Don't ask! Come quick!" Dad raced from downtown to Jewish Hospital (now Einstein Northern Hospital) in northeast Philadelphia. The thirty to forty-five-minute drive seemed to last forever. Trying to imagine what the emergency was that Grandmom couldn't

• • • • • • • • • • • • • • • • • • • • • • • • • • • • •

talk about on the phone, his mind must have been a blur, wondering what could have happened.

Upon arriving at the hospital maternity ward, he was met by Grandmom, who by this time was more than upset. She was hysterical, pacing the floor, crying, and trying to communicate in two languages, Yiddish and English. Nobody seemed to understand what she was saying.

"Irving. Thank God you're here!" Grandmom sobbed in heartbreak. "The doctor, Irv, you'll talk to the doctor. He'll tell you everything!" By this time she was falling into his arms.

"Mom, Ruthe—is she all right?" He was almost afraid to ask again.

"She's sleeping. She doesn't know."

"She doesn't know what?" he persisted. "Where is the doctor?" His worst fears were turning to panic, and then to anger. He wanted some answers. My father was the kind of man who was always in control, and yet now he felt so out of control.

Almost as if on cue, Dr. Androsciere, Mom's gynecologist, arrived at the nurses' station. A short, thin, bald man with a mustache, who spoke with a French accent, he had been Grandmom's gynecologist and had delivered my mother as well as my oldest sister Linda.

"Mr. Steinberg, your son has a serious problem." That was probably the easiest way to begin.

"What kind of problem?" Perhaps now Dad would get answers.

"He was born with multiple birth defects." He paused. "The medical term for what your son has is Phocomelia. In simple language, he was born with no arms and deformed legs. And there are other complications, mostly internal. Frankly, the prognosis is not good. We're not even sure at this time if he will live, how long he will live, or what to expect. He is alert and appears to be trying. He is fighting hard to make it, and we are doing everything for him."

His worst fears were confirmed, though no one could

have anticipated news as horrifying as this. "Ruthe—how is she? Does she know?"

"She's resting. She knows only that she has a son." A nurse told her in the recovery room. "I wanted to wait until you came before I told her." Dr. Androsciere felt that Dad should be there for support, and he knew that Mom had had problems with her nerves in the past.

What inward tortures and searchings my thirty-one-year-old father must have experienced! I can only speculate.

How much he confided to Dr. Androsciere is anybody's guess. I assume they had a discussion about what might have caused this birth with so many deformities. Dr. Androsciere must have quizzed him about the family history. My cousin on Dad's side who now lives in Switzerland had been born with a clubfoot. Dad knew of nothing else.

In spite of a multitude of unanswerable questions, there were more questions. How did this happen? Was it a drug? Thalidomide? Dad insisted that Mom not be told. I can only suppose that he wanted to protect her from pain.

From that brief meeting, the doctor escorted my Grandmom and my father to the nursery to have a look at me. Shock is the only word to describe his reaction. It was then that Dad affirmed that he would not tell Mom, and that he would make all of the decisions as to my care. He felt that perhaps Mom would not be able to handle the situation emotionally, and perhaps he thought that he was strong enough for the both of them. A sort of chivalry, I suppose, a love affair, a king so in love with his beloved queen that he would do anything to shield her from hurt.

Dad hurried to Mom's room and bent over her bed. "Ruthe, Ruthe," he whispered gently.

Still benumbed by the anesthetic, Mom stirred and instinctively brushed at her dark brown hair. She opened her eyes slowly and sleepily and saw the familiar fringed head above her; dark brown eyes peering anxiously from behind square, black, horn-rimmed glasses.

"Well? . . . Have you seen our son?" she mumbled, smiling faintly.

Dad shook his head yes, not knowing yet what to say. He tried to be reassuring.

"I want to see him . . . , Jeffrey David. I want to hold our son." I was named after my great grandfather on my mom's side of the family. He had been killed by the Nazis during World War II.

"Ruthe," Dad interrupted. His soft and soothing voice had a foreboding tone. "There is something . . . I must tell you." He paused, struggling for the right words. "There are some problems."

"Irv? Irv, what's the matter? What kind of problems?" she kept prying.

"We don't know, yet. The doctors are running tests now. It will be a while before they can tell us anything."

"Is . . . he . . . dead?" She pressed for an answer.

"No, Ruthe, he's alive." This time he ventured a faint smile.

"Irv, there's something you're not telling me." The creeping fear that something was very seriously wrong was clearing her mind and she was noticeably agitated.

"The doctors are doing all they can. Honey, you need to rest."

"He's retarded, isn't he?" she persisted. She tried to sit up. "Tell me, Irv. What is wrong with my son? Is he . . . retarded?"

"The doctors are doing all they can." Dad finally managed to mumble. He tried to help her to lie back down.

"He's got a funny face. I know it. He's a Mongoloid."

Grandmom slipped into the room behind Dad and tried to console her. "Ruthe, his face is gorgeous. He has a beautiful face. Ruthe, he's a sick boy. Your son, he is very, very sick."

Mom continued pleading.

A nurse came in and gave Mom something to help her rest while Dad and Grandmom retreated to the waiting room. They agreed that Dad would stay at the hospital while Grandmom went back to check on Grandpop who was terminally ill with stomach cancer.

I was much older when I learned that, during her pregnancy with me, Mom had a problem with spotting and that Dr. Androsciere had given Mom a medication to help her not to lose the baby. This medication might have caused the cellular metabolism in my development to go awry, as happened to the thalidomide babies of almost a decade after my birth. This information came to me secondhand in the fall of 1981, long after the doctor had died and his records presumably destroyed. I had also heard that another doctor told Dad my defects could have resulted from a bad sperm.

"You shouldn't blame yourself, Mr. Steinberg," he reportedly said. "It's probably something that will never happen again to you and your wife."

As consoling as this news was intended to be, there was little relief in their present circumstance. What was he to do about me? After all, I had already happened to the Steinbergs.

The medical records were grim. Phocomelia, the word they used to describe my "multiple congenital defects," means "seal limbs." There was no trace of a left arm, although the shoulder was in place. A bulbous stump stuck out from my right shoulder like a tiny pink cucumber. My thin legs were scissored and turned inward at the knees. My left foot was considerably smaller than my right and had only three toes. Nails were missing from these toes and the five toes on my right foot.

"He may have other shortcomings that we haven't found yet," the pediatrician informed Dad. "But, he's taking nourishment and he is alert. He should survive."

Mom knew none of this—only what Dad had told her the first day—that I wasn't expected to live. And when she sought to walk down to the nursery to catch a glimpse of me, the nurses would see her coming down the hall and shut the curtain.

The time soon came for Mom to leave the hospital.

"Irving, when will you tell Ruthe about the boy?" Grandmom pestered.

"If I do, she'll have a nervous breakdown."

"She has to know. Look, he's her son."

Dad looked at her, hard and flinty. "No!"

The hospital psychiatrist agreed with Grandmom. "You shouldn't take all the worry on yourself," he told Dad.

Dad had another reason, which would come out later. If Mom learned the truth, she might be afraid to have another child. Dad desperately wanted to try again. Perhaps he wanted to prove that he could have a normal son.

Grandmom kept fussing. "How are you going to care for the child?" she demanded to know.

"I can't," Dad said wearily. "I have a hard enough time keeping up with the bills by working three jobs."

The decision was made to contact the Child Welfare Department. I became a ward of the courts at the age of one month. For Dad, there was no other choice. After all, they could provide better care than he could. However, Grandmom insisted that he was wrong in not telling my mother about me. She felt that any decisions made should be made by both of them.

"Then I'll tell her!" Grandmom ventured.

"Stay out of our affairs." Dad ordered. "You've got enough to do with a sick man at home."

I try now to put myself in his place. He was reeling from the birth of a child with multiple defects. His wife was very nervous and had a four-year-old waiting for her at home. He was working three jobs—clerking in a shoe store, sorting mail in a post office substation when postal workers were paid poverty wages, and teaching Hebrew to children in a synagogue on Sunday and giving private tutoring lessons during the week. With all this, he was having trouble making ends meet. It appeared that every time they tried to make the ends meet someone moved the ends!

Dad saw relatives on both sides as being no help. His

· · · · · · · · · · · · · · · · · · · · · · · · · · ·

mother-in-law was threatening to tell his wife. His father-in-law was terminally ill with stomach cancer. He knew his own parents would not come or offer help. They would likely say he was being punished for his sins.

I don't know all of this for certain. I'm just speculating from what I know of the situation at the time. Judgments are easy to come by and often much harder to live by. We must either live up to them and their expectations or live them down and their reputation. Too many times those who are quick to judge could not stand up under the scrutiny of a similar judgment. I believe that under the circumstances my father felt his only recourse was to make me a ward of the courts.

Grandmom knew I was in the downtown Children's Shelter at 18th and Parkway, and she came frequently with Dad and my sister, Linda, to see me. They wanted to be sure I was well cared for. Grandpop could still get about. She begged him to come, but he refused.

"He's the namesake of your poor dead father," she pleaded. "The least you could do is go see your grandson."

Grandpop would not budge. It was as if he never had a grandson.

Did Dad's parents, Bubbeh and Zayde, in New York City, know about me? I assume they eventually heard. Bubbeh would see me for the first time years later. Zayde never laid eyes on his grandson, for he died two years after I was born.

Grandpop Vedatsky begged Grandmom to take him to Los Angeles and escape the miserable Philadelphia winter. "I'll feel better out there, and I can see my son, Morty," he said. She sold their home and moved. Grandpop was there only a few days when he wanted to come back to Philadelphia. By the time Grandmom got him back he was so weak he had to be cared for in a nursing home.

I still don't know the length and frequency of Dad's visits at the Children's Shelter, though I was later told that he and Grandmom came every weekend. I believe he came fairly often because in later years I felt closer to him than Mom.

Child health specialists are now finding how important the emotional and physical bonding with a parent is for an infant.

How skillful Dad must have become in keeping his visits to the Shelter from Mom, who assumed I had mercifully died shortly after birth! Did he tell Mom he was going somewhere else on Sunday when he was bound for the Shelter to see his son? I only know that he was there.

The thalidomide tragedy, which shocked the world in the early 1960s, stirred a flurry of research and publicity about infants born with multiple congenital defects. The doctors didn't see many babies like me in the early fifties and I became a curiosity to the medical fraternity in Philadelphia.

One of the physicians who saw me in the Children's Shelter was Dr. John Royal Moore, chief of Orthopedic Surgery at Shriners Children's Hospital. "Bring this poor little fellow out and let us check him over," he urged the social workers. "Maybe something can be done for him."

Pauline Martin, a welfare department social worker, took me to the outpatient department of Shriners Hospital on Roosevelt Boulevard, just a mile or so from where my parents then lived in northeast Philadelphia. I was one day short of being eleven months old when Dr. Moore and Dr. C. J. Wagner examined me. The terse medical record for July 17, 1952, states:

Chief Complaint: *Deformity of legs and absence of arms.*
Family History: *Obtained from social worker. Mother is living and extremely nervous. Father is living and well. One older child is perfectly normal. No family history of congenital anomalies available.*
Past Medical History: *Born in Jewish Hospital, Philadelphia. No details as to pregnancy or delivery available.*
Provisional Diagnosis: *Multiple congenital anomalies of both upper extremities and both lower extremities.*
Pediatric Examination: *Patient is a well-developed and*

. . . . . . . . . . . . . . . . . . . . . . . . . . . . . .

*nourished white, male child, who is alert and not acutely
ill.*
Recommendations: *Continue at Children's Shelter. Return in
one year for checkup. Prefer to postpone correction of
deformities until as near the end of growth as possible.*

Mom did become pregnant again. Sheryl Rae was born
January 16, 1953, almost sixteen months after I made my
traumatic entrance into this world. Dad's disappointment
over not having a son was overcome by the sight of a
healthy, normal daughter. This time he had forbidden
Grandmom to come to the hospital. He called her and
crowed, "Everyone's fine. This one's got everything. Two
good arms and two good legs."

Grandmom was delighted. "But, Irving," she reminded,
"when are you going to tell Ruthe that she's got another
child in the Children's Shelter? Irving, you can't keep Jeffrey
David from her forever."

"You just mind your own business," Dad shot back.
"When the time is right, I'll tell her. Just remember, no one
is to talk about this around Ruthe. I will be the one to tell
her."

When Mom got home and was up and around,
Grandmom could stand it no longer. While Dad was at
work, she said gently, "Ruthe, would it be worth hearing?"

Mom got the message. "It's Jeffrey, isn't it? What's the
matter? Is the baby living?" The words tumbled out in a
torrent of pent-up longing.

"Yes, honey, he's alive. Jeffrey is alive and he is beautiful. I
see him all the time. He's at the Children's Shelter."

Mom sat back, reeling from the shock.

"Ruthe, Ruthe, you're all right? Ruthe, you had to know
sometime. He's your son. I wanted to tell you at the
hospital, the psychiatrist thought we should, but Irving—he
wouldn't let me tell you. He was afraid you'd have a
nervous breakdown."

"Mom, what is so wrong with my baby? Why won't they

let me have him? Mom, is Jeffrey retarded? That's it. He's
retarded, isn't he? He's got a funny face. I knew it, I knew
it." By this time she was almost hysterical. "And Irving lied
to me!" she sobbed.

"No, no, Irving loves you. He was afraid to hurt you,
afraid you'd have a nervous breakdown. We were wrong in
not telling you he was alive, Ruthe. Jeffrey David has a
beautiful face and gorgeous chest. He eats like a horse, and
he's smart. He's got a real *yiddishe kopf* (Jewish brain), that
boy."

"Why can't I see him?" Mom demanded. "What's wrong
that I can't see my son?"

Grandmom drew back, fearing to look Mom in the face.
"Ruthe, Irving said I was not to tell you anything. I've said
too much already. Ask him when he comes home."

Mom confronted Dad. "Mom told me that Jeffrey's alive,
Irv."

Dad stiffened in anger. "I gave her instructions . . . I
ordered her, I'll. . . ."

"Irving, I had to know sometime. If he doesn't have a
funny face, what's he like? Tell me, Irving. I can take it."

Dad looked at her in apprehension. "You promise not to
carry on and scream? You promise?"

"I promise, I promise. What is wrong with Jeffrey?"

Dad blurted it out. "He's got no arms and bad legs. He'll
probably never walk. I kept this from you because I didn't
think you could take the shock. You can't care for him here,
not with a normal baby. They're giving him special help at
the Shelter. Doctors, nurses, medicine—they give him
whatever he needs. So help me God, that's the truth,
Ruthe," Dad sobbed. "That's what I've been afraid to tell
you all these months. Oh, Ruthe, I wanted another baby, a
baby that we could be proud of, and I knew you wouldn't
try again if you saw Jeffrey." Dad cast a glance at little
Sheryl, sleeping snugly in her crib. "Thank God, she's
normal."

Mom was pale. Dad rushed to support her.

· · · · · · · · · · · · · · · · · · · · · · · · · · · ·

"Get the doctor," she gasped.

They rushed Mom to the hospital with a nervous collapse. Poor Grandmom, with Grandpop dying in the nursing home, did the best she could with her new grandchild, Sheryl, and our older sister, Linda, now starting school.

Mom recovered, as she had before. Grandpop died a few days later, without ever having seen me, his only grandson.

Dad finally took Mom to see me at the Shelter. She held me and then put me back in the playpen.

"Take me home, Irv," she said to Dad in resignation. "I didn't nurse him. I can't care for him. Keep him here. We've got to get on with our lives."

With both Mom and Grandmom knowing, as well as Dad, the truth inevitably spread to friends and acquaintances. I wasn't talked about as a son, a person, a little black-haired boy growing and saying my first words. I was that terrible thing that happened to the Steinbergs.

*". . . an artist starts painting on a blank piece of canvas . . ."*

# CHAPTER TWO

• • • • • • • • • • •

# AT DEATH'S DOOR

If a family had applied to adopt me, Mom and Dad might have gladly said, "He's yours." The chance of that happening was about as great as the earth stopping on its axis. Who would want a kid who looked like he would be a basket case for life?

My parents didn't want to abandon me. They shared the Jewish commitment to family and reverence for life. Mom, with two young children at home, though she did not keep *kosher*, involved herself as much as she could by singing for Jewish social and charitable productions. Dad continued to teach Hebrew in the Sabbath school at a synagogue.

It was simply that the extent of my defects were overwhelming. They didn't know what to do with this severely handicapped child.

Dad and Grandmom did come to the Shelter often. I knew who they were and cried when they left. Mom had the pressures of a baby and a four-year-old, plus her secretarial job and occasional musical performances, and visited only once in a while when she felt she was emotionally up to it. It didn't take me long to learn who she was.

Dad brought me home on occasional weekends and took me to Shriners twice during the next year for more extensive examinations. Dr. Moore wrote on my medical record, "It's hard to get a name that describes all these defects."

Besides the obviously missing arms, he could not find quadriceps—the four-headed muscle in the front of the thighs, hamstrings—the powerful muscles used to flex the legs—or knee caps. He also noted that the joint was frozen on my right knee.

I was a worse mess below the knees. I had a normal fibula on the right, while the inner tibia was stunted and fused to the femur where the ball socket should have been. This was why my right leg was frozen at the knee.

On my left leg, the tibia extended abnormally above the knee joint, while only a tiny stump dropped below the knee where the tibia should have been. Consequently, I could not swing my left knee beyond a ninety-degree angle.

My right foot turned inward and was five-sixteenths of an inch longer and eleven-sixteenths of an inch wider than my left—quite a difference for a three-year-old. I couldn't bend either foot backward at the ankle, and the absence of nails on my eight toes was plain to see. X rays showed I was missing the metatarsal bones on the left foot leading to where the missing two toes should have been. I didn't know what they were doing, yet I got used to being poked at, speculated about, and examined by anybody and everybody in a white jacket.

I did have all the muscles in my lower legs, my ankles were mobile, and I could wiggle all eight toes.

I didn't know that all of these things were wrong with me or I might have given up, after all the talk about what I could not do because of what I didn't have. I concentrated on what I could do with what I did have. For instance, eating was no big deal. My feet became my "hands" to swing a spoon or fork to my mouth. Also, by using my great toe as a thumb and my second toes as forefingers, I could pick up and take apart almost anything.

I could get around, after a fashion, extending first one foot and then the other, and swinging my fanny up to my heels, I slid across the floor on my backside, shifting from cheek to cheek. The doctors and nurses didn't know whether to cry or laugh.

The medical records say they explained all these shortcomings to my parents and told them to bring me back to Shriners in six months, after I had time to grow some more. Mom is described as "extremely nervous." I expect almost any mother would be at seeing such a child as I.

Dr. Moore saw me as a challenge. In many ways he came across as a miracle worker, building great hopes in Mom and Dad, almost beyond belief. Due to unexpected responses, and necessary surgical procedures, these hopes for a level of normalcy may have fallen far short of the goals. Perhaps it was wrong to build such hopes. However, without hope, we only tend to give in to defeat and to despair.

Disputing the pessimists, he thought I could be improved. It might take a few years and extensive surgeries, but eventually, he believed, I could walk, and with an artificial arm, make my own way in the world. "But you'll have to get him admitted to Shriners," he told Dad.

Dad made all the decisions, mainly to protect Mom. He could have left me with Welfare to vegetate in an institution. He cared enough to find a Shriner who persuaded his temple to serve as my sponsor. He wanted me to have the best care available. After I was admitted, Dad joined the Shriners in gratitude and was a loyal member for the rest of his life.

Shriners Hospital for Crippled Children, in northeast Philadelphia, admitted me as a resident patient, August 24, 1954, six days after my third birthday. The sprawling H-shaped complex of two-story stone buildings surrounded by an expansive green lawn served as my childhood home. But the doctors, nurses and other people who cared for me never quite became my family.

Shriners Hospital of Philadelphia is one of nineteen orthopedic and three burn facilities which the Shriners operate in the United States and Canada. I am just one of more than 300,000 crippled and severely burned kids whom they have helped since opening their first hospital in Shreveport, Louisiana, in 1922. Not one of these kids or their families have ever been charged a penny. Not a cent of government money has ever been received. The Shriners themselves give and raise more than $160 million a year to fund these twenty-two hospitals. The determination of the medical staff matches the commitment of the supporters. "The difficult," they say, "we do right away—the impossible takes a little longer!"

My case ranged somewhere between the difficult and the impossible.

I was admitted to and stayed in the boys' ward—a long room on the first floor accommodating about thirty beds rowed along each side of a wide aisle with a sun porch on the east end facing Roosevelt Boulevard. The girls occupied a similar ward down the long hall at the other end of the building. The variety of orthopedic problems was mind-boggling. Shriners' patients were kids who could not get the help they needed anywhere else. The main difference between myself and the other children was that I had more apparent disabilities, and I was more mobile and aggressive.

Dr. Moore planned to have my legs in casts much of the time. I wouldn't be able to get my feet to my mouth and would need another way to feed myself. He also wanted to start getting me accustomed to having a prosthesis—an artificial arm.

My stump hadn't grown enough for a conventional arm and hook. Frank Malone, the prosthetist, rigged up a stopgap contraption. He cupped a nifty little gray cardboard-like "sock" over my stump, then attached a figure-eight harness which he looped around my upper torso and across my left shoulder muscles. By flexing the muscles and lifting my stump toward me I could rotate a device on the end of the sock that would hold a spoon or fork. He slipped in a spoon and showed how I could "swing" the utensil to my mouth. It took a little practice, but in a few days I was scooping up soup and cereal about as quickly and efficiently as any ordinary three-year-old.

I still preferred eating with my feet. Before a cast was put on, the nurses frequently tied my feet down so I had to use the sock. As soon as they turned me loose, I reverted to my old tricks. I also loved to take things apart with my toes. Miss Morrison, the head ward nurse, made the mistake of leaving her watch beside my bed. By the time she came back to look for it, I had it almost disassembled. "Jeffrey Steinberg!" she yelled. "Get your toes out of my watch."

My favorite game was "hide and seek." A nurse would come by for bed check and find only my sock and harness. She would walk up and down the aisle peeking under beds and calling, "Jeffrey!"

Finally, "Ah, there you are. Come out, Jeffrey."

When I didn't come out, she reached under to grab me. I would scoot out of her grasp and across the floor like a cockroach to the next bed.

This game ran on and on with kids hollering, "There he is!" "He's over here, Miss Morrison." A second nurse, Mrs. Cook, joined the chase, then a third, and finally they trapped me. Even then it was hard to get a hand on me. Have you ever tried to pick up an armless three-year-old?

There is no such thing as quickie care at Shriners. The doctors take their time, poking, feeling, peeking, ordering X rays and other tests, then consulting and discussing alternate approaches with outside specialists before scheduling surgery. When a parent wanted Dr. Moore to get on with it, he'd say, "Your child will have to live with this for a lifetime. We want to be sure that he's getting the best possible correction."

Weeks dragged into months. Mom and Dad weren't in any hurry. Every Monday morning the doctors, residents, interns, and visiting physicians trooped by on rounds. The nurses had me in my bed, clean and ready for inspections.

Dr. Moore always began the same way: "This is Jeffrey Steinberg. He was born with multiple congenital anomalies of both upper extremities and both lower extremities. He has an abrachius on the left and a humerus stump on the right . . ."

I sat up and got close to the side of the crib. "Hi, Doctor Moore," I chirped, watching for a change of expression.

He always had time for a friendly "Hello, Jeffrey, and what are you up to today?"

Dr. Moore described my situation so many times that I learned to parrot him. One day I was ready. He started, "This is Jeffrey Steinberg. He was born . . ."

I picked up the patter ". . . with multiple congenital anomalies of both upper extremities . . . ," and recited it back with every pause and "uh" of Dr. Moore's. The doctors roared. When I saw that they enjoyed it so much, I started doing it every time they came by, until finally Dr. Moore remarked, "This little fellow knows as much about himself as I do."

It was my first experience of being in the spotlight and making people smile and I loved every minute of it.

Dr. Moore ultimately chose to start with my left knee. He put this leg in a cast, hip to ankle, and began wedging the knee a few degrees further to the left every week. He didn't want to inhibit the interaction of my feet. The cast became hot and the pressure of the wedging material irritating. I couldn't scoot around fast enough to get away from the nurses. I didn't let even a cast keep me down. I took just long enough to get used to it, and then kept going.

Dr. Moore removed the cast every few days to check the degree of rotation. In a month, I had twice as much "swing" as before. I had been in the hospital five months when Dr. Moore said I could have the cast off for awhile. "We're going to try and help you walk a little," he promised.

He attached an orthopedic brace vertically against my right leg and lifted me to my feet. Slowly and cautiously, with Dr. Moore holding my shoulders, I pushed my left foot forward while dragging my right foot behind. I took another step and another. The nurses patiently "walked" me along the aisle. Then they removed the brace and took me back into therapy and exercised both my legs, as they had done so many times before.

Again and again they repeated this procedure until I could actually shuffle slowly along by myself.

"C'mon Jeffrey, you can do it," they cheered.

"Wait until Dr. Moore sees you," Miss Morrison said happily. "Will he ever be proud of you!"

I looked up at my admirers and took my eyes off the floor and my feet. My left leg caught under my right foot. Before anyone could catch me, I fell face first onto the floor.

Miss Morrison reached down to pull me up.

"No, no," I protested, shifting my fanny until I was flush against a bed post. Slowly, I extended my left leg, then my stiff right one and tried to lurch to my feet. "I can do it. I can do it," I squealed. But I couldn't and she had to help me back up.

Hospital life was bearable because Dad, Grandmom, and my older sister, Linda, came every Sunday afternoon for a short visit. Sometimes he brought Mom when she was able. She began to come more often and, as time passed, it became easier to hide her emotions, to act out a part for my benefit as well as the family's. I'm not sure that she ever really learned to cope with me.

Visitors were not allowed in the ward. I could only talk with them through a screen. I remember many visits with them standing on the lawn, even in the snow. Most of the kids were in the hospital for weeks, some there for months, and a few, like me, were patients for years. The doctors felt then that if a kid got too close to his parents he would be more discontented with living in the hospital.

Thankfully, they later decided it was OK for the family to visit with their child on the sun porch. Every visit was about the same. "Hello. How are you, Jeffrey? What did you have for lunch? What have you been doing?"

And I would tell them I loved it when they would come to visit, but all I wanted to know was, "When can I go home?"

"We don't know, Jeffrey. It's up to the doctors. When they tell us you can go home, you'll come home."

The Saturday after I learned to take a few steps on my own, Mrs. Cook dressed me in a little sailor suit. I had the leg brace on and when they came in I lifted my left leg forward, while dragging my stiff right leg behind as usual. Dad and Mom were smiling.

"Very good, Jeffrey," Mom said.

Dad knelt down and hugged me. "I'm proud of you," he agreed.

I took a few more steps and shuffled my body against the wall below the screen. "Take me home," I begged. I saw, from watching TV, what a real home was like—a family eating together, kids running and teasing one another, a boy with tousled hair snuggled in his father's lap before a crackling fire while his Dad read an exciting story.

"Take me home, Daddy. I don't want to stay here any longer. Please take me home." I wanted to be like "normal" kids.

Mom turned her face away. Dad looked at me smiling. Was his lip trembling? Did a tear of sorrow for me trickle down his cheeks? I don't remember. All I know is that I begged and cried and all he said was, "Jeffrey, this is the best place for you now. The doctors know what is best."

Still, their Sunday visits were the highlight of my week. "How many days until Sunday?" I would ask the nurses over and over. "Mom and Dad are coming to see me on Sunday."

Yet, the conversation was so perfunctory and bereft of feeling. "Hi, Jeffrey, how are you? What did you have for

lunch today? Are you doing what the doctors and nurses tell
you?"

I saw other parents visiting with their children. I heard
them say, "We love you, Darling. We're looking forward to
when you can come home."

Though they often told me that they loved me, I don't
recall Dad or Mom ever once hoping that I could come
home.

Grandmom did say the magic words, "I love you, Jeffrey.
I wish I could see you often." She bragged on me, too.
"You've got a real *yiddish kopf*, Jeffrey. I'm proud of you."

My older sister Linda came fairly often with Mom and
Dad. Tall and pretty with soft brown curls, she was ten years
old. "Hello, Jeffrey," she said sweetly.

I fell in love with her from the first visit. We didn't have
much opportunity to really become family because of the
visiting hours and regulations. It would be many years later
that we would become close. I saw her, and later my
younger sister Sheryl, regularly.

Leaving was always the worst. "Jeffrey, we've got to go
now. We'll be back next Sunday."

"Stay, stay," I begged, after they had told me for the
umpteenth time that I couldn't go home with them.

"No, Jeffrey, we have to be on our way. Good-bye."

Each time I watched them walk down the hall as far as I
could see. Then I hobbled toward the sun porch where I
waited to see their orange '57 Pontiac with a white top and
the Indian on the front of the hood coming out of the
driveway and turning onto busy Roosevelt Boulevard. I
stood there, balanced against the window sill, streaking the
glass with my tears, long after the orange car had turned
into the stream of Boulevard traffic.

Dr. Moore cleared every major treatment with Dad. He
presented the options for my right leg where the knee
remained frozen. "We can amputate just below the knee
and fit Jeffrey with a prosthesis. Or, we can do an overlap
osteotomy on his knee and try to unfreeze the joint. I'll

· · · · · · · · · · · · · · · · · · · · · · · · · · · · · · · ·

excise the little tibia stump, then overlap and fuse the
normal fibula to the femur that will help balance the weight
on his leg below the knee."

"What are the chances of success for the osteotomy?"
Dad asked.

"Very good. I'd say 99 percent. I've consulted with the
professor of orthopedic surgery at Stanford and he thinks it's
worth the effort."

Dad reluctantly gave him the go ahead. He had noticed
my unique ability to use my feet like hands and he didn't
want the surgery to interfere with that. Perhaps he felt that
was my claim to normalcy.

How do you explain such complicated surgery to a four-
year-old? Dr. Moore tried. "We're going to do our best to fix
your right knee, Jeffrey. If it works, you won't have to drag
that leg when you walk. We'll put you asleep and you won't
feel a thing. When you wake up, the job will be done."

If wishes were horses we all would ride. If hindsight was
foresight we'd all be right. The thought of the operation
terrified me. I fought the ether, screaming and squirming
wildly until I finally succumbed. Dr. Moore took out the
tibia stump and fused the fibula to the femur as intended.
But he destroyed the growth tissue in my knee. Not only did
my knee remain frozen; the surgery doomed my right leg to
be four inches shorter than my left leg.

At four o'clock, on the morning after surgery, the night
nurse heard me moaning, "My tummy hurts!" She ran and
checked my vital signs and found my pulse racing at 140
beats per minute.

I was bleeding internally, gasping for breath, and turning
yellow. Years later I learned that I had had a reaction to
some of the anesthetics. The resident on duty started giving
emergency oxygen. The nurse called St. Christopher's
Hospital and asked for an immediate transfer, since Shriners
was not equipped to handle cardiac emergencies. A doctor
and nurse rode in the ambulance to St. Christopher's,
keeping me alive with continuous bursts of oxygen. By some
miracle, I survived.

• • • • • • • • • • • • • • • • • • • • • • • • • • • • • • • •

Dad was furious at Dr. Moore.

"Ninety-nine percent chance! That's one hell of a 1 percent! You ruined my son's leg and almost killed him in the process."

Dr. Moore wearily shook his head. "Mr. Steinberg, we're not God here at Shriners. With our best knowledge and hopes, things sometimes go wrong. We haven't given up on Jeffrey. I believe with all my heart that we can help Jeffrey and we won't give up easily. With your permission, we're going to help your son make it yet."

Dad later cooled down. There seemed to be no alternative. The doctors at Shriners were the best in their field. There wasn't anyone more qualified to treat and care for crippled children than Dr. Moore and the staff at Shriners. He told Dr. Moore to do what he thought best. So long as I was in Shriners, Mom was protected.

# CHAPTER THREE

· · · · · · · · · · · ·

# THE LONE RANGER

The surgical disaster ended all hope for mobility in my right knee. Dr. Moore still thought he could straighten my right leg and foot by wedging. This procedure would have to wait until the incisions from surgery had healed.

While the cast remained on my right leg, he went back to work on my left knee. He put it back in a cast and resumed the wedging to improve the swing.

There I was—four and a half years old with both legs in casts and recovering from cardiac failure. Sixteen months in the hospital and parents who gave me no promise that I could ever go home with them!

With both legs in casts I had to stay in a crib. I could reach out only with the little quasi prosthesis to which Miss Morrison attached a spoon at meal time. I scooted around in the crib, calling to anyone who passed by. On the outside I was playful and carefree, paying no attention to my limitations and circumstances. Yet in other ways I was like any other four-year-old. Inside, I was crying, "Hey, world.

Look at me. I'm Jeffrey Steinberg. I just want somebody to love me."

Miss Morrison could never resist my call when she came by my crib. Whenever possible, she picked me up and pressed her cheek against mine. "There now, Jeffrey. It isn't that bad. You're not going to be here always. One day, we'll have you fixed up and you can go home. You'll go to school and one day marry a beautiful girl who'll be lucky to have you."

"I wanna marry you when I get out of here," I replied confidently.

"Oh, you do, do you?" she said saucily.

"Yep. Would you be lucky to have me?"

"I sure would. And, maybe I'll wait for you—if you're a good boy and don't throw your food as you did last night."

"I'll be good," I promised.

Miss Morrison kissed me full on the lips. "You darling little boy." Then she rushed away, perhaps so I wouldn't see her tears.

Today I thumb through the inch-high stack of my medical records from Shriners. The words sound so cold and foreboding:

"Multiple congenital anomalies of both upper extremities and both lower extremities. Continue dynamic splinting, left knee, dorsiflexion wedging, left foot, abduction wedging, right foot . . ."

Page after page, day after day . . .

"Continue abduction wedging on right foot: a four-degree gain is reported on the last wedging. Motion in left knee is reported to be ll5 degrees to l60 degrees—ten degrees extension over last week's report . . ."

Monday mornings, Dr. Moore and his entourage continued their rounds. He'd look up my chart, "This is Jeffrey Steinberg, age four years and seven months . . ."

I picked up from there, ". . . multiple congenital anomalies of both upper extremities and both lower extremities . . ." Then they'd stand around and poke and measure and discuss degrees of knee flexion and possible surgeries and future treatments.

Finally, "We'd better move on. Hang in there, Jeffrey. I'll be seeing you again."

"Not if I see you first, Dr. Moore," I piped back. I always had some smart remark. I wasn't born in Philadelphia for nothing.

One morning Dr. Moore pulled the sock off my stump and tickled the tissue that had overgrown the bone. "How'd you like to have a real arm with a steel hook, Jeffrey?"

"Like Eddie's?"

"Yeah, like Eddie's."

I had often watched Eddie, who had lost his arms in an auto accident, pick up books, switch channels on the TV, and even open doors.

"When, Dr. Moore?" I asked eagerly.

"Soon as Mr. Malone can come and take new impressions and measurements."

Mr. Malone was in the ward every Friday. The next time I saw him I yelled, "Dr. Moore says I can have a hook."

"That's what I'm here for." He removed the sock and wrapped my stump in bandages soaked in plaster of paris. When the plaster hardened, he cut the plaster mold in half with a cast cutter and pulled off the mold which would harden into a cast of the stump.

"Your stump has grown, Jeffrey. Your chest is bigger. Been eating your Wheaties, I guess."

"Yeah. When do I get my hook?"

"I'll tell my little elves to get right to work and make Jeffrey a new arm. It'll take a little time. Possibly in a few weeks."

The next time I saw him I yelled, "Where's my new arm?"

"They're working on it."

"Tell your little elves to hurry. I want to pinch the nurses. I saw Eddie do that."

A couple of weeks later Miss Hampton plopped me in a

· · · · · · · · · · · · · · · · · · · · · · · · · · · · · · · · · · ·

wheel chair and rolled me down the hall to the prosthetics
department. Mr. Malone stood at a table grinning, my new
arm and hook under his hand.

He first placed soft cotton stump sock on my stump and
shoulder in order to soak up the sweat and to keep my skin
from direct contact with the plastic. He then cupped the
shoulder end of the arm tightly over my stump. "This may
be bothersome for a while, Jeffrey. You'll get used to it, just
as you did the little sock, and forget that it's there."

He put me in a new harness and curled a stainless steel
cable, wrapped in plastic, around my left shoulder. Then he
showed me how to move the muscles there, to lock and
unlock the mechanism in the elbow that manipulated the
hook. "Practice every day," he advised, "and you'll soon get
the hang of it."

I got the new arm just before Valentine's Day, 1956.
Lifting it was like lifting a lead pipe. The cup irritated my
stump until I cried. Miss Morrison asked if I wanted to take
it off. "No, no," I protested. I was very determined to get
used to it. And I became good at using it, when it was
convenient. After all, this was a major step toward
"normalcy."

Eating with the hook was cumbersome. I kept spilling my
food and turning my plate over in the crib. Mrs. Cook saw
the problem and ordered suction cups and plates which I
could not turn over.

My stump ached and throbbed. Dr. Moore pulled the
arm socket away and saw that it was red and swollen. "Let
him keep it off for a few days, wash the stump twice a day
with pHisoHex soap, then we'll try it again." I had to go
back to feeding myself with my feet.

Dr. Moore wanted me to try the arm again. The swelling
and pain came back and the socket had to be removed once
more.

I came down with a fever and a rash all over my body.
The pediatrician diagnosed German measles and sent me to
Philadelphia General Hospital for treatment. I stayed a
week and was brought back to Shriners.

Dr. Moore put the arm back on. Same problem. With the arm on, my stump became inflamed. Off, the redness disappeared in a few days. Off and on, off and on for the next four months. One week feeding myself, the next being fed by the nurses.

Dr. Moore reported to Dad, "This isn't working. I recommend that we excise the bursa, the little sac that is swollen over the end of his stump, apply a skin graft from his chest; when the stump heals he should be able to use his arm without hurting."

Dad wasn't happy about more surgery, but what could he say?

I quivered with fear as Dr. Moore tried to explain the procedure.

"Don't worry, Jeffrey," he assured. "We're going to send you to St. Christopher's first and have them make sure you'll be OK."

St. Chris kept me a week and gave the green light to Shriners. When the anesthetist came with the mask, I screamed and yelled and squirmed and wriggled, trying to break away. He kept pressing the mask over my mouth. I felt myself slipping, slipping once more into the dark void.

The next thing I knew, my stomach was violently churning and I was throwing up all over the bed. My heart raced, my breathing became heavy and labored, and my skin turned deathly ashen. The medical team gave me oxygen and other emergency aid, and in a few hours I was sleeping peacefully.

While my stump healed, Dr. Moore kept casts on both legs for wedging. When a boil mushroomed on my right knee, he had to take the cast off for a while. With a cast only on my left leg, I could stand up against the crib rail. It felt good to be vertical again.

With treatment, the boil dried up and he put the cast back on my left leg. I broke out with a skin rash and he took it off again. He treated the rash and replaced the cast. The rash came back. The cast came off. The rash healed. Another cast. Another rash.

Mr. Malone gave me back my arm. Within two weeks my stump was too sore to bear the arm. Puzzled and frustrated, Dr. Moore refused to quit. "You're a tough little nut, Jeffrey," he said. "Hang in there and we'll make it eventually."

Gradually he was straightening my immobile right leg and foot, but he couldn't keep wedging the left knee because of the skin rash, and I was developing a new bursa on the end of my stump.

After extensive consultation and research in the medical literature, Dr. Moore identified my postoperative reaction as dysautonomia—a breakdown of the autonomic nervous system which controls the involuntary bodily functions, including heart beat and respiration. Susceptibility to dysautonomia is a hereditary weakness known only to occur among Jewish children. He also found that I was allergic to chocolate.

Undaunted, Dr. Moore next did a posterior capsulotomy on my left knee. He cut the tendons and hamstrings in hope of loosening the tension and making the knee more amenable to wedging. He was afraid to do more because of the potential dysautonomia. I still suffered the same miserable postoperative symptoms. He immediately put me on intravenous fluids and my breathing and heartbeat quickly slowed to normal.

When the incision healed, he started wedging again and the left leg moved a few more degrees.

Mr. Malone reattached my arm. I broke the cable above the elbow. The prosthetist sent it out to be fixed.

Dr. Moore had both leg casts taken off for awhile. My arm came back with the cable repaired.

What a relief! I walked up and down between the beds. I could go watch TV in the big day room at the end of the hall without having to be carried there. I could play with other kids on the back lawn. Green grass between my toes and a warm sun on my back was heaven.

This was my best summer after four years in Shriners.

The only upsetting experience was being transferred to Temple University Hospital for eleven days of genitourinary tests. They decided that my frequency of urination had probably been a nervous reaction to the troubled surgeries.

Every time Dr. Moore saw me walking, he said, "We've got to do better with that left knee." With Dad's permission, he had me prepped for more surgery. Dad knew he was taking a risk with my susceptibility to dysautonomia, but let him go ahead.

This time, September 12, 1958, Dr. Moore fractured and realigned the misgrown tibia where it extended abnormally above the knee, in hopes this would make a realignment possible. Once again, I went into severe postoperative shock. They didn't take any chances and rushed me back to St. Christopher's. After ten days of emergency care at St. Chris, I came back to my old home at Shriners.

When the knee healed, Dr. Moore reapplied the wedging and increased the mobility a few more degrees. My fourth surgery had been at least partially successful.

I was now seven years old. Dr. Moore said he was through with my right knee. "We've done all we can here. We've gotten the leg as straight as we can."

But the surgical mishap on my right knee had destroyed the growth tissue there. My right leg was now conspicuously shorter than the left. To correct the imbalance, Dr. Moore had the brace shop place a "second foot," which would be added as an extension of my leg brace on the right. This would even up my stance. However, I made a curious sight ambulating with "three feet."

He gave me another vacation from the cast on my left leg. He ordered a new arm socket for my still growing stump.

Hospital life fell into a happier routine. A therapist exercised my left knee twice a week. I attended school on the premises Monday through Friday. Our class schedule was kept as close as possible to that of the public school schedule in spite of the interruptions for surgery, recovery, and therapy sessions. I watched a lot of TV, played games with the nurses, and looked forward to the weekly visits with my family.

I badgered Dad every week about when I might get to go home. "I don't know," he said, and he didn't. "The doctor will tell us."

Linda and Sheryl now came with Mom, Dad and Grandmom every Sunday.

Dad and I did most of the serious talking. Mom was good at small talk and appeared to show more interest in me, but she still seemed a bit nervous and ill at ease around me, though she hid it on the surface. I drew closer to Dad than to her as though I needed his approval. He was my authority figure. He made all of the decisions on my behalf. But if she had just made a move, just one move, I would have flung myself into her arms. I wanted to be wanted by her, too. Perhaps she was afraid of becoming too closely attached for her own sake. I always watched them until they disappeared down the hall. Then I hung by the window to see the old orange Pontiac come down the side street, turn into the traffic on Roosevelt Boulevard, and disappear until the next weekend. The hurt and deep longing to be with my family continued.

My visitors came on Sunday afternoon. Saturday afternoon I never missed Dick Clark's "American Bandstand" record hop which originated from Philadelphia. I loved the music of Frankie Avalon, Fabian, Bobby Rydell, and other "rock and roll" stars of that era. I sang along with the records, spun around on my left foot (when the cast was off), and dreamed I was whirling with the teenagers before the cameras doing "The Stroll," "The Walk," "The Fish," "The Slop," and other dances of the fifties.

"C'mon, dance with me," I called to Miss Morrison.

She took my hook and what a pair we made! Eat your heart out Fred Astaire!

The Lone Ranger, Superman, and Zorro ranked as my TV adventure favorites. After a show I'd get up shows with the other kids and nurses. A kid who couldn't get out of bed or a wheelchair said his part from where he was. I was usually the hero, and sometimes the narrator, too.

On this eventful Thursday night, Miss Morrison helped me put on a black mask which she and I had made. I crouched before the screen . . . waiting. Then came William Tell's blood-stirring overture and the dramatic voice. . . . "From out of the past come the thundering hoofbeats of the great horse Silver. . . ." I clicked my tongue against the roof of my mouth to give a near-perfect imitation of hoofbeats. ". . . A fiery horse with the speed of light, a cloud of dust and a hearty 'Hi-yo Silver,' . . . the Lone Ranger rides again."

I imagined myself on the great white horse, galloping into the wind, chasing a mean crook through a rocky canyon. "Come on, Silver, come on, big boy," I yelled.

"Get 'em up, Scout!" screamed Mike Higgins, a cerebral palsy victim in a wheelchair.

One afternoon, Mike and I were acting out a Lone Ranger drama when one of the nurses hustled us to our beds. "A very important visitor is coming," she said. Suddenly the door opened and a tall figure strode into the ward. White hat, black mask, blue shirt, red scarf, and silver bullets in his gunbelt. Our mouths hung open. It was Clayton Moore who played the masked man on TV! He strode down the aisle, talking to first one kid, then another. Finally, he leaned down to shake my hook.

"Hello. What's your name?"

"Jeffrey Steinberg," I said confidently.

"It's a pleasure to meet you, Jeffrey. I'm the Lone Ranger."

"You're my favorite. Where's Tonto?" I thought to ask. "And Silver?"

"They couldn't make it. Maybe next time."

He gave me a photograph of himself, autographed it, and then he moved on to the next bed and in a few minutes was gone.

"Wow!" I yelled at Mike. "The Lone Ranger!"

To this day I enjoy watching and even collecting those old TV adventure shows.

Mrs. Guido, a peppery little dark-haired woman, taught about twenty of us in a school room down the long hall between the wards. She came to the beds of those who were not ambulatory.

I learned to write with my mouth and could take the written tests, but I conned her into asking me the questions orally. It didn't always work. I just wanted more attention. She had told my parents that I was a very good student.

I continually made demands on Miss Guido, Miss Morrison, and others on the staff. "Teach me how to draw a giraffe." "Hey, look, Miss Hampton, I can pick up this glass with my teeth." "Oh, Mrs. Cook, did you bring the comic books you said your nephew was through reading?"

There were not enough personnel, even at Shriners, to give personal attention to every kid all the time. I learned to get what I wanted by speaking up, by hollering above the others if necessary, by badgering someone until they gave me what I wanted.

Fall slipped into a cold winter. We couldn't go outside to play on the back lawn again until spring. We saw on TV the first passenger jets taking off from Philadelphia's Municipal Airport. Alaska became the forty-ninth state on the second day of January, 1959. I had not been off the hospital grounds, except for emergency trips to other hospitals, for over four years. The Children's Shelter was a dim memory.

I kept asking, "When can I go home?"

Dad kept saying, "The doctors will let us know."

Two days after Valentine's Day, 1959, Miss Hampton had us all on our beds for rounds. Dr. Moore entered the ward, trailed by his usual entourage of interns. I waited for him to come to my bed.

He picked up my chart and started droning the particulars. This time I ignored him, my thoughts were on

• • • • • • • • • • • • • • • • • • • • • • • • • • • •

Superman. Suddenly he mumbled something about "letting him go home awhile."

"Home?" Boy did I become alert! In four and a half years I had never heard that before.

"I can really go home, Doc?" My lower lip was trembling.

"You heard me right, Jeffrey. You're getting around pretty well. You're using that hook like a pro. I want to do a little more work on you, but you need time to grow some more. Think you can make it at home for a few months?"

"Yeah!"

"Good. I've already arranged for your Dad to pick you up the day after tomorrow."

The rule was that we had to stay in our beds and be quiet until the doctors finished rounds. I could hardly contain my excitement. I had to tell it. Finally, the last white coat disappeared through the door.

"I'm going home!" I screeched. "Dr. Moore says I'm going home day after tomorrow."

I was out of bed, bubbling up and down the aisles, hollering to anybody in sight, "I'm going home!"

Miss Morrison picked me up and hugged me tight. "Didn't I tell you, Jeffrey? Didn't I tell you? You're going home!"

# CHAPTER FOUR
· · · · · · · · · · ·

# HOME!

Wednesday morning, February 18, 1959. Seven and one-half years old. A cold day in Philadelphia, but warm in my heart.

"Yippee! I'm going home, I'm going home," I kept yelling as Miss Hampton gathered up my things. I was eager to go, yet there was a certain sadness. After all, Shriners had been my home for five years.

"Calm down, Jeffrey," Miss Morrison laughed. "They won't be here for another hour."

I had a longer wait than that. They had to sign papers and be briefed on my care. How to take off my arm and shoulder harness at night. Remove my leg brace and extra foot. Bathe me and wash my stump. And we were to continue using pHisoHex liquid soap. Put me back together in the morning.

Finally, I could leave. "Don't pamper the boy," Dr. Moore urged Dad. "Let him do as much as he can."

Dad offered to carry both me and the suitcase. "No, I can walk," I insisted.

I followed them down the ramp and across to the parking lot. With a little help from Dad, I scrambled into the front seat of the old orange Pontiac. Mom slid in beside me and Dad pulled out of the lot and turned the corner toward Roosevelt Boulevard. I looked over to see Miss Morrison, Mrs. Cook, and many of the other doctors and staff that I had grown to love, waving from the sun porch, the place from which I had tearfully watched my folks drive away so many times. These wonderful people at that Shriners Hospital were the family I had grown up with. I would always be grateful to them for their love and constant devoted care.

But now I was going home with my mother and father and natural family, a new family, to a new world, a new chapter in my life. It was scary, and yet exciting.

As Dad edged into the heavy traffic, I cast a side glance at Mom. She appeared as excited for me as I was, or was I just nervous over the future of our relationship? I slid in close to her. She put her arm around me and appeared to be glad to see me. What's she thinking? Is she really glad to have me coming home? What would it be like being a part of a real family, a brother to three sisters? Would I belong? Would I have friends like they did? Where would I go to school? There seemed to be a million unanswered questions, but for now, nothing was more important than the excitement and joy of sitting where I had only dreamed about, in the front seat of my parents' car on my way home.

I had imagined our house from their descriptions—a little gray stucco duplex, with my family occupying one side and renters the other.

Dad tried to be jocular as he pulled up to the curb in front of 1823 Placid Street. "Home sweet home," he said. "Ruthe, I'll help Jeffrey and then come back for his suitcase."

"I'll go in and get some lunch ready." Mom opened the door as I shifted my body over and stuck my stiff shorter right leg over the side. Placing my hook against the edge of the seat, I swung my left limb out and stood as straight as I could.

"Better hang on to me, Jeffrey," was all Dad said.

"I can walk by myself." I handed him the crutch which the hospital had given me to be used for support.

Mom pushed back the crutch. "Mom, I can do it. I'm not crippled."

Dad took me to the room next to my sisters'. I sat down on the bed and watched Dad put my clothes and toys into the dresser drawers.

Mom poked her head in and forced a smile. "Are you guys hungry?"

"I've got to get back to work," Dad said, and hurried out of the house.

Mom gave me a peanut butter and jelly sandwich and poured me a glass of milk. She sat down across the table from me.

"Jeffrey, would you like a straw for your milk?" she asked.

"I can handle it." I then grabbed the edge of the glass with my teeth and swung it up to my lips.

Mom, as if by instinct, reached out for the glass.

I gulped down a big swallow and set the glass back down. "Mom, I do it all the time at the hospital." I must confess that I was showing off, and enjoying the attention. Mom, however, was a bit uncertain. Maybe, a part of me was trying to prove that I could be as independent as other "normal" kids.

After lunch I set out to explore the rest of the house and check out the neighborhood. I went down to the basement which had been made into a den, watched a little TV, played with some of the toys, and then went outside to look around and to meet some of the neighbors, and maybe even make some new friends. The afternoon wore on. After I asked for the tenth time, "When are Linda and Sheryl coming home?" I heard a rumble from the corner, a squeak of brakes, then a babble of voices. The girls came running into the room. They had come with Dad and Mom many times to visit me in the hospital. I recognized them immediately.

"Linda! Sheryl!" I squealed. "I'm home."

Both gave me quick hugs and kisses. Linda, almost a teenager, ran off to call her friend. Sheryl, who was six, wanted to see my arm, all the way to the stump. She took off my shirt and inspected the mechanism. Linda heard Sheryl talking and came to see. I did all the hook tricks I knew and also wrote their names with a pen clenched between my teeth. They were impressed. All this time, Mom was in the kitchen, getting dinner ready, I guessed. Later, I realized many of Mom's trips to other parts of the house were to get away from me. Out of sight, out of mind, I suppose.

While talking to my sisters, I felt the urge coming on. There was no nurse I could tell. I couldn't ask one of my sisters to take me to the bathroom. Finally, I went into the kitchen and whispered to Mom, "Can you take me? I need to go."

"Come on, Jeffrey." She took me in, pulled down my trousers, stood back and waited for me to finish. She then zipped up my pants and that was that. It was easy to notice that this was a new and perhaps a difficult experience, but she was patient. "You'll have to learn to do this yourself, Jeffrey." She was smiling.

Grandmom Vedatsky came over after supper and lightened up the atmosphere. She laughed and clapped her hands when I demonstrated skills with my hook. "Didn't I tell you, he's got a real *yiddish kopf?* This is one *schmart* boy."

My sisters grinned, and Mom smiled, "You're right, Mom. He's a smart boy."

Dad came home from work around five with a newspaper under his arm. The girls were in their room doing homework, so he paid a little attention to me. We had supper together. We were a family.

A little after nine, Dad volunteered to give me a bath and

help me get in my pajamas. He stripped off my clothes in the bathroom and removed my arm and harness just as the hospital had instructed. He took off the band that secured my brace to my right hip, then pulled away the brace and the extra foot on the end.

He already had the water running. "In you go, Jeffrey." He sat me down nice and easy and began washing me down with a soapy cloth.

"Hey, Dad, you're pretty good at this," I chuckled as he was toweling me off. "They should hire you at Shriners."

I think he liked it that first night.

I wasn't home very long before Dad had changed jobs to become a letter carrier for the U.S. Postal Service. He would leave for work at five in the morning, before we got up. Mom had to put me together, dress me, and feed all of us. The girls walked to the corner to catch their bus. A little while later I would walk out to the front of the house where I would catch the bus for Widener Memorial School, a school for physically handicapped children and kids with special learning disabilities. Dad had already enrolled me and given them my records from Shriners.

I was not the most severely handicapped student in the school, but I might have been the most assertive and demanding. As at Shriners, I conned the teacher, Mrs. Stennhouse, into giving me tests orally instead of having me write the answers with a pencil stuck between my teeth.

When I didn't bring any papers home, Dad called and gave my teacher a piece of his mind. "I want to see the work he does!" Dad demanded. At first she thought Dad was cruel and uncaring, so she refused. It was an argument that was taken by my father to the Philadelphia Board of Education.

She made me do written work after that.

The cold snowy winter surrendered to a warm spring. My sisters and I wanted to get out and play. Mom ruled that we had to have our homework done first.

Home wasn't working out as I had imagined. She

restricted me to the yard. "You're handicapped, Jeffrey," she reminded. "You can't do what other kids do."

I didn't want to be handicapped! I didn't want to be treated like I was different. So, I rebelled. When Mom went back inside, I shuffled into the street. Sheryl ran and tattled. Mom ordered me back into the house and I sat on the living room couch sulking and feeling sorry for myself with the shouts and yells of other kids at play ringing in my ears.

I kept going back into the street until Mom gave in and told Linda to watch me. A couple of days later I went out without doing my homework. Mom came and marched me back inside. "Stay in your room until your Dad comes home," she ordered.

Dad led me into the bathroom and took off his broad mailman's belt. As he reached to pull down my pants, I looked at the belt and shrieked, "No, Dad! Don't!"

Grasping me by my right shoulder, he brought the belt down hard on my naked behind. I screamed and hollered as if I were dying.

I was careful to do my homework first after that.

I couldn't be satisfied just watching the other kids. I wanted to prove that I was normal and could do what they did—like riding Sheryl's tricycle.

The first time my feet got tangled in the pedals and I fell on my chin. I was rushed to Philadelphia Children's Hospital. It took twelve stitches to sew up the wound.

"Hey, you oughta be a little more careful," the doctor said sympathetically. I told him I'd probably be back, if the tricycle didn't cooperate.

Same challenge, same injury, same hospital. Dad was furious and almost belted me.

The third time I actually pedaled a few yards. Then having proven I could do it, I extricated my legs from it. I haven't been on a tricycle since.

Off and on I had been plagued with incontinency at Shriners. Part of the cause was a mild form of spina bifida which my parents were never told about. The other part

• • • • • • • • • • • • • • • • • • • • • • • • • • • • • • •

was probably the feelings of hostility I developed toward my mother.

The second time I wet my pants, Mom told Dad when he came home. He warned me once and when I did it again, he pulled me into the bathroom, jerked down my pants, and slapped my naked bottom with the belt.

The next time, he increased the force and the number of swings.

Mrs. Stennhouse at Widener saw me squirming at my desk and asked the problem. I told her. She called Dad and read him the riot act.

Dad got the principal on the phone. "You people don't know what it's like to care for a kid like Jeffrey," he stormed.

The spankings didn't control my urinary misfortunes. Dad thought I was wetting my pants deliberately. "You're much too old for this, Jeffrey," he declared grimly. "I have to teach you a lesson." I can't help but wonder if Dad didn't worry that he was a failure in that department.

I still can't excuse Dad for the way he whipped me, although I can understand him a little better now. He was coming home from his second job, tired and hoping for a little relaxation. The first thing he heard when he walked in the door was, "Jeffrey wet his pants again. Can't you do something with him, Irv?"

Mom became pregnant again, making family life for me even more uncomfortable. Dad tried to limit her activities, hoping to protect her, meaning she could do less for me.

One of the few happy times came when we went to New York and celebrated the Passover Seder with Dad's relatives. Zayde had died two years after I was born, but Bubbeh was there to welcome her large family of children and grandchildren.

I had never seen a Seder before. Two tall candles flamed in Bubbeh's worn silver candlesticks at the center of the dining table. The Seder foods—the bitter herbs, the shankbone, the greens, and the charoseth—were spread on the Seder plate.

"We praise you, O Lord our God, King of the universe," Dad prayed. "You have kept us alive, sustained us, and brought us to this good season."

The grown-ups raised the first cup of wine. Dad broke off a piece of matzoh bread and held it up to pronounce the blessing. "We praise you, O Lord our God, King of the universe. You have sanctified us through your commandment that ordained we should eat unleavened bread."

I stood quietly among a group of cousins whom I had met only an hour before, trying to understand what was happening, hearing the clink of glasses as the adults took more sips of wine.

*"Shulkan arukh.* The table is ready," Dad announced. Two of the women brought in a great bowl and began to ladle out the matzoh ball soup. Dad came around and stood protectively beside me, making sure I had no problems in eating. I looked up at him and grinned shyly.

After the meal, everybody sat around the table and chanted and sang Psalms of thanksgiving for the deliverance of the Jews from Egypt. I knew I was Jewish, but it was all quite strange to me. There was a corner synagogue just down from our house in Philadelphia, but Mom and Dad never went there while I was home. Dad couldn't stand the garish chartreuse paint on the outside. He called it "puke green." He went to a synagogue across town where he taught Hebrew to young children, but he never took me there. Mom attended Jewish social events, and she continued to act and sing in local musicals for Jewish charities.

The family gathering was over all too soon. We climbed into the Pontiac for the two hour drive back to Philadelphia. Dad had to be at the post office early the next morning to sort the mail for his route.

We had just crossed over into New Jersey when someone proposed that we sing to make the trip go faster.

Dad led out, *"Ha-vah Na-gi-la, Ha-vah Na-gi-la . . ."*

• • • • • • • • • • • • • • • • • • • • • • • • • • • • • •

somewhat awkwardly. Mom came in with her beautiful
mellow alto to help Dad out, or was it to rescue him? We
kids in the back seat quickly picked up the tune and the
words. *"Ha-vah Na-gi-la vemis mechah . . ."*

I raised my voice the second time around, and was really
enjoying myself. I may have even screeched a little. When
we finished the stanza, Dad began laughing.

"Jeffrey," he said, "if you ever decide to sing for a living,
please don't do it while I'm around." Everyone laughed.

I broke my leg brace the next week and Dad had to cart
me back to Shriners. They checked my shortened right
leg—it was OK, and put the brace in the shop for repairs.
They decided, at the same time, to lengthen it to
compensate for my left leg which was longer. I could walk
and get around pretty well, and would be no trouble at
home the next week. Dad would have to take more time off
from work to go back and pick up the brace.

My stump started hurting next. Mom pulled off my
prosthesis and saw that the flesh was red and swollen on the
end of the stump. She called Shriners and they told her to
clean it with a certain kind of antiseptic and water.

"Leave the arm off a few days and see if the stump
doesn't get better," they advised.

This worked, temporarily. The swelling went down, but
within a few days after resuming use of the prosthesis, my
stump was aching again. This time it was infected and Dad
had to take me back to Shriners. They readmitted me a
month before my eighth birthday.

They cleared up the infection and Dr. Moore put my left
knee back into a cast for wedging, in hopes of increasing the
mobility. After three months, the swing had widened only a
few degrees. Doc got Dad's permission to amputate the
troublesome end of my arm stump and while I was on the
operating table to go back into my left knee and slice off the
extended tibia that had apparently been hindering mobility.

Dr. Moore cut off about two centimeters of the stump,
inserted a control button on the smooth end of the bone,

and grafted skin over it from my chest. While I was still "out," he sliced off the spike end of the tibia and turned my leg and foot more outward.

I didn't suffer the life-threatening postoperative symptoms experienced in previous surgeries. A consultant beforehand had suggested feeding me blood sugar through the muscles before the anesthesia was administered. This apparently held back the dysautonomia.

The new knee surgery helped straighten my left leg, but did little to improve mobility. A couple of months after trimming my stump, Doctor Moore reattached my prosthesis. I had the same old hook, but a new socket for the stump and a new control wire for the shoulder harness. As a going-away present they put skid-proof soles on my soles and added a three-eighths inch lift to my left heel.

Exactly five months before my ninth birthday, Dad checked me out of Shriners for the last time. I had spent over five years of my life there.

I went out with a stiff right leg, four inches shorter than the left. My left knee was more mobile than when I went in. I still had only three toes on my left foot and no nails on any of my existing eight toes. My left sleeve hung flat against my side, and on the right I had an artificial arm. Hardly a beautiful body by the world's standards, but good enough to get by.

Dr. Moore, who had never stopped believing that I would walk out of the hospital, was still not satisfied. His last entry on my medical record read, "He walks well but I am constantly reminded that I would like to straighten the (left) knee."

I went home with the thought that I was out of an institution forever. No more casts and surgeries. No eating from plastic plates and cups held down by suctions any more. No intercom blaring, "Dr. Williams, please come to prosthetics." No dinging bells and rustling white coats. Freedom, family and new life, though I had no idea how new my life would be.

• • • • • • • • • • • • • • • • • • • • • • • • • • • • •

This time my expectations for living at home were more realistic. I had learned to control my bladder better during the last hospital stay. Mom now had a new baby, Harriet. She would have even less time and patience for me. Dad still had two jobs, besides his teaching at the synagogue. I had to be on my best behavior.

Harriet and I slept in the same room. She was beautiful, with jet black hair, and big brown eyes.

Mom still could not allow herself to show much affection to me. I think she was afraid of becoming too attached. I enviously watched her cuddle the baby, though I was grateful to be a part of the family. I yearned to feel her warm arms around my neck. She would kiss me and say, "That's very good, Jeffrey. I'm so proud of you." But those times would overshadow those comments that made me feel as though I just didn't measure up. She encouraged me, though not very often. I later learned that she feared that if they encouraged me too much I would hurt myself. They wanted me to be safe. Those incidents would simply upset her more.

The old ambivalence of love and hate began to build. I did little things on purpose to get her attention, if not her approval. The more I did, the more she complained to Dad, and the more he spanked me. Yet I wanted to please Dad. Even with the spankings, I sensed that he loved me. I think I now understand why I felt so differently toward my parents. Dad was the only one I knew for the first seventeen months of my life. He had visited me regularly and played with me in the Children's Shelter. Mom, not knowing I was alive, had not. Unconsciously, I felt she had never cared for me.

I can better see now the ordeal of Mom when I was home. Dad left for work at 5:00 A.M. not to return until 4:30 P.M. We would have supper, and then he would leave to teach Hebrew in a Hebrew school two nights a week. Some nights he wouldn't get home until 10:30. Four children, with a new baby and an assertive, hyperactive, nine-year-old severely handicapped son. Cooking. Warming bottles.

Settling fights. Wiping noses and bottoms. Giving baths. Getting me and the baby ready for bed.

When Dad didn't always get home in time to give me a bath, Mom, nerves frazzled and body exhausted, had to do the honors. She admits today, "There were times when I wanted to drown you in the tub and put you out of my life forever." She might well have if Dad hadn't given her a breather by arranging for me to attend the Philadelphia Variety Club's month-long summer camp, outside the city, for handicapped children.

Camp was a blast. We went to bed and got up to the sound of bugles. We had to clean our bunks and get ready for inspection every morning. Each of us was responsible to have clean bunks for inspection. We all had to work feverishly to get our cabin ready for inspection so that ours would be selected as the neatest.

Shriners mostly treated kids with orthopedic problems. Here at camp were blind and deaf kids also. Nobody talked much about limitations. Everybody talked about what we could do with what we had.

I went out for softball. A counselor helped me balance the bat between my chin and right shoulder. The deaf pitcher threw the ball gently and I "swung." Crack! The ball bounced over the pitcher's head and my runner took off for a double. That was fun. Great fun.

I learned to communicate with the deaf. I didn't have any fingers to "sign" with, but I got to where I could understand the language and became pretty good at reading lips.

We went swimming. A big burly coach plunked me in the water with a life jacket. I paddled around yelling, "Hey, look at me, I can swim! I'm swimming!"

On Sunday, we could go in a bus at 6:00 A.M. to either a Catholic or a Protestant church. I got up and went with the Catholics. When we got there, I must have been the last one in the building, and the shortest one, because I couldn't see the front. My nose caught the strange, sweet smell of burning incense. A guy with a high-pitched voice up front

was speaking in a strange language—Latin. I was too short
to see over those standing in front. I craned my neck on
both sides and couldn't see through the crowd. What was
going on here?

I heard a moan that sounded like an organ. A choir came
in, slow, soft, sad and in Latin also. Though I did not
understand the lyrics, the music was beautiful. I enjoyed
going and watching the service, anyway. That was the last I
saw of church for a long time.

When the bus dropped me off at the end of the month,
Mom and Dad came and met me at the bus. I chattered
about the ball games, the swimming, the picnics, and the
contests. Sheryl wanted to know how I swam and played
baseball. Mom said only, "I'm glad you enjoyed camp,
Jeffrey."

I wet my pants again. Mom laid this and a pile of other
woes on Dad when he came in from work. He thrashed me
hard. I screamed loud enough for the neighbors to hear.
Dad just kept right on beating me.

One afternoon of the next week, Dad came home
unexpectedly from work. He wanted to talk to me, and so I
followed him into my bedroom; he sat on my bed and faced
me, looking serious. He tried to explain to me that he and
Mom couldn't take care of me. "I'm taking you to stay with
a new family for awhile," he said.

In a way, I felt relief. In another way, I was confused and
hurt. It wasn't what was said that bothered me as much as
what wasn't said, and Dad's spankings to the contrary, I
didn't want to leave my family. Protests did no good.

"Let's get your things together, Jeffrey." Dad began
carefully packing clothes into a suitcase, while Mom helped
to gather up my toys, and in a half hour we were on our
way.

Bill and Doris Johnson, my foster parents, were a solid,
pleasant, middle-aged couple. Mr. Johnson was a school bus
driver. They lived in a neat brick row house on Huntington
Ave. closer to downtown Philadelphia, about ten miles from

my folks. They had a teenage daughter, Rosalie, who suffered from cerebral palsy.

Dad and the social worker who had been following my case believed they could handle me.

Dad shook hands with the Johnsons, introduced me, carried my suitcase to my room. He then came into the living room and they spoke briefly before he turned to leave. I stumbled behind him as he strode toward the door. "Wait, Dad, wait." I was in tears trying to be brave. "Will you come and see me? And why can't I stay home? I'll be good. I won't wet my pants."

He stopped, knelt in front of me, took me into his strong arms and held me close. "You know Mommy and I love you very much and we want what is best for you. We will come and visit as often as possible."

"When? Will you come back tomorrow? I don't want to stay here. I want to go home with you."

"I'll be back to see you in a few days. You be a good boy."

He hugged me and held me tight for a few moments, kissed me, then got up and left. As the door closed behind him, I raced to the screen door and saw him get in the old orange Pontiac and drive away.

Mrs. Johnson knelt beside me and placed her arms around me. "There, there, Jeffrey, they'll be back often. You'll see. Come and watch TV with Rosalie. I'll have supper ready in a few minutes."

Later in the evening Mr. Johnson undressed me in their bathroom. "Jeffrey, how did this happen?" he gasped.

"I wet my pants . . . and . . . Dad spanked me . . ." I was afraid to continue.

"How many times has he whipped you?"

"I don't know. Lots of times." I tried to hold up a brave front and pretend that it didn't hurt.

"Doris, come in here," he yelled.

Mrs. Johnson came running. "Oh, my God. What have they done to this child? Oh, my God!"

• • • • • • • • • • • • • • • • • • • • • • • • • • • • • • • • • •

"I'm going to wash him with soap and warm water," Mr. Johnson said. "Get some salve."

He cleaned the bruised area, then Mrs. Johnson gently spread on some soothing salve. She helped me into a pair of clean cotton pajamas and Mr. Johnson carried me gently to my bed. They both hugged me good-night and I turned over and fell quickly asleep.

Mr. Johnson called the social worker the next day. She agreed that under no conditions would the Welfare Department allow me to return home.

During the three months I was with the Johnsons, Dad came almost every Saturday and occasionally brought Mom and my two oldest sisters. My conversation with him and Mom was little more than at Shriners, "Hello. How are you doing?"

"OK, I guess."

Just the chitchat of casual acquaintances.

All the time, Dad was trying to find a place where I could receive long-term care at public expense. He looked first for a Jewish agency and, finding none, began to search elsewhere. A friend of a friend took Dad's dilemma to the mayor of Philadelphia. Mayor Dilworth pulled strings to have the Lutheran Children's Bureau pay for institutional care in the Good Shepherd Home of Allentown, Pennsylvania, sixty-five miles northwest of Philadelphia.

I had no hint of any change until Mrs. Johnson told me on Monday morning, October 3, 1960, that I was to stay home from school that day. "Your parents are coming for you," she said.

I brightened, figuring they were coming to take me home. Mr. Johnson had already left on his bus route.

Around eight o'clock they drove up in the Pontiac. Peeking through the window, I saw Dad take an old suitcase from the car that I recognized as belonging to Grandmom Vedatsky. Mom came trailing after him.

"I'm going home!" I said expectantly.

"No, Jeffrey, we're taking you to a place where they can take better care of you."

For a few seconds I stood in shock. Then I began to tremble and cry. "Please, take me home," I begged. "I want to live with my sisters."

Mom hung back, looking at the wall. Mrs. Johnson busied herself in the kitchen. Rosalie had already been picked up for her school.

"Jeffrey, we're doing this for your good," Mom said. "You're only going to Allentown, about an hour's drive from Philadelphia. We can visit you there."

I stamped my left foot. "No! No! I won't like it. I'll hate it. I won't stay there! You can't make me stay there!"

Dad called to Mrs. Johnson. "If you'll show me where his clothes are, I'll start packing."

# CHAPTER FIVE
· · · · · · · · · ·
# LAMB AT GOOD SHEPHERD

Mrs. Johnson held me close for a few moments, then kissed me good-bye as Dad waited at the door.

"C'mon, we have a long drive and Mommy is waiting in the car."

Dad placed my suitcase and my playthings in the trunk and opened the front door. I clambered in and sat between Mom and Dad.

"Take me home," I sniffed, without any hope.

Dad looked back over the seat. "Jeffrey, I've explained to you we're going to the Good Shepherd Home in Allentown. They can care for you there. They have other handicapped kids there. You'll be happier there."

"I want you to take care of me," I sobbed.

Ignoring me, Dad started the motor. I buried my face in the back.

"Jeffrey, you're upsetting your mother. Do I have to stop and use my belt?"

At the sound of that word I froze. My eyes stopped

leaking. I sat very still for a long time, not daring to say a word.

Dad turned onto Roosevelt and sped north. I fell asleep and awakened when Dad pulled off the highway at a diner. We went inside and I sat sulking in the booth across from them. "What do you want, Jeffrey?" Dad asked.

"I'm not hungry."

"Suit yourself." He ordered coffee for himself and Mom, and a Coke for me. I, deep in thought, swirled the straw around in the glass.

"Drink your Coke," Dad ordered.

I didn't think he would use the belt in the restaurant.

They finished their coffee and Dad drove on. I climbed back in the front seat, dreading what lay ahead, and the time when I knew they would leave me again.

Dad stopped at a traffic light and turned left. We passed blocks and blocks of row houses, crossed a bridge over a small creek. Then Dad stopped on a street across from a big red brick building that looked like a school, at the corner of Sixth and St. John Streets.

I looked up at the top of the structure and saw the sign:

*GOOD SHEPHERD HOME*
*FOR CRIPPLED CHILDREN AND AGED PEOPLE*

"We'll take you in to meet Reverend Raker, the superintendent, and get you settled," Dad said. He went around to the passenger side and opened the door for Mom, then let me out and we walked across St. John Street to where concrete steps led up to a fancy white door. Dad saw me drawing back.

"Take me home," I begged again. "I hate this place."

"Jeffrey, you haven't even seen the inside yet." Dad lifted me to his shoulder and carried me up the steps with Mom trailing after.

I saw the cross above the door. "Dad, this is a Christian place. I thought we were Jewish."

· · · · · · · · · · · · · · · · · · · · · · · · · · · · · ·

"It's the only institution we could find that could take care of you," Dad explained as he set me down inside the door.

"Dad, I don't want to live here. I want to live with you and Mom and my sisters."

"Shhhh." Dad bent close to my ear to hold his voice down. "You're going to be happy here, Jeffrey. These are good people. You'll be much better off than with us. They can do more for you than we can."

We stepped into a long hall. A small elderly woman greeted us from in front of the switchboard as if we were expected. She introduced herself as Miss Hammer, the administrative assistant. "You're the Steinbergs, aren't you? And this must be Jeffrey." She bent down and shook my hook in a firm but kindly way.

She continued speaking to me, "Hello, Jeffrey. I think you're going to like it here. There are lots of other handicapped children here to play with and be friends with." She straightened and spoke to Mom and Dad, "Reverend Raker has your papers and is expecting you. I'll let him know you're here."

A minute later a tall bespectacled man with straight slick hair parted near the middle and wearing a dark suit came out of a set of offices across the hall. He shook hands with Mom and Dad and bent down to take my hook. "Come on in," he invited.

Scared, hostile, and confused, I vowed not to like this Reverend or anyone else here.

My parents took side chairs. Rev. Raker patted the slick seat of a big, black leather chair directly in front of the desk. "You can sit here, Jeffrey." I slid down in the leather, dangling my feet over the edge. Rev. Raker caught sight of the artificial foot below my regular foot, but he didn't blink.

"Did you have a nice drive up?"

"Very nice," Dad replied cordially. Mom agreed.

"Would you care for some coffee?"

"Yes, please."

"Did you tell Jeffrey what we have here?"

"A little. We didn't know much of what to expect ourselves."

"I'll take you up to his room as soon as we finish the paperwork." Then looking at me. "I think you'll like it here, Jeffrey."

I started to open my mouth, but thought better when I saw Dad looking at me. I merely drew in my lips and frowned.

Rev. Raker read some mumbo-jumbo. Dad kept nodding and when the Reverend thrust the papers across the desk, he and Mom signed. I wanted to yell, "Don't I have something to say about what you're doing with me?" But what good would it do now?

Years later I would read from Good Shepherd's records:

*Jeffrey came into Good Shepherd able to walk with braces. Nothing in his physical condition warranted institutional care. Attempts to keep him at home resulted in emotional upsets for his mother. It was felt that Good Shepherd Home would offer him more continuity, stability, and emotional security and better peer group relationships than other considered options.*

The paperwork completed, Reverend Raker came from behind the big desk. "Now let's go upstairs and see Jeffrey's room." The minister led the way to the elevator, carrying Grandmom's old suitcase. I trudged along between Mom and Dad, unspeaking and unsmiling.

The number 3 glowed on the panel and the elevator stopped. "Our younger children live on this floor," Rev. Raker explained. "Boys have rooms at one end of the floor and girls at the other in what we used to call the Baby Cottage. Our older residents live up and down the ramp from here on the other side of this building." He rattled on, telling about the kind nurses, the good food, the Christmas parties, the Valentine's Ball, and "uh, we have only Lutheran services here, although we have guests of various faiths. We want everyone to attend some kind of religious services. Jeffrey may go to the synagogue if he desires to. We can arrange for someone to take him. I assure you that nobody on our staff will put any pressure on him.

"Down here is the little dining hall where the boys and girls eat together. We have only a half dozen boys and a few more girls. Up the hall is the boys' bathroom." He walked us inside where a washing machine and dryer stood between the toilet and the wall. "The staff wash the kids' clothes here. Cheaper than sending out."

As we came out of the bathroom, the Reverend called to a buxom red-haired lady of medium height, dressed in a white uniform and white shoes, walking casually down the hall.

"Oh, Mrs. Remaley, come and meet the newest member of our family. Grace Remaley is the house mother, Jeffrey. All the kids love her." He then turned to another lady of about the same height, also dressed in white, thin, with short white hair.

"And this is Mrs. Boyle, her aid," he said. I later learned that Jimmy Boyle, Ruth's husband, was head of the maintenance department.

"Hi, Jeffrey." Grace bent down and took my hook and spoke to me before she did to my parents. "You can call me, Grace. Everybody else does. We'll get along great, I'm sure. Have you seen your room?"

"No, we're just going there. Come along with us," the Reverend said.

"Oh, you're wondering where the other kids are," she continued as we walked along. "They're in the TV Room on the boys' side. You'll see them in a little while, Jeffrey. Gives us a little breather," she said in an aside to Mom who offered up a little smile.

My room looked quite different from Shriners, more like home. The walls were painted a pale institutional green, a plain orange spread neatly covered the bed that was to be mine. I glanced across at the other bed, with the stuffed animals piled below the pillows. Cats! And on the small dresser were cat pictures and figurines.

"Your roommate, Gary, loves cats, as you can see," Mrs. Remaley noted.

I saw Dad glance at his watch. "We'd better be getting on the road. We know you'll take good care of Jeffrey."

I followed them to the elevator, with Rev. Raker and Grace walking a discreet distance ahead.

"How long will I be here?" I asked.

"This is your home," Dad said, "but we'll be coming to see you, just as we did at Shriners. Maybe not as often, because of the distance."

"We'll come as often as we can, Jeffrey." Mom was trying to reassure me.

"I don't want to stay here," I insisted again. "I hate this place." I started sobbing again.

"Jeffrey, Mommy and I can't take care of you at home, and here you'll have friends and the best of care. We'll try and come and see you next Sunday afternoon." He bent down to hug and kiss me. Mom followed suit, kissed and hugged me good-bye.

"Do you promise you'll come and see me next Sunday?"

"We'll do our best. We can't make any promises. You be good for these people."

Rev. Raker was holding the elevator door open. I stood and watched them walk down the hall and get into the elevator, feeling hollow, abandoned, alone. Angry at the world.

Rev. Raker stepped in behind them and the door closed. I stood there a long time, fresh tears trickling down my face.

Finally I felt a tug at my shoulder. It was Grace. "Jeffrey, honey, they'll be back Sunday. Come on and let's put away your things. Then you can go in the TV room and meet the other kids."

I turned around and saw a window in a room that looked out to the street. Ignoring her, I shuffled there as fast as my bent leg and brace could carry me. There, there was the orange Pontiac. Now they were coming out of the building and crossing the street. Now they were getting in the car. Now they were driving away, farther away than they had ever been from me before. The awful finality hit me. This was not a hospital. It was a "home for the handicapped," and my parents intended for me to be here forever.

Mrs. Remaley gently put her arms around my shaking shoulders, her auburn hair brushing across my streaked face. "It'll be all right, Jeffrey. You'll get used to it. You'll make friends. There will be lots of things for you to do here. Let's go put away your clothes."

I walked with her into the room. She opened Grandmom's old bag and began taking out my clothes.

In frustration, I banged my hook against the wall. "I won't stay here! I won't! I hate this place."

Again, she came over and put her arms around me. "I understand, Jeffrey. I know you'd rather be at home. But you'll make new friends here. I'll be your friend."

A whoop pierced the hall. "Some of the kids are coming," she said.

I stood there shyly and defiantly as Grace introduced me to three of the boys. I met my roommate, Gary Smotherman, the cat freak, a dark-headed, slender kid with a butch haircut. He had muscular dystrophy, but could walk, though awkwardly, and many times his legs would give out from under him. Gregory Clements, with sandy blond hair and heavy build, also had muscular dystrophy, however, his condition was further advanced and he was confined to a wheelchair. Eddy Orlando, who stood tall and appeared to be "normal" until you took a close look at him, was harder to look at. Holes with little flippers were where his ears should have been, and his face was disfigured.

I was told that Eddie's father took one look at him at birth and walked out claiming that this "ugly" baby was not his child. I was also told that Eddie was taken from the hospital against the doctors' wishes by his mother, who informed hospital officials that if he was going to die, then he would die at home. He was raised mostly by his mother. She later remarried. Eddy attended school at the Home, but lived a few miles away with his family in a nearby twin community called Bethlehem, Pennsylvania.

Eddie was pushing Ricky Bachman in a wheelchair that had a tray in front. A polio victim, Ricky wore braces all the way up to his chest, with a corset around his waist. If it were possible for Ricky to stand he might have reached all of three feet tall. His hands flattened due to the polio, he could barely hold a spoon between his thumb and index fingers. Ricky smiled at me in a way that no kid ever had before. I didn't smile back. I was determined not to like anyone.

Mrs. Remaley busied herself straightening the clothes in my drawer. "If you're tired you can lie down and rest. Or you can go into the TV room with the others until supper."

Gary took me down and I sat there with about two or three other kids saying nothing. Ricky tried to make conversation, but I wasn't budging.

At 4:30, the supper bell rang. We all went down to the small dining room where the wheelchair kids clustered around one big table and walkers sat at the other. I was introduced to the girls who occupied the other end of the hall: Rachel, in a wheelchair, unable to speak due to cerebral palsy. Maxine, also in a wheelchair due to spina bifida. She had an enlarged head due to fluid on the brain at birth. Miriam, also in a wheelchair, whose speech was unclear due to CP. These were just a few of the girls. It appeared that I was one of two residents in the Baby Cottage that could walk.

A redheaded girl of about sixteen was helping Ricky cut his meat loaf. Grace saw me looking and called the girl over. "This is my daughter Lucy, Jeffrey. She comes in and helps me after school. My husband Bill works in another department, maintenance, so our whole family is here."

Lucy Ernst just said, "Hi," and went back to the wheelchair table. No apparent sympathy or concern for me.

A skinny girl, she had the same auburn red hair as her mother, a red discoloration on her left cheek, which I was informed was a birth mark, and a thorough dislike and distrust for the opposite sex. She had made it clear on many occasions that she would never marry. If I had a chip on my shoulder, and I did, then she carried the whole tree!

Grace clapped her hands. "OK, everybody, let's bow and say our grace."

They recited the prayer:

*Come Lord Jesus be our guest;*
*Let these Thy gifts to us be blessed.*

Grace saw my puzzled face. "This is how we thank God for our food. We also have a Psalm at the end of the meal. You don't have to join in, but I hope you will."

The Psalm sounded more Jewish:

*Bless the Lord, O my soul; and all that is within me, Bless his holy name. Bless the Lord, O my soul, and forget not all his benefits (Psalm 103:1, 2).*

After dinner we all went back to the TV room. A young man of about twenty-five, swinging on crutches, came to the couch where I was sitting and introduced himself as Curtis Peterson. He said he lived down the ramp in another part of the building with the men. I stared at him stonily, mumbling only what was absolutely necessary, determined not to be friendly. It wasn't easy, and my obstinacy did not last for very long. Soon, I was sitting on his lap, and deeply involved in whatever discussions and stories were going on. Curtis later became one of my best friends.

The next morning, I joined Eddy, Ricky, Gary, and the other kids in school. Mrs. Hoffman, the teacher, a merry little chirrupy woman with snow white hair, tried hard to get me involved. I just sat there staring daggers at her and anyone else who made attempts to be friendly, daring them to knock the chip off my shoulder.

That evening at supper, I sat there playing with my food while everybody else at my table finished. Suddenly, a shadow fell over me. "Start eating, Jeffrey."

I glared up at Lucy. "Mind your own business. You can't make me!"

"You are my business, now eat your food."

I raised my hook menacingly. "Try and make me."

"Stop it, both of you!" Her mother came running over. "Lucy, let me help Jeffrey." Grace pulled a chair up beside me and started asking questions, about my sisters, if I had ever gone to camp, what kind of TV shows I liked. After awhile, I looked down and my plate was clean. "I knew you were hungry," Grace said as she walked me back to the TV room.

Grudgingly, I fell into the routine. Breakfast, dash to brush my teeth, comb my hair, and get ready for school. I wanted to go in the GSH station wagon with a couple of kids who were allowed to attend public school.

"We'll have to wait and see how you get along here," Mrs. Hoffman said. For some of the kids like Gregory, who had muscular dystrophy, after school hours on alternating days there was physical therapy, where they would work with the lower extremities to get or keep them working. Others of us would attend art or ceramic classes in the occupational therapy department, where they also work to restore full use of the upper extremities. Using my mouth, I got to be pretty good on a typewriter and painting landscapes.

Saturday, we had a swarm of visitors. Some were folks who had heard about the Good Shepherd Home and wanted to see for themselves, while others were parents and family of the guests (That's what we were called instead of patients). I didn't expect my folks, though they had said that they would try to come Sunday afternoon.

Sunday morning began for all of us with breakfast, then Sunday school at the little red-brick storefront Mennonite church, less than a half block down Sixth Street. At approximately nine-thirty, between five and ten very pleasant men and women came to escort us (some to push those in wheelchairs, including Gary and Ricky) over to the church. The small auditorium looked so barren, compared to the Catholic church I had visited while a camper at the Variety Club camp.

Immediately upon arrival, I was greeted by a very pleasant lady and was asked my name and age. I was then taken and introduced to Erma and George Long. Erma, I was told, would be my Sunday school teacher. A direct opposite of their name, both George and Erma were short in stature and of somewhat stocky build.

George, you could easily tell at first glance, was a hard worker with traces of grease on his hands. He had a receding hairline with most of his deep brown hair in the center combed back and parted on the side. He appeared to be a man of few words, at first. At that first meeting, he seemed friendly enough, although in time I would come to know that he was a man who cared very deeply for me and could become quite animated, enjoying a good laugh or funny story with the best of us. He would appreciate and encourage talents and abilities that I could only dream of showing off.

Erma, on the other hand, though soft-spoken, was a much warmer and friendlier person, an almost motherly personality. She wore a plain dress with a matching bib, her dark brown hair, also parted on the side, pulled back, and rolled into a bun with a lace bonnet on the back of her head. I was told it was a prayer covering. George and Erma had one daughter, Dolores, also short and stocky, with long brown hair parted in the middle and combed into pigtails.

Dolores was about my age. I was told at that first meeting that she played the piano. She sat between her parents during the services.

The Sunday school began with an opening assembly. I entered the auditorium and walked somewhat awkwardly up the aisle trying to give the appearance of "normalcy," which is difficult enough for me to do, without trying. For that opening exercise, I sat close to the rear, still being uncertain of the situation. A tall and lean gentleman with blond hair hanging across his forehead, Henry Musselman, the song leader, walked up on the platform at the front and announced, "Let's start our worship this morning with, 'Leaning on the Everlasting Arms.' "

He took a small round wafer-like object with holes along the sides, from his pocket, which later I learned was a pitch-pipe, blew into it and sounded a single note. "Mmmmmmm," the leader intoned. "Mmmmmm."

"What a fellowship, what a joy divine. Leaning on the everlasting arms . . ."

There were only thirty or forty people in the little church, but could they sing! Boy, could they ever sing! They needed no instrumental accompaniment—their voices clear, enthusiastic, and their harmonies were perfect, almost angelic. The rhythm wasn't quite "American Bandstand," but it was happy singing. A warm feeling crept over me as I listened. I enjoyed the singing and realized that these were very special people. They were contented with themselves and their relationship to their God, though I still knew nothing of who God was or what he meant to them. They sang several little short songs—choruses, the song leader called them.

Then we were directed to our classes in another room, with Erma as our teacher, there were several other kids. She set up a display board she called a flannel graph. She slapped several cut-outs on the board of people in strange garb and started telling a Bible story. I loved it. I had never heard a Bible story before.

Following the Sunday school hour, those of us that wanted to could stay for the morning worship service at the Mennonite church, while the others were required to attend the Lutheran worship services, conducted in the main auditorium in Old Folks building at Good Shepherd Home. Those services were conducted by Rev. Raker, the superintendent.

I decided that I wanted to stay at the Mennonite church,
if I could sit with my new Sunday school teacher. The
pastor, a rather tall, hefty man named Al Detweiler, with
thick gray, almost white hair, slicked back, and wearing
black round glasses, read a long passage from the Bible in a
loud voice. Then he put the Bible down and started
"preaching" . . . loudly. I sat between Erma and George on
the right of the auditorium down near the front, almost
under his pulpit. He pointed a long bony index finger
my direction and shouted, "The Bible says, 'all have
sinned . . .' "

I jumped in fright. He walked up and down the platform
still preaching loudly for awhile, then he came back to the
pulpit and pointed that finger again. By this time I knew he
wasn't going to push it down my throat, so I busied myself
with reading Erma's Bible, beginning at the point where the
preacher left off. That became our Sunday morning routine.

It wasn't more than three or four weeks after that first
Sunday that Erma invited me to their home for lunch. This
would be the first of many such visits. She was a good cook,
and I always loved her pot roast and homemade creamed
corn. George was a mechanic at the Collegeville Farm
Equipment Company. After lunch one particular Sunday, he
took me there to give me a ride on one of the tractors. I sat
on his lap to ride.

"Can I drive the tractor?"

I saw George looking at my hook.

"I can hold the steering wheel, I know I can," I said.

"Well," he was a bit reluctant. But I was convinced I
could do it, and I believe I convinced him, too. Or, at least I
persisted to the point he was willing to let me try, if for no
other reason than to find out for himself. I would steer the
tractor, sitting on his lap, while he operated the throttle and
the brake. We were quite the team. Of course, to me, this
wasn't a tractor at all, this was a car and I was the driver in
my own car with my own driver's license.

As I mentioned, this was one of many visits for the day. I

went home with them for lunch, participated as a part of their family in reunions, trips such as the one to the Bowery Mission, a rescue mission in New York City, to participate in a special service, or just stayed at their house playing games. And then, they would take me back to the Home when they went back to church for the evening service. It was wonderful being wanted. I was somebody.

But this first Sunday after church, George and Erma took me back to Good Shepherd in time for Sunday dinner. They served us pork chops, mashed potatoes, gravy, and hot apple pie over a white tablecloth with a bouquet of fresh flowers in the center of each table.

I banged my fork on the tablecloth and hollered at Lucy at the next table. "Come and cut my meat."

She shot daggers back. "I don't respond to orders, Jeffrey. You say, 'Please, come and cut my meat,' in a nice way."

"Not to you, I don't. You don't work here." She was a volunteer.

"Then you can very well get somebody else to slice up your old meat."

Lucy's mother moved in to break up our little fight and cut my meat.

Grace asked if Mom and Dad were coming for a visit.

"Yeah, Dad promised to come this afternoon. I don't know what time."

"After dinner, you go in the TV room and wait," she said.

Ricky and I had become pretty good friends by this time. He asked me to push his wheelchair there.

"Are your parents coming, too?" I asked him.

"They never come," he said sadly. "I just thought I would wait with you."

My folks brought all three of my sisters. Sheryl, almost eight, came running from the elevator to give me a hug. Linda was fourteen. She pecked me on the cheek as Mom always did. My baby sister, Harriet, now two years old, toddled toward me, trying unsuccessfully to say my name.

They didn't stay long. While the girls wandered around looking things over, Mom and I exchanged a little chitchat. Then Dad quizzed me about my activities and if I liked Good Shepherd Home.

"It's OK, but I'd rather be home with you and Mom and my sisters. How long do I have to stay here?" I knew the answer without waiting, but held on to a glimmer of hope.

He handed me the same old routine. "This is the best place for you, Jeffrey. You know your mother can't care for you."

We talked about the other kids, like Eddie, Ricky, and Gary and the school. I told them about Sunday school and my teacher, and I told them about Lucy. I didn't like her and I knew she didn't think much of me. After they left, I rushed to the window to watch the old Pontiac drive down St. John Street. I stood there, face pressed against the glass, a long time after they had left.

Then I heard strange voices and turned to see a tall, elegantly dressed woman come in with a couple of very pretty teenage girls, one blonde and the other dark-haired, who could have walked right off a magazine cover. The woman was gorgeous! She took a book from her bag and sat down on one of the couches. The blonde girl wheeled Ricky over to where a couple of other boys had already gathered around the woman I presumed to be the mother. She began reading a story. Ricky, leaning across the tray over his wheelchair, was beaming.

I stood there, eyes on the floor, frowning and pretending not to be interested. Finally, I edged over in curiosity, and she stopped reading.

"Hi, you're Jeffrey, aren't you?" she said.

I nodded, melting a little under her smile.

"I'm Wanda Gensemer and these are my daughters, Patricia, the blonde, and the other one is Jo Ann."

"Her name isn't Wanda, it's Quacky," Ricky piped. "That was her camp name last summer."

"I went to camp once," I volunteered stiffly.

"Oh, did you?" the lady said, wryly. "I'm sure you had fun."

"Yeah. I played softball and went swimming. It was called the Variety Club Camp. What's the name of your camp? And who can go to your camp?" I was trying to be hard to get, still playing the wise guy, but inside afraid of being alone.

"Oh, it isn't until next summer." Quacky continued cordially. "It isn't my camp, the Easter Seal Society sponsors it for handicapped kids. My Girl Scouts and I just help out. I'm sure you can go. It's called Camp-With-A-Grin."

"That's a dumb name."

"Uh, yes, well, let me finish our story. You're welcome to come over and we can talk later." I was still standing across the room at the window, keeping my distance.

My armor was pierced. I slowly eased closer and listened to the end of the story and hung around afterwards. She even said I could call her "Quacky." And her daughters were so nice! Not at all like Lucy.

Before leaving, Quacky gave me her phone number. "Any time you want to talk, Jeffrey, just call me up."

"Yeah," I breathed. "Maybe I will."

Quacky had won my heart.

# CHAPTER SIX
· · · · · · · · · ·
# QUACKY

My family came to visit me the next three Sunday afternoons, then skipped the following Sunday. Dad called to say not to expect them. "Sunday afternoon is the only time I have off," he said, "I hope you understand, Jeffrey." I didn't.

During my second year at Good Shepherd they came once every couple of months. They didn't write much either.

On one of the times they did come, Mom talked to me more than usual. She said she was singing in a musical for the Variety Club.

"Sing something for me, Mom?" I asked, extending in my hook the microphone of a little tape recorder that one of Good Shepherd's benefactors had given me.

I'll never forget it. She opened her mouth and sang, "The Shadow of Your Smile." I sat there entranced, listening to her beautiful alto voice, watching the little blinking light on the tape recorder, making sure that I got it all.

After they left, I played the song back over and over.

"Hey, that's my mom singing," I told everybody. "Isn't she terrific?"

When they didn't show up again for several weeks, I got this bright idea of taking Mom a gift for Mother's Day. I found an employee of Good Shepherd who would drive me to Philadelphia and back.

Grace said I could go, but she advised, "Be sure and call before you leave. Your parents might not be home."

I phoned and Dad answered the phone. I told him about my ride and that I wanted to surprise Mom. He didn't sound too thrilled.

"Mommy hasn't been feeling well lately, Jeffrey. She wouldn't be up for company. You better make it another time."

"She doesn't want me to bring her a gift for Mother's Day, or does she just not want me to come?"

"Jeffrey, I told you, she isn't feeling well."

"Dad, I want to come."

"No, Jeffrey." Then in a softer voice, "There will be other chances to visit."

My ego was bruised, the hurt constricted my throat.

I went back to my room to cry, and lay on the bed a long while.

I waited a whole month before telephoning again.

On another occasion, in August, my birthday was on a Sunday afternoon and I arranged it with George and Erma to take a Sunday afternoon drive to Philadelphia to surprise my parents by visiting for my birthday. The only possible hitch was that they might be coming to visit me at Good Shepherd for my birthday. I decided to risk it.

This time no one knew except the Longs. However, this time the surprise was on me. Surprise is a mild word for what happened. When we arrived at the house, 1823 Placid Street, they were not home. They had not gone to Allentown for my birthday. Instead they took a leisurely drive to New Jersey! Why? Had they forgotten. . . ? My sister Harriet and Grandmom were the only ones at the house. Grandmom talked and visited with us for a while, telling George how much she loved me and letting them know how she felt about the way my father had handled the situation from the beginning. She gave them an earful, and most of it was hostile toward my father. Now she was upset because they were somewhere else on my birthday. I felt hollow inside, forgotten, and angry. I would have understood if they had gone to Allentown, but they had not. This was the ultimate insult. I had tried to ignore the comments of those who wanted me to believe that my parents wanted me out of the way, that they didn't want me or love me. But here I was with all the proof I needed. I just didn't want it to be true.

No one made any comment on the way home. I didn't know whether to yell in anger or cry.

The next day, I received a birthday card signed in my mother's handwriting, *Love Mom & Dad, Linda, Sheryl, Harriet, and Grandmom.* Inside the card was a check for $25. I did not want money. I wanted them! I wanted to be wanted! Loved! Important and special. All of the things I couldn't be.

Later that day, I went downstairs and talked to the social worker, Mrs. Wilcox. I told her everything about the situation that I knew and how badly I wanted to go home.

"Could you call Dad—help him understand how I feel?" I pleaded.

"Sure." She smiled.

Dad really let her have it. He let her know that Good Shepherd was not to let me come to Philadelphia until they were ready for me. "His mother is not up to it," he warned. "She could have another breakdown that would send her to the hospital."

"Couldn't Jeffrey come for just an afternoon? We have a very responsible person to drive him."

"No," Dad thundered back, "and I wish you wouldn't permit Jeffrey to call here unless it's a real emergency."

The social worker sugarcoated Dad's ultimatum, but I

saw that I wasn't wanted. I cried far into the night. Ricky tried to brighten me up, but this time he couldn't.

I survived until the next Sunday when George and Erma Long took me out to their home for the afternoon. George lifted me up in his lap and let me steer the tractor with my hook, again. Boy, did I feel like a million bucks!

When they brought me back to Good Shepherd, I called Quacky. "Hey, could you, do you mind?" I pressed. I told her about my visit home. "I need someone to talk to. Well, uh, Ricky said he'd like to see you, too."

She was a wonderful listener, and very supportive. Quacky came when she could. "I'll be there in twenty minutes, Jeffrey. I'll ask them to let me take you boys out to get some ice cream."

I trotted down the hall to tell Ricky. By the time she got there I had pushed Ricky in his wheelchair downstairs and signed us out. I had learned that you didn't have to ask twice to go somewhere with Quacky. Everybody at Good Shepherd knew and trusted her.

Monday morning always came and with it another week to face. It wasn't like Shriners. Good Shepherd had a small staff of doctors, nurses, therapists, and counselors. The two doctors didn't come on rounds and stand by our beds, discussing all the horrible things wrong with us. Nor did a nurse saunter into the room without knocking and puncture your anatomy with needles. We did get regular checkups and treatments for minor problems. For surgery or some other major need they sent us to the Allentown General Hospital.

The extent and frequency of therapy depended on the handicap. The staff spent more time on Ricky than me, although I had to do leg exercises twice a week, and I was expected to participate in occupational therapy as well as keep up my schoolwork.

Nobody made a big deal of our handicaps at Good Shepherd. The Home was our home, and we were treated as family, and encouraged to do all that we could for ourselves. Jimmy Johnson, a teenager with severe cerebral palsy, typed with a stylus attached to a band around his head. Billy Lupold, who had CP and had little or no use of his arms, did marvelous sketches of famous people by manipulating a brush with his toes. Billy was a perfectionist and sometimes did a dozen or more drawings of a subject before he got what he wanted. Mrs. Watkins, his teacher, sent his sketch of the president to the White House. A few days later he got a personal letter of thanks signed, "John F. Kennedy." The news was all over Good Shepherd in an hour. Bill Anderson, who had no arms or legs, took up sign painting, holding the brush between his shoulder and jaw. He was awarded the Pennsylvania State Employee of the Year trophy.

We didn't sit around thinking of ourselves as the poor, unfortunate handicapped. Too often, people view the handicapped only in the light of the physical accessories needed to help them to be normal. Ricky Bachman was more than a wheelchair and braces. Curtis Petersen, who came over almost every evening from the men's quarters to watch TV, wasn't just a pair of crutches and two somewhat lame legs. There was more to Jeff Steinberg than a hook and a brace with an extra foot. To many, I was Jeffrey, often loudmouthed, obnoxious and pushy, trying to get attention. But to me, I was more. Jeffrey Steinberg, with big plans and dreams, a lot of determined potential just waiting, sometimes impatiently, to be unleashed.

In occupational therapy I learned to type more proficiently with a pen in my mouth, took ceramics classes and art classes. I learned to paint landscapes holding a brush between my teeth. Under the supervision and training of Mrs. Whitherow, my art instructor, I painted four 8″ x 10″ oil paintings, "free-mouth." On one occasion, we had an art show, and I was offered $100 for one of my pictures. I was flattered and thrilled that someone liked my work enough to want to pay for it; I liked my pictures too much to sell. I did enjoy showing my work. What eleven-year-old kid doesn't like to show off? I knew I wasn't dumb. Actually, I thought I was pretty smart.

I always felt that there was nothing I couldn't do if I

wanted to badly enough. I might have to work a little harder, or find an alternative way to get the job done, but if I persisted I would succeed. All too often we quit at the threshold of success. Years later I found that the Welfare Department psychologist, who tested me periodically, agreed. She wrote on my record:

*Jeffrey is an alert, outgoing youngster. He's extremely extroverted, personable, and does not seem to miss a trick.*

I didn't miss a trick, nor would I be left out of anything if I had my way.

I hated to be patronized, even by well-meaning people. I remember one such "goodbody" visitor, an elderly lady, about ninety-nine years old, patting me on my hard little head and clucking, "Tch, tch, you poor child."

"Don't feel sorry for me," I replied sarcastically, "I'm a young man and you have one foot in the grave!" She was none too thrilled. In fact, she was indignant.

Rev. Raker didn't like people pitying us either. He often said, "I wish the word 'cripple' could be stricken from the English language."

Everyone around the Home called him, "Dr. Raker," since he had been given an honorary Doctor of Divinity by a Lutheran college. I learned that he could act up and joke around with the best of us. One day, he answered the hall telephone in the girls' building with a Brooklyn accent, "Kelly's Pool Hall." The voice on the other end was the Chairman of the Board, Tilghman G. Fenstermacher. We all cracked up laughing, and Ricky almost fell out of his wheelchair.

During my first five years at Good Shepherd, Dr. Raker was administrator, public relations man, fund raiser, social worker, chaplain, and surrogate parent all rolled into one. It was easy to see when he was around us that the latter was his most enjoyable role.

He would put his strong arm around your shoulder and

you would feel secure, or he would whack you on the back like your best friend, only, you felt his "friendship" long after he left. Ouch! Whenever possible he would listen, and really care when you talked to him. You could tell that he hurt when parents didn't write, call, or visit one of his kids for months at a time.

I felt hurt for the way I thought my parents had avoided me, but I knew other kids with more to complain about. Johnny Wilkerson, paralyzed from the waist down and seven years older than myself, didn't know where any of his relatives lived until he learned about a cousin in Baltimore. The cousin gave him the address of his mother in New York. Johnny got someone to take him there. They arrived to find that his mother's apartment was on the third floor of a building with no elevators. John's friend went up to tell her that her son was downstairs. She refused to come down and see him.

Dr. Raker had heard too many such stories to be surprised anymore. "Someone who doesn't have the capacity to care," he remarked, "is more greatly handicapped than someone without arms or legs."

A blue collar residential neighborhood of row houses surrounded Good Shepherd. Dr. Raker encouraged us to make friends in the neighborhood. Any of us, he said, could bring a friend back to dinner at no charge.

One afternoon a bunch of us were sitting on a porch across from the traffic signal at the intersection of St. John and Sixth. Some of our neighborhood friends, including Jerry Zinner, a former orphaned resident, thought it would be great fun to sit in wheelchairs awhile. They would help those handicapped guys, who were able, to get out of their wheelchairs and sit on the steps in the front of the main building. They then got in their chairs and pretended to be crippled.

A middle-aged woman with her hair in a thick bun stopped to wait for the light to change and glanced our way. Her focus caught the boys in wheelchairs. "You poor, poor children," she clucked. "May the Lord bless you poor creatures." Jerry had an inspiration and lifted his arms and eyes skyward. "I see the light!" he shouted, as he slowly rose from the chair to stand upright.

The woman's mouth widened and eyes bulged. "Glory, Hallelujah! It's a miracle!" The light turned green and she kept hollering. The drivers behind her began honking. Jerry danced around, still shouting, "I see the light! I see the light!"

Dr. Raker didn't approve of such irreverent shenanigans, but he sympathized with our reaction to pity.

The neighborhood was considered safe and no one counted noses until supper. Then, if a staff member noticed a kid missing, he would tell Dr. Raker, who lived in a house on the corner. Dr. Raker would start calling around the neighborhood until he located his charge.

One evening I came up missing. "Where's Jeffrey? Have you seen Jeffrey?" Dr. Raker kept asking. Finally, he walked out on the street to look for me. He found me standing in the intersection at St. John and Sixth waving my hook up and down and playing traffic cop. His face reddened and he yelled, "Jeffrey Steinberg! Get out of that street!"

"Just a minute, Dr. Raker," I yelled back, motioning for the cars to stop in front of me. I calmly walked across the street to where he was standing. "Did you want me for something, Dr. Raker?"

I thought he would explode.

Dr. Raker knew everybody who was anybody in Allentown, a city of more than 100,000, and everybody knew him. He had friends always on the lookout for any big celebrity or political figure who came into town. These friends brought the VIP straight to Good Shepherd to meet us. I met Pennsylvania Governor David L. Lawrence, novelist Pearl S. Buck, cowboy stars Dale Evans and Roy Rogers, band leader Lawrence Welk, and many other famous names.

Roy and Dale came to the Sunday morning Lutheran

services at Good Shepherd. Lawrence Welk and members of his band entertained in the auditorium.

I sat by Dr. Raker when Welk and his group performed. When they finished their first number, I leaned over and whispered dramatically, "Dr. Raker, you should be on TV, too."

"Arrumph, you think so, Jeffrey?" He threw his shoulders back and straightened his tie. "You really think so?"

"Yeah."

"Why?"

I turned my mouth up at him and grinned, "So I could turn you off."

His face fell a foot.

Dr. Raker's and Good Shepherd's biggest day came on the summer anniversary of the founding of Good Shepherd by his father in 1908. The Allentown Parks Department put up a big tent on the lot across St. John Street from the Home and trucked in hundreds of folding chairs. The Allentown City Band played, politicians made speeches, special guests were honored, and Dr. Raker talked about how wonderful we Good Shepherd residents were and how much we appreciated the financial support from the community.

The women and girls wore Sunday dresses and men and boys decked out in suits and ties, with a little help from the staff, who rolled the wheelchair people along the front. A few of us were drafted as tour guides. I enjoyed that. It allowed me to meet a lot of people and feel like a big shot.

I usually sat just in back of Ricky and beside Curtis Petersen. Curtis was older than Ricky and I put together and suffered from spina bifida and arthritis. He couldn't use his legs and walked swinging on crutches. Even with arthritic hands, he was a fair artist and a mediocre piano player. He was a classical music buff, and while he knew a lot of theory, his arthritic finger would not allow him much flexibility and skill. He brushed his hair up in the style of Elvis Presley and raised it high over the forehead in a slicked back pompadour. Curtis had been at Good Shepherd since he was a small child. I guessed he knew everything there was to know about the Home.

Dr. Raker told about the founding of the home by his father. Curtis sat there knowingly, anticipating every word, as Dr. Raker related the story in his usual formal manner:

*My late father was a Lutheran minister who took in orphan children at a place not far from here. One day a woman came to him in tears saying her husband and seventeen-year-old son had been killed in a railroad accident and her fourteen-year-old boy crippled. She begged him to take the crippled boy, since she had to work and couldn't care for him. But Dad had to say no because the state charter for his orphanage wouldn't allow him to take in handicapped children.*

*Dad never forgot the look on that mother's face. Later he accepted a pastorate in this neighborhood, with the understanding that if he ever had the opportunity to care for handicapped children, the congregation would let him do so.*

*Before I was born he and Mother had a little daughter named Viola who was taken to the Heavenly Father when she was just three months old. Dad and Mother had come home from the funeral home and were trying to console one another when the mailman brought a letter from a pastor who knew they were interested in handicapped children. "I have a little crippled girl in my church whose mother has died," the pastor said. "She has nowhere to go. Could you folks take her in?"*

*The pastor happened to mention that the crippled girl's name was Viola. Dad and Mother thought that providential. They took her to raise as their own child. When news got around, people began asking him to take other handicapped children. He and my mother couldn't handle them all in the parsonage, so Dad located an old farmhouse on the spot where our main building is today, which he could buy for $7,500. About that same time a man handed Dad a half dollar, saying that was all he could give, but he wanted it to go for the home for crippled children. Dad took that coin and*

* * * * * * * * * * * * * * * * * * * * * * * * * * * * * *

*on faith signed an agreement to buy the farmhouse. That's
why we say Good Shepherd was founded on faith and fifty
cents.*

*It wasn't long until people began bringing handicapped
adults, some of them very old. As long as he had a bed, Dad
wouldn't turn anybody away. The home grew very rapidly
and kept growing until today we're caring for 180, from
babies still in cribs to some adults in their nineties. We're
doing as much as we can, but we desperately need
additional facilities to better provide for them and help more
people.*

Dr. Raker was at this time, the early 1960s, trying to
raise $730,000 for a modern rehabilitation center and
convalescent hospital to be built on the property between
the main building and the Old Folks' Building facing
St. John Street. Besides limited medical facilities, it would
include departments for hydrotherapy, physical and
occupational therapy, pre-vocational testing, vocational
counseling, audio and speech therapy, prosthetic and
orthotic areas, classrooms and an "Activities of Daily
Living" apartment where handicaps could learn to care for
themselves before moving into their own home in society.

"We don't intend to care for all the handicapped for the
rest of their lives," Dr. Raker said. "Of course, we'll always
have room for those who must have custodial care or have
nowhere else to go. But our main thrust will be to prepare
residents to leave Good Shepherd and become producing
members of society."

Curtis wasn't happy about the advances of Good
Shepherd. "I guess Good Shepherd has to change with the
times. Still, I don't like it. There will be more machines,
more people with fancy titles, more rules, and less of the
family atmosphere that we enjoy now."

"Don't you think Good Shepherd ought to be getting
people ready to leave?" I asked. "When I finish school, I'd
like to go out on my own."

"Sure, but some of us will never leave. Even if we could,

we've become too dependent on the institution. I tried living by myself in an apartment once. I had a job, operating an answering service. I couldn't make it. I was too institutionalized. I asked them to let me come back here."

I thrust forth my chin. "I'm going to make it. I'm not spending the rest of my life in this place."

"I hope you can. Just don't wait as long as I did."

Curtis and I were a strange pair. He was much taller and older and swinging on his crutches. I hobbled beside him, dragging my stiff right leg up to follow my left. Saturday mornings, we hitched a ride into downtown Allentown. We window shopped along Hamilton Street, the main drag, then poked around in the Liberty Bell Museum in the basement of the old Zion Reformed Church. Allentown's main claim to historical fame is hiding the Liberty Bell which was secretly brought from Philadelphia during the Revolutionary War to prevent it from falling into the hands of the British.

Curtis had an oddball sense of humor. Once when we were walking downtown, he caught his crutch in a sewer grate and tripped, falling backwards on the sidewalk. A passerby saw him and asked, "What are you doing down there, young man?"

"Lady, I always wanted to see the city from this angle," Curtis retorted, "and now's my opportunity."

Curtis believed that the funniest part of the world is in us. We can take ourselves too seriously and become almost paranoid, or we can laugh at ourselves and get on with becoming. Maybe I acquired my sense of humor and perspective from him.

Curtis had quite a few years on me. I was still maturing. For one thing, it irritated me to have people stare. I noticed that if I looked back, an adult would turn his head and pretend not to have seen me. A child would keep right on staring. One day a fellow who was old enough to know better kept his eyes riveted on me. I turned around and yelled, "Take a picture. It'll last longer." That turned his eyeballs over.

I was caustic and sarcastic with a lot of people, especially

• • • • • • • • • • • • • • • • • • • • • • • • • • • • •

Lucy Ernst, the house mother's redheaded daughter. One evening at supper I snapped at her, "Why don't you get married and go away and leave me alone?"

"Nobody would have me!" she shot back in mock hurt.

I hit the ball right back. "No wonder, the way you act." I could be cruel, too.

Strangers didn't quite know how to take me. It was fun catching new people off guard. Like an elderly couple, Mr. and Mrs. Roy Houseman, who came over one Sunday afternoon and invited me to go for a drive with them. Mrs. Houseman stood a very thin six feet tall, and had snow-white hair. She must have been at least one hundred and ten years old! I was always ready to go anywhere to get out of the Home. We were heading down the hall toward the elevator when I saw the door starting to close. I ran and stuck out my hook between the door and the wall. Slam! "Yeooooww! Yeooooww!" You could have heard me scream in New Jersey.

The woman turned white. "Jeffrey, Jeffrey, are you all right?"

"Yeah," I said, "but I think I bent my fingers."

My craziness didn't seem to faze her husband, but the poor woman could have died of cardiac arrest. They soon got used to my sense of humor and we became very close friends. I went out with the Housemans on many Sunday afternoons since then. Dr. Raker saw that everybody got out as often as possible. He and Mrs. Raker had a farm outside of the city which they used as a retreat from Good Shepherd. One special Saturday they took us all on a bus to "Raker's Acres" for a picnic. We had been told we could go swimming in the spring pond that was reputed to be 187 feet deep. I jumped in with an inner tube and Dr. Raker almost keeled over in fright. It was sheer bedlam before the counselors could get things organized.

Just as Quacky promised, I got to go to Camp-With-A-Grin, held in a park along the Lehigh River. According to custom, they divided all the handicapped kids into units with each choosing the group's name. My bunch of about twenty decided to call ourselves "Pirates." Quacky was our unit leader with her Girl Scout troop, including daughters Jo Ann and Pat, serving as counselors.

"Oh, good," she said when she chose the name the Pirates' Den. She probably planned on getting rid of the name "Quacky."

"No such luck!" I yelled back. "We can call you 'Captain Quacky!' " She was always "Quacky" while I was at Good Shepherd, and she will always be Quacky to me.

After camp she brought her group over to her house for cake and ice cream. We met her husband, "Speed," who worked for the Mack Truck Company, a quiet man, extremely devoted to television sports, and a very special guy for sharing his family with us.

After the refreshments, we went across the street to a playground for a softball game. A Girl Scout stood behind me and helped me swing the bat. Another Girl Scout ran for me. Hooray for the Girl Scouts!

During the weeks before Christmas, local businesses and service clubs hosted parties for Good Shepherd residents. The deejays of Radio Station WAEB, for example, came and distributed gifts which listeners had paid for, then they presented a two-hour show of music and interviews, "Christmas at the Good Shepherd Home."

Oh, man, did I love it! I had no trouble talking before a mike. I asked if I could do it again and the deejays—Kerm Gregory, Jay Sands, Don Bruce, Joe McLaine, and Ernie Stiegler—all said, "Sure. Come on down this summer. We'll be doing a remote at Dorney Park Amusement Park." They even promised to let me read a commercial.

Curtis, Ricky and I took the transit bus. I announced records and read a pitch for the Holiday Inn.

"Terrific," Kerm Gregory said, clapping me on the back. "Do another one."

One evening I came back late by myself and found Dr. Raker wearing a frown. "Jeffrey, we don't mind occasional trips away from the home, but this is getting to be too much of a habit. The staff feels responsible for you and when they can't find you in the building or in the neighborhood, they begin to worry. We didn't know where you were tonight until somebody said, 'Turn on WAEB.' There you were, giving a commercial!"

I handed him a big smile. "Aren't you proud of me, Dr. Raker?"

"Yes, I'm proud, but we're responsible to your parents. From now on, get permission to go and get back at the expected time."

Our biggest social event at Good Shepherd came on Valentine's Day when the Student Council of the Good Shepherd School sponsored the Winter Ball. The girls and women came in long dresses, the boys and men in tuxes or dark suits and ties. No one was too young or old or too handicapped to come. There was music and dancing and we elected a King and Queen for a Night.

When I was twelve, the Ball featured a Caribbean "limbo" dance in which the dancers try to pass beneath a crossbar at varying heights to the tempo of fast music. People were ducking and screaming, wheelchairs whirring, and crutches clacking, as the music played. It was wild and hilarious.

The next year, I called Quacky, "Hey, how about letting Jo Ann come to the ball with me and you come with Curtis? Do you think that will be OK with Speed?"

"I'm honored that you'd ask me," she trilled. "I'll ask Speed and call you back."

He said, "OK!" Quacky drove herself and Jo Ann down. Curtis came out with me following. Balancing on one crutch, he opened the car door for them, then the two of us walked our "dates" into the recreation room where the Ball was being held. Jo Ann was gorgeous and stole the show. "And you look terrific," I told Quacky.

After the ball, Quacky took us out to eat. Wow! We had a wonderful time.

Years later I learned that Quacky and Speed had lost their first child, a boy. Maybe she saw in me a little of the son they couldn't keep. Maybe her interest came because she is just naturally a caring person. Maybe it was because she and I could communicate so well. She always knew what I was thinking before I said it and I could read her mind pretty well, too.

Wanda and Clarence Gensemer had a beautiful home in a nice neighborhood. She had a good husband, two gorgeous daughters, and a lot of wonderful friends. She had a full life without coming over to the Good Shepherd Home so much. Still, she dropped everything and came whenever I needed her.

If Jo Ann or Pat couldn't come with her, Quacky drove over by herself, leaving poor Speed to watch the ball game. Every week or so, as often as I dared, I'd call the Gensemer house and say, "Quacky, this place is driving us crazy. Can you come and get us out of here?" "Us" being Ricky and me, or Curtis and me, but I was usually the instigator.

She'd say, "Hold tight, I'll be there in a few minutes. Meet me downstairs."

I gave Ricky's wheelchair a push and we raced to the curving ramp that descended at a pretty steep grade from the second to the first floor. At the top of the ramp, I jumped on behind the chair. "Geronimo!" we screamed. "Wheeee! Lookout, here we come." Anybody coming up the ramp would have thought we were going to crash, but we never did.

We seldom had long to wait. Quacky would get out of her car and lift Ricky from his chair and into the front seat. "Oooh! Aahhhh!" he complained, pretending she was hurting him, sometimes before he was even touched. "Ooooh!" I squirmed in beside him. And away we went to MacDonald's or some other favorite spot.

Wanda "Quacky" Gensemer was a gracious lady and my local "Mom" all the years I was in Good Shepherd. I could always count on her. She helped fill the aching void left by the long absences of my real parents.

She never asked for anything in return except the opportunity to share and give her love.

God bless Wanda Gensemer, always Quacky.

CHAPTER SEVEN
· · · · · · · · · · · ·

# SPIRITUALLY SPEAKING

*"O little town of Bethlehem, how still we see thee lie . . ."*

The Bethlehem I knew was neither little nor still—
Bethlehem, Pennsylvania, with its great steel furnaces
belching smoke and fire, adjoined Allentown.

Quacky and her family lived in Bethlehem. On the first
Sunday of Christian Advent, a switch was thrown and the
city suddenly glowed with 85,000 glittering white lights.
Above the banks of lights, the great Star of Bethlehem
beamed down on us from South Mountain. The lights and
the star could be seen for many miles around, but every
Christmas I wanted to see them up close.

"Quacky, can you take us to see the lights?" I asked. I was
surrounded by names and symbols from the New
Testament. Towns named Bethlehem, Nazareth, and
Emmaus. Stately, steepled Moravian churches rooted in pre-
revolutionary America. Choirs caroled for us on the nights
before Christmas, beginning at the bottom of the ramps and

circling up to sing along the hallways until they were just outside our rooms.

The next morning, I was awakened with shouts of, "Merry Christmas," and more singing. Then after breakfast, we hurried down to the tree to unwrap our gifts.

For Easter, the great Christmas Star on South Mountain was converted into a cross. At night, I could look across the rooftops and see this shining symbol of the Messiah's victory over death. There was just no way I could escape the testimonials of Jesus, whom Christians acclaimed as the Messiah and the Savior of the world.

The church visitors came on Saturdays and Sunday afternoon. One type would pat me on the head and cluck, "You poor child. God bless you," as if to show forth their spirituality and Christian love.

I hated it every time one of these well-intentioned self-righteous "saints" reached out a hand to mess up my hair. I'm amazed that their Christian love shows but once or twice a year for a fifteen minute tour, but is never there to ease the hurt or pick you up when you've fallen.

A second kind carried a ninety-seven pound Bible and beat you over the head until you repented in utter exhaustion.

"Jeffrey, do you know what the Bible says about you?"

"Nope. What does it say?"

"Read this verse on which I have my finger, 'For all have sinned and come short of the glory of God.' That's from Paul's Epistle to the Romans in the inspired Word of God."

"All includes you, doesn't it, Jeffrey?"

"I guess so. If you say so."

"What does it mean to sin, Jeffrey?"

"I don't know. Be bad, I guess,"

"Have you ever done anything bad? Like lie to your house mother or say something mean to a friend?"

I twisted around to see my roommate, Gary, who was sitting on his bed, trying to look solemn. He offered no solace.

"God knows you've sinned, Jeffrey."

"Not me!" I egged him on.

"Do you know where sinners go when they die, young man?"

"To Philadelphia?" I cracked.

"Jeffrey, you're not being serious! Sinners go to hell! You don't want to go to hell, do you? Wouldn't you rather go to heaven and be with Jesus?"

I shook my head no.

"Jeffrey?"

"I don't want to go to either place right away. I'd rather go to Philadelphia." I was pretty determined not to let him have the last word.

"Well, you could die at any time. Tonight, even."

"I don't think so. I'm only ten years old. But, I suppose it's possible."

He read to me about Jesus dying on the cross for sinners.

"Jesus was the Jewish Messiah, Jeffrey. Did you know that most of the Jews rejected him?"

"They did? I'm a Jew."

"You're Jewish? That's wonderful! You're one of God's chosen people."

"That's what I've been told."

"Oh, Jeffrey, you're one of God's very, very special people. A member of the chosen race."

"Well, what do you know. Hey, Ricky, I belong to the chosen race. Do you belong to the chosen race?"

"Jeffrey, you're not being serious again. Whether you're a Jew or Gentile, you need to be saved."

"Saved? Saved from what?"

"Saved from sin, as I just read to you. Jesus will save you, if you'll repent of your sins and invite him into your heart. Would you like to do that, Jeffrey?"

By this time, I was willing to do a cartwheel, anything to get rid of the pest.

"Yeah, I guess so."

"Very good. Then bow your head and repeat this prayer after me . . . "

I repeated the words because that was what he wanted me

to do and doing what he wanted me to do was the fastest
and easiest way to get rid of him. He gave me a couple of
tracts and said, "I'll come by and pick you up Sunday
morning and take you to my church. We have a fine
Sunday school class for you and you can talk to the pastor
about being baptized. Will you be ready?"

"Well, no, uh, I've promised Mr. and Mrs. Long I'd go to
the Mennonite church with them."

"Oh, you did. Well, that's wonderful. Be sure and tell
them what you did this afternoon. How you prayed to
receive Jesus as your Savior. You won't forget that, will
you?"

"Nope. I guess not."

"You 'guess not.' You'd better not."

Then with a pat on the head and a shake of my hook, he
was gone.

I had a lot of visitors like that. I went to church with
some of them and that brought more people back to see me.
Good, well-intentioned Christians who tried to help me
from the Bible. I understood in my head what they were
saying, but not in my heart. I said the words they wanted to
hear in hopes they would go away and leave me alone.

Quacky attended an Episcopal church, she said, but she
never tried to evangelize me. That I was Jewish didn't
make any difference with her. She loved me for who I was.
Dr. Raker didn't make any distinction between the three
of us who were Jewish at Good Shepherd and the Gentile
residents. It was quite all right with him for me to attend
Jewish services, but no one ever offered to take me. As it
was, I attended different churches with people who took the
trouble to pick me up.

David Esh was one of several Mennonite and Amish
young men who worked at Good Shepherd, serving their
country in that type of work in lieu of military combat duty
because of their religious convictions. Once a year, David's
parents had the Good Shepherd family out for a picnic
at their farm, about fifty miles south of Allentown in a

small Pennsylvania Dutch farming community called
Churchtown.

The Eshes were "old order" Amish. They did have indoor
plumbing, thanks to the windmill that they assembled to
pump water, though they had no electricity or telephone.
They lit their way with gasoline lanterns in the barn and
lamps in the house; however, having no phone did not stop
them from catching all of the latest gossip.

David's father prayed and read the Bible at the end of the
day. With his thin long white beard, wide-brimmed black
hat, and tenor voice and stooped shoulders, he reminded me
of a biblical prophet. Though Dave's father and mother
belonged to the "old order" Amish, an extremely
conservative denomination, and drove horse and buggy
everywhere, Dave, at an early age "kicked the traces," and
joined a more progressive Mennonite church nearby. Davey
and I became close friends. It was special having a friend
right there that I could confide in, and we talked about
everything. In addition, I went home with Davey several
weekends and attended services with his family.

In 1964, Dave and his family chartered a bus, took the
Home's old pickup truck, and gathered a bunch of the guys
and girls along with the staff and some of our neighborhood
friends and took us to a giant town picnic at the Esh farm.
The whole community of Churchtown was there to help
serve food, provide hayrides, and just become friends. We
were then told about the time in 1961 when the Esh barn
burned to the ground and in seven days was rebuilt and
painted because of the "community" spirit of the neighbors.
The men would build and paint while the women cooked
and cleaned. Whenever there was a need or cause, they were
always ready to come together to help. Now they came
together for us. They wanted to show us a good time out in
the fresh air on the farm. And they did. It became an
annual treat for several years.

During my years at Good Shepherd, I went to the
Mennonite Church on Sixth Street more than anywhere

else. I sang "This Little Light of Mine" loudly along with the rest. When we came to the part, "I'm gonna let it shine all over Allentown," I waved my hook in the air as they waved their hands. Their beautiful a capella singing, rich with harmony, was very much a part of their tradition, but I didn't fully understand why they didn't have an organ or a piano. They didn't think that human voices, when blended together in song, needed instrumental accompaniment.

The Longs lived about a half hour southeast of Allentown, on the Old Philadelphia Highway, Route 23, just outside Telford, Pennsylvania, near Souderton. For the forty-minute drive out, I sat between George and Erma, with Dolores, their daughter, in the back, and we sang Sunday school choruses like, "Climb, Climb up Sunshine Mountain." I sang too loud and sometimes off-pitch, but they didn't seem to mind. I felt so warm and secure that the ride to their house could have taken all day and I wouldn't have complained.

The Longs let me borrow some of their Christian books to read. I read *Foxe's Book of Martyrs*. I had never imagined people were willing to die for religious faith. They also gave me Carol Kaufman's *Search to Belong*. I identified with the orphan trying to ferret out his past.

That night, after the Longs took me back to Good Shepherd, I lay awake a long time, reading and thinking about my family and Grandmom and trying to piece together some of the unknowns in my life. Paul Lutz, a young man in a wheelchair because of CP, who lived at Good Shepherd, brought his girlfriend, Betty Lou Snyder, and her parents touring through Good Shepherd Home on a Sunday afternoon in February 1962. They were very friendly and in many ways reminded me of the Longs. With the assistance of one of the orderlies, I was playing around with a friend's guitar when I was introduced. I told them about my interest in radio and ventriloquism. I had a small dummy that I used for practice.

Several months later, in June 1962, Paul approached me

about a graduation party being thrown for Betty Lou by her parents and several members of their church, the Pilgrim Holiness church in Lehighton, Pennsylvania, a town about thirty miles up the Lehigh Valley from Allentown. I was asked to entertain with my dummy. However, because this was a church group, I was told to be careful selecting material for the show in order not to offend anyone.

Betty Lou's parents, Mr. and Mrs. Arthur Snyder, came to pick me up. Mr. Snyder, who told me to call him Art, a tall distinguished looking gentleman with thin snow-white hair, was quick with a joke and very happy-go-lucky. Often, he was mistaken for a doctor, preacher, or funeral director due to his distinguished appearance.

On one occasion, in an ice cream parlor, the cashier looked at Mr. Snyder and asked, "You look like Rev. Hosann."

"Why, thank you," he replied with a smile.

She continued almost without hesitation, "He's dead!"

He laughed so hard his face turned beet red.

I quipped, "You do look like a dead preacher!"

We all got a big laugh from that.

Mrs. Grace Snyder, "Betty," as everyone in town knew her, had long wavy deep red hair, combed straight back and rolled in a bun. She sang with a strong rich alto voice that could be heard clearly from anywhere in the room. She was the one person everyone called for help, whether it was for nursing, clothes (her car stopped at all rummage sales!) and even helping missionary families a half a world away. There was never any doubt about her love for people.

Once, thanks to "Betty," a native resident from British Guiana, attending Bible college in Allentown, was able to have his wife come to the United States to be with him while he studied. Mrs. Snyder personally sponsored her and her children, paid the fares and fees and then drove with her family to New York to greet them when they arrived. She truly was a special lady.

The Snyders were to take me back to Good Shepherd

that evening, but because of a severe rainstorm, they invited me to stay at their house and go to church with them the next morning. Mrs. Snyder called and got permission for them to keep me overnight and bring me back the next afternoon.

The next morning, we returned to Lehighton for services at the Pilgrim Holiness church. The Pilgrim Holiness denomination later merged with the Wesleyan Methodists and the Lehighton church became the Lehighton Wesleyan Church.

When Mr. Snyder learned I was interested in music, he introduced me, after Sunday school, to Helen May, the church organist. I plopped down on the bench beside her and we talked while waiting for the worship service to begin.

Suddenly, I felt an uncontrollable itch. "Hey, will you scratch my back?" I asked. "My arm isn't as flexible as yours."

"Oh, it isn't? Any time," she laughed as she raked her fingernails across the trouble spot.

I took a seat three rows back in the congregation beside Mrs. Snyder while Mr. Snyder got up to lead the singing. They enjoyed singing as much as the Mennonites, but with piano and organ accompaniment. Their singing was alive and refreshing, filled with enthusiasm. I had never heard anything like it. I was just overwhelmed.

The Snyders and I came to be really close. I started spending two and three weekends a month with them, becoming active in the Lehighton Wesleyan Church, going to camp meetings, revivals, gospel music concerts and family functions. In fact the first Christian music concert I ever attended was with the Snyders. "Mom" and "Dad," as they let me call them, and daughter, Betty Lou, sang in a family trio. I went with them for several church engagements, then at the third, I asked if I could do a number with them. I learned the songs by singing with them in the car on long trips. Dad Snyder said, "Come on." I loved it, even if I wasn't very good. I was just beginning.

Dad Snyder was an electrical engineer for the Bethlehem
Steel Corporation. Mom was a nurse at the Allentown State
Hospital. Even more than Quacky and the Longs, they
became my surrogate parents.

Dad Snyder gave me a copy of the *Living New
Testament.* This was a Bible I could understand, and I read
it through in two days.

They took me that summer to what they called a camp
meeting, sponsored by Brethren in Christ churches. Rev.
Simon Lehman, the short, bald teen director for the week,
was one big grin, and spoke like no other clergyman I ever
heard. When he talked to God, he didn't say, "Heavenly
Father" in some pompous or pious tones. Instead, he leaned
in close to the microphone as if to whisper in God's ear, and
said softly, "Now, Lord," and spoke to God as though he
were his best friend.

John Rosenberg, the camp evangelist, tall and lanky with
fringes of gray hair, reminded me of Bozo the Clown in a
black clerical suit without a tie. He kept us entranced when
he spoke. He had the ability to make us laugh one minute
and cry the next. Hearing him, I got an even deeper
impression that God was not some impersonal cosmic
being, but someone with whom I could walk and talk day
by day.

He told about a missionary in desperate need of ice and
how the Lord provided through a deliveryman, who
happened to be an atheist. When the delivery man heard
the missionary thank God for bringing the ice, he said,
"God had nothing to do with it. I delivered the ice." The
missionary declared, "Well, the Lord sends even if the devil
delivers." I laughed out loud. Then I started thinking about
John Rosenberg's point: "God provides for his people even
through unbelievers."

I felt comfortable going up to Simon or John or anyone
else and asking any question on my mind. Lovingly,
carefully, painstakingly, they explained God's love in
language that I, an eleven-year-old Jewish boy, who had been

deeply hurt, could understand. They told me and showed me in the Bible, in the Psalms, that "I am fearfully and wonderfully made." But they never pressed me as some well-meaning visitors had at Good Shepherd Home. Any commitments to be made were mine to make in my own time, and in my own way.

One afternoon I was sitting on a bench by myself, mulling over what I had been hearing from John, Simon, and the Snyders. A little lady came over and asked, "Jeffrey, wouldn't you like to give your life to Jesus? Invite him into your heart as your Savior and allow him to make you 'a new creature'?"

I was ready. "Yes, I would." I bowed my head and prayed with her, right there on the bench. I didn't realize then the far reaching impact this would have in my life and those whose lives I touched. But I did know that I wanted what these people had, a personal working relationship with the God who created me and a lifelong love affair with the King of the universe. A deep peace engulfed me, and I felt good about myself as I realized that God, the Creator of everything, loves me! It was no accident that Jeff Steinberg was born handicapped. I was getting a better view of the Masterpiece beginning to unfold. I sought out Mom and Dad Snyder and told them I had been "saved." They wrapped their arms around me and we cried and praised God together.

These wonderful people loved me to their Lord. When I stayed overnight with them, Mom Snyder undressed me and bathed me as she would her own child. She did it lovingly and with never a complaint.

I was "saved" in August 1962. I returned to Good Shepherd from the church camp on a Saturday. The next morning I ran to Erma Long as soon as I saw her. "Hey, I got saved at camp. I asked Jesus to come into my heart and forgive me."

She started to cry. "That's wonderful, Jeffrey! Wonderful! Let's go and tell George." I did, and we all had a great day of celebration.

One Christmas, an Allentown businessman heard that I was interested in ventriloquism and gave us dummies. When Quacky came over on Sunday afternoon, naturally I ran to her and said, "Quacky, you've got to help us work these things."

"I don't know anything about a dummy," she protested with a smile.

"The trick is to make the audience think the dummy is doing the talking." The challenge of ventriloquism is to learn to speak without moving your lips. You apply pressure to your diaphragm to push air through the vocal cords, bringing the sound up to the front of your mouth. It is important that you be looking at your dummy when you talk so that the audience's attention is focused on the dummy.

With Quacky helping and correcting, Ricky and I practiced breathing, sounding out syllables until we could speak whole sentences without moving our lips. We became quite good at it.

My dummy was a Christmas gift from the Snyders, and just the kind of dummy I had wanted. It was large and took two people to operate and had eyes that opened and closed and moved from side to side, a mouth that opened and a head on a pole that came completely off. Quacky attached to my hook the string that hung out of the base of "Professor Joe Smith's" neck, controlling his mouth. While I moved his mouth by pulling on the string, she maneuvered the "pole" (the dummy's backbone) up and down to make the eyes move.

Ricky and I practiced with Quacky. Then she took us out for ice cream and we laughed over our lines.

I got good enough to be asked to perform for a group of Cub Scouts. Quacky dressed Professor Joe in a Cub Scout uniform and the routine ran like this:

"How do you like being a Cub Scout, Professor?"

"I love it. I do lots of good deeds."

"Oh, you do good deeds? Have you done any good deeds, lately?"

"Why yes, yesterday I helped an old lady across the street."

"Wow, that's wonderful, Professor."

"Yeah, I thought it was. There was just one problem."

"What's that?"

"She didn't want to go!"

Corny? Certainly. But kids loved it, and our routines were directed mainly to kids.

I had loved music since my days at Shriners where I never missed watching Dick Clark's "American Bandstand" on TV. At the Mennonite church in Allentown and the Wesleyan church in Lehighton I discovered gospel music. The gospel songs struck chords of praise and joy deep within my heart. I sang with the Snyders, at the Longs, and to anyone who would listen to me.

One weekend I went with George and Erma to the Bowery Mission in New York. I saw drunks lying in alleys and on the street with people walking around to keep from stepping on them. Looking back now, I can see that these men's lives were pretty much like mine—the hopeless feeling of not being wanted or loved. They had given up. I hadn't.

We went into the mission and George, who knew the man in charge, asked permission for me to sing.

"Sure," he said. "The men will be touched."

Dolores Long played the piano and I sang "Until Then," an arrangement by Stuart Hamblen. Every eye in the audience focused on me, as I sang and balanced on my deformed legs beside the piano:

*My heart can sing when I pause to remember,*
*A heartache here is but a stepping stone,*
*Along the path that's winding always upward;*
*This troubled world is not my final home.*

*But until then my heart will go on singing*
*Until then with joy I'll carry on . . .*

An old white-haired fellow in a sleazy denim jacket grabbed my empty left sleeve as I went to sit down by George and Erma. "You wuz ter-r-r-iffic, kid, ter-r-r-iffic. Praise de Lord!" He and many others, including George and Erma, were wiping away tears.

I got a mixed reaction when I told my friends at Good Shepherd I had been saved. Curtis Petersen never liked that kind of gospel music. His tastes went toward the classical. But he was my best friend and he wanted me to be happy. He told me, "If that's what you want and it makes you happy, that's what I want for you." I could tell he was a little skeptical. Curtis had been exposed to a lot of different churches and slants on the Bible. He preferred the more formal services of the Lutheran church, and he certainly was not going to leap into anything before taking a long hard look.

Ricky said, "That's great, Jeffrey. I want to know God." Ricky and I had some long, long spiritual talks. We became closer than ever. About a year and a half after I was saved, Ricky joined a confirmation class led by the neighborhood Lutheran pastor. I went to the confirmation services in the Good Shepherd chapel, and seven other people in wheelchairs were "set apart," as Lutherans say, to live for Christ.

Ricky had an almost angelic look on his face as he held his hand on a Bible and answered the pastor's questions. I wasn't aware that any of his relatives were there, although his Polish grandmother might have been.

Ricky was confirmed on Sunday, May 17, 1964. That same night after the ceremonies and festivities, while we were all lying in our beds, Ricky called out to me, "Jeff, do you think God would take me to heaven?"

"Of course he would," I was quick to respond. Ricky was no angel, but if anyone were to get into heaven, I was convinced Ricky was a definite yes. That night I prayed for my friend, though I didn't know why.

The following Friday he started coughing. Knowing he

had only one weak lung because of polio, the staff kept him out of school and in bed watching him very closely.

Sunday morning, I went out with friends for church and didn't get back until late evening. When I came on our floor, I asked about Ricky.

The charge nurse said, "They took Ricky to the hospital today. He's real bad." I had an uneasy feeling about my friend.

The aide undressed me for my bath as I prayed silently, "Lord, you've got to help Ricky."

I was sitting on the edge of the tub when the nurse in charge stuck her head just inside the bathroom door, "Jeffrey, I don't know how to tell you this, but they just called from the hospital. Ricky is dead. I—I'm so sorry. We all loved him so much. I don't know what to say except that maybe he's better off."

I heard the words but I couldn't accept them. It was all so final, so cold. Ricky couldn't be dead. Not Ricky. Anyone but Ricky. The harsh reality of Ricky's death did not hit at that point. I sat down in the warm bath, too numb to say anything. I had known others at Good Shepherd who had died. Miss Winnifred Hammer, Dr. Raker's assistant, the first person I had met at the Home, had passed away a few months before. But she was older. Ricky was young, barely fifteen, too young to die. Ricky was my little brother, my closest friend.

The nurse's aide helped me get into my pajamas. I went into the television room and tried to watch TV. Curtis came over from the men's quarters and sat beside me.

"You're white as a sheet, Jeffrey," he observed. I felt like a ghost, empty and afraid inside. I didn't feel like talking much. Curtis did not push. He stayed for a long while just for support. He was a good support and a great sounding board. I don't remember what we talked about, except that it was about Ricky. When he finally left, I went back to my room where my roommate was already asleep.

I lay there for what seemed an endless time. When I

finally drifted off, I had a horrible nightmare. I was riding in
the hearse for Ricky's funeral and I decided I would lie
down in an extra casket to be close to him one last time.
They were trying to close my casket, only I was not dead! I
woke up shaking and didn't sleep another wink that night.

The next night was almost as bad. Every time I closed my
eyes that same nightmare came back. I'd wake up and try to
get my mind on something else. This horror went on for
seven or eight nights, until life slowly came back into focus.

I had never told Dr. Raker or my folks in Philadelphia
that I had received Jesus. The Snyders didn't push for me to
join their Wesleyan church, nor did the Longs urge me to
become a Mennonite. My parents knew only that I had
been going to church with the Snyders and the Longs. They
weren't happy about this and told Dr. Raker so.

I was now nearing my thirteenth birthday, when Jewish
boys are expected to become bar mitzvahed, a Jewish ritual
defining the passage from childhood to adulthood. Dr.
Raker was approached by a local Jewish couple about
arranging for that very important event for me with their
synagogue, Congregation Sons of Israel. When he offered to
make all the arrangements, I said, "Go ahead and set things
up with the rabbi." I couldn't see that believing in Jesus as
my Messiah made any difference.

I was transported in the GSH station wagon every
Thursday afternoon immediately after school. Cantor
Samuel Weiss taught me the Hebrew words and prayers I
needed to learn. Dr. Raker was very proud and encouraged
me. He talked the event up around the Home and most of
the staff went to my Bar Mitzvah on that very special
Sabbath morning, *Kee Tetze,* the fourteenth day of Elul,
5724, August 24, 1964 at the Sons of Israel Synagogue.

My Dad and Mom had nothing to do with the
preparation. Still they came and my father stood by my side
as I read from the great scroll of the Torah the familiar
verses.

Dad sat down and I spoke to the congregation of my

friends, family, and community of the responsibilities of adulthood and how proudly I would assume the responsibility of being a Jew. I read from the Torah, a great thrill, chanted the prayers and read the Haftorah portion, all of which were written in Hebrew. When I completed the service, Rabbi Rosenberg announced that I was Bar Mitzvah. He then invited my friends to come and congratulate me and share in a special reception downstairs in the *Oneg Shabbat.*

Mom and Dad kissed me on the cheeks. My sisters and Grandmom hugged me, as did Dr. Raker, the Snyders, the Longs, Quacky, and many, many others. The Rabbi looked pleased. I received many gifts, including my Bar Mitzvah suit given to me by Mom and Dad and money from friends that did not know how to buy for me. I felt pretty important myself.

When it was all over I rode back with my family to Good Shepherd. Dad began to pack my suitcase and when I asked the reason, he announced to me, "Mommy and I are taking you home for the weekend. We're very proud of you and we decided to surprise you." I was delirious with excitement. That was the best gift. Maybe now I could show them that I was ready to live at home. I wanted this to be a beginning. And that weekend was the best time I ever had at home. Perhaps because there were a lot of people to visit with, places to go making a short weekend. No matter. For that weekend, I was the "son" and "brother" I had not been.

I never went back to the synagogue in Allentown. Though I desired to learn conversational Hebrew and Yiddish, and though Cantor had offered to teach me, he never followed up. I made several calls to him and then gave up. I was not hostile—just indifferent about what I didn't know about being a Jew. I could read what I had rehearsed, but could not be one of them. In fact, I could be shut out if they started speaking Yiddish or Hebrew. To anyone who asked, I readily admitted my ethnic identity. I honestly saw no contradiction in being a Jew and in accepting Jesus as my Messiah.

CHAPTER EIGHT
· · · · · · · · · · ·

# CLIMBING THE MOUNTAIN

The thalidomide disaster hit the headlines while I was growing up in Good Shepherd Home. The pictures and stories of deformed babies, born with little flippers for arms and legs, triggered feverish research on the effects of tetratogenic drugs in fetal development. This was still years before I learned that my mother's doctor had probably given her one of these drugs, but I identified with the thalidomide children. Many looked like me when I was born.

The thalidomide babies helped the fund-raising campaign at Good Shepherd for the new rehabilitation center. The stories gave Dr. Raker a talking point to explain his hopes and dreams for the physically handicapped.

He wrote in *The Lutheran* magazine (May 22, 1963) about a young mother in Belgium killing her thalidomide child. "The Belgian mother," he said, "rejected her child with an overdose of barbiturates. Others reject by withholding love." The article continued:

*The building blocks of a child's personality are the love,
confidence, affection, and inner support given it by those
closest to it, most frequently the parents. If a physically
normal child needs these to attain an inner security and
strength, how much more does a child born with a physical
handicap? Instead of even thinking of denying them life, it
should be clear that they need all the love, the assistance, all
the support it is possible for us to give. They know beyond
a shadow of a doubt that they are not only loved and
respected, but wanted.*

*As horrible as the thalidomide incident was, it is time that
we realize that the greatest crippler in the world is not
accident, disease, or even thalidomide. It's the denial of love.
More children go through life deformed and twisted inside
because of this than anything else. Really the only truly
deformed child is the one born without love.*

Dr. Raker and the people at Good Shepherd saw this deep
need in the lives of kids like myself who had been hurt by
parents and society. The ambivalence I felt toward my Mom
and Dad never left me. The occasional bitterness and anger
from feeling rejected and left out shifted quite often to love
and desire for them, depending on my needs and
circumstance at the moment.

As I got older, I came to understand that Dad was
trapped by circumstances. With his work schedule, he
couldn't care for me, and because of Mom's reaction to
emotional stress, he felt that she couldn't handle me while
giving my "normal" sisters the bringing up they deserved.

As for Mom, at times I felt she just didn't want to be
bothered by her handicapped child, but now I realize that
she just couldn't cope. She had never had to cope with her
own feelings. Dad did all of the coping. Neither one was
willing to talk it out with the other, and each felt as if the
entire load rested on his or her own shoulders. I can
understand both Mom and Dad better now, but in my
childhood all I felt was deep, deep loneliness and rejection.

• • • • • • • • • • • • • • • • • • • • • • • • • • • • • • • • •

Good Shepherd sought to fill the emptiness and ease the
hurt, while training us in some meaningful skill or job. Carl
Odhner, Good Shepherd's Director of Rehabilitation, who
was also handicapped, told us, "We're not dropping coins
into a beggar's cup. We're trying to help you stand and gain
the means to earn your own living. We're not looking at
your disabilities but your abilities. We don't consider anyone
pitiful or hopeless but everyone valuable and capable of
contributing to society."

Carl was a living testimony of his own message. He came
to Good Shepherd as a small boy after being crippled by
polio in both hands and legs. He lived in a wheelchair,
graduated from high school and college, took a master's
degree in rehabilitation counseling, married a girl in a
wheelchair, and had a child. Carl and Rowena lived outside
Good Shepherd and Carl drove himself to work every day.

Carl, a big, handsome man, with thick brown wavy hair
combed back, was always telling us in occupational therapy,
"Look, I did it. You can make it. You can climb the
mountain. . . . If you can't do it in an ordinary way," Carl
said, "then improvise."

We did a lot of improvising at Good Shepherd. One of
the guys, for example, had crippled hands and couldn't
sharpen a pencil. He rigged the sharpener up to the motor
from an old electric typewriter and sharpened all our pencils
automatically.

I brought to Good Shepherd the same problems I had
at Shriners. Dr. Alfonso Mueller, the head doctor, like
Dr. Moore at Shriners, was always trying to figure out a way
to improve my ambulation, my walk. He called my
ambulatory pattern, "quite bizarre. His right knee doesn't
bend, but his hip goes into forward propulsion with marked
pelvic tilt." Dr. Mueller feared that degenerative joint disease
might develop in my frozen right knee or that my hip
might give out a few years down the line.

After consultation with other doctors, Dr. Mueller
proposed that my right leg be amputated at the knee and

replaced with a prosthesis, followed by new surgery to
straighten and balance my left knee. The artificial right leg
would be extended to the length of my left leg, eliminating
the need for the extra foot I had been carrying on the right.
If my left knee could be put in shape, then I wouldn't have
to swing my hip at every step. These ideas were not new.
Dr. Moore had wanted to do much the same at Shriners,
but time was not in his favor.

I called home to tell my Dad about the proposed surgery.
He drove to Allentown and met with the doctors at the
clinic and was filled in on the plan for the possible surgery.
We consulted the orthopedic specialist, Dr. Richard White,
recommended by Dr. Mueller, and awaited his opinion.
Dr. White was certain that the surgery would improve my
appearance, but could not guarantee to improve function.
He reminded me that I was presently able to use both feet
for walking, writing, and various other functions, and that
with the surgery they would amputate my right foot and I
would lose the use of that foot. He wanted me to be aware
that if the surgery failed and I were not able to use an
artificial leg due to skin breakdown, etc., that I would have
lost my functional abilities for the sake of cosmetic
appearance. The importance of cosmetic appearance was a
decision that could only be made by me and my family.
Dad told me that the choice was mine to make. It gave me
a lot to consider. I decided to reject the surgery. I did not
mind my appearance. After all, I have been "me" all of my
life, and I knew that my capabilities were not to be limited
by what others could see. Looks aren't everything. There
were many people that I would meet who would look better
than I, but there was no one I would meet that would be
comfortable with themselves and their abilities better than I.

Dr. Mueller had replaced my right arm with a new
prosthesis and hook a couple of years after I came to Good
Shepherd. This was an improvement over the old one in
that it gave me action at the wrist, as well as at the elbow, to
manipulate the hook that served for a hand. But the cap on

my right stump didn't fit well and the stump became irritated. The arm was on and off for a couple more years, making it an aggravation for me and the staff. Without the arm and hook, they had to spend more time feeding and doing for me—although I was pretty adept at picking up a glass with my teeth—and giving more assistance in dressing and bathroom duties. Mom Snyder performed these extra chores when I was at her house, and again, she never complained.

Dr. Mueller ordered a new prosthesis. Good Shepherd's Rehabilitation Center was not yet open, so he sent me to the Pennsylvania State Hospital for Crippled Children at Elizabethtown, a hundred miles southeast of Allentown, for their amputee clinic and subsequent fittings. It seemed that the hospital took their merry time in building the arm and getting it back to me. When it did come, I had the device only a few days when the flexer cable at the elbow broke. Dr. Mueller sent it back to Elizabethtown through the mail. Another month's waiting without an arm. By the time they mailed it back again, I was sick of people helping me and they were sick of me pestering them so much.

A week or so later the cable snapped a second time. Dr. Mueller mailed the arm back to Elizabethtown with an angry letter for not fixing it right before. I didn't see it again for another month, but this time the cable held and the cap fit snugly on my stump.

I continued to practice and perform my ventriloquism routines with the dummy that the Snyders gave me that memorable Christmas. With a little help from Quacky, Professor Smith and I were a blast:

ME: *What direction does the Lehigh River flow?*
PROFESSOR: *Downhill.*
ME: *Where was the Queen crowned?*
PROFESSOR: *On her head, Dummy.*
ME: *Where was the Declaration of Independence signed?*
PROFESSOR: *At the bottom.*

• • • • • • • • • • • • • • • • • • • • • • • • • • • • • •

ME: *Professor, I heard you are going to be the judge of a dog
     show. What do you know about dogs?*
PROFESSOR: *You think I don't know anything? You should
            have seen the girl I was out with last night. She
            was a real dog.*

I wasn't quite a Edgar Bergen or a Paul Winchell, but I
could make audiences laugh. I especially enjoyed making
my audiences laugh.

I also continued to help WAEB's deejays when they did
remotes from Good Shepherd and at other places in the city.
But what I began to like most was singing. I practically
drove the staff at Good Shepherd crazy. They were all pretty
patient with me except Lucy.

"Jeffrey, did anybody ever tell you that you couldn't
sing?"

"No."

"Well, they should. You can't."

Lucy and I always antagonized each other, like brothers
and sisters. Though we never quite got to be close, we did
learn over the years to respect each other. She continued to
call me "Jeffrey," while I preferred Jeff, now that I felt grown
up. When she really got on me, I headed for the elevator
and rode it up and down, singing at the top of my voice
until Grace, Ruth, or one of the other staff members
stopped it and told me to clear out.

In the back of my mind was the memory of Dad saying,
"Jeffrey, if you ever decide to sing for a living, please don't
do it while I'm around."

Mom and Dad Snyder thought I had talent. They
continued to let me sing with them and Betty Lou. One
Friday afternoon they picked me up for a concert in
Glassboro, New Jersey, by the Eastmen Quartet, a southern
style gospel quartet from Lansdale, Pennsylvania, near
Philadelphia, and The ViCounts, a trio specializing in a soul
gospel sound. The ViCounts were from Harrisburg,
Pennsylvania, not exactly the soul capitol of the country. I

didn't breathe until intermission. What perfect pitch, blending, and harmony! Beautiful! When the audience applauded, I beat on my chair with my hook, kicked my three feet, and hollered, "Yeah! Yeah!"

The next morning, we went to hear the Eastmen Quartet in a smaller church in the area and after speaking with them before the service, was surprised to hear them announce that they were going to sing a song just for me, "He Touched Me." The Eastmen Quartet, Ron Landis, tenor, J. R. Damiani, their manager and baritone, Frank Sanchez, second tenor, Richard Sterban, bass (now singing bass for The Oak Ridge Boys, a country music group), and Nick Bruno, pianist and arranger, would have a strong and profound influence on my musical ambitions and my life. J. R. Damiani would become a chief source of encouragement giving me some of my earliest major performance opportunities at their own concert promotions, and a lifelong friend.

There were other concerts. We went to hear the Couriers. They were even smoother, three men with a vocal sound similar to the pop group the Lettermen. They were different in still another way. They would often perform many of their songs with orchestrated sound tracks, or "canned" music. Dave Kyllonen, the tall skinny baritone singer and manager, Duane Nicholson, tenor, and Neil Enloe, lead singer, composer and arranger, the Couriers, pioneers of gospel music in the great northeast, added a level of maturity to my music tastes and added a sense of professionalism to Christian music. I dreamed of having my own group.

"Good evening, ladies and gentlemen. Welcome to our concert. For our opening number . . . 'Give the World a Smile Each Day . . .' Now, 'Let Us Have a Little Talk with Jesus, let us tell him all about our troubles . . .' " The crowd was cheering and . . .

"Jeff, turn that stereo down! We can hear it and you all through the building." It was Grace.

There was still one other group that would make a big impression in my life. It was on an unusual Sunday afternoon at the Home when I met the mother of one of the new patients, an accident victim. She was coming to visit her son, Wayne, and was being trailed by three men dressed in matching suits. They called themselves the Envoys and they were from a small town in north Jersey. They had sung in her church that morning, and now they were coming to visit Wayne. They invited me to come with them. They sang some of their songs and then visited for what seemed like a very long time and then boarded their customized GMC bus and drove away. I had made more new friends in gospel music, in the Envoys: Don Storms, their soft spoken, somewhat stately manager and lead singer, Ron Kelly, their jovial little tenor, and Dallas Henry, the tall baritone singer, pianist and arranger. I thought I was the luckiest kid that ever lived, to have personal friends who were professional entertainers and who cared about me.

Curtis Petersen and I had known each other since my first year at Good Shepherd, though not well until after Ricky's death. With Ricky gone, we had become closer than ever. I convinced him on many occasions to go with me to hear the Envoys when they came into the Allentown area. "How did you like them?" I asked when the concert was over.

He screwed up his face and twisted his upper lip under his brown mustache. "You don't want to know."

"I do want to know. Tell me."

He broke into a grin. "Well, they're not quite my cup of tea. But if you like them, I guess they're OK." That was Curtis!

Good old Curtis. He preferred classical music and he made no bones about it. He tried to make me appreciate Bach and Chopin and, whether he realized it or not, I helped him to appreciate simple gospel music in four-part harmony. One evening I put on a new album by the Envoys and sat enraptured until the last strain of the last song faded into the plastic. "You know, Curtis," I breathed. "I think God wants me to be a gospel singer. What do you think?"

My best friend handed me a long quizzical look. "Jeff, if that's what you think God wants you to be, who am I to question you?"

Curtis never insisted I had to like his type of music. He did say, "If you're going to be a gospel singer, be a good one. Learn all you can. You'll have to work at it, but if I know you, you'll make it." Then he told me about his struggle to learn to play the piano with arthritic hands, how his hands ached from practice, how people discouraged him.

"I don't kid myself, Jeff. I'm not a very good pianist, as comparisons go. But I think I'm the best I can be and I enjoy banging on the ivories. You know, there's much more to a career in music than performing. You've got to love what you do with all your heart."

I was now attending public school at South Mountain Junior High in Allentown. Curtis urged me to take vocal music and become involved with the school's choral groups. I became active in the choral groups and all of the musical shows I possibly could, and at the end of the year, I was presented an award for vocal music. I also made friends with the instrumental music teacher, Albert Geary. Now there's a challenge for a good instructor. Teach a man with no arms to play an instrument. Since I never had the handicap of being bashful, I ventured confidently up to him one day and asked him if he would teach me.

He didn't bat an eye. "What would you like to play?"

"Well, I'm not too good on the piano. I'm a bit short-handed and I have lousy finger dexterity."

He looked at my hook and laughed. "Yes, I guess you do. What do you have in mind?" His curiosity and interest was piqued.

"Maybe I could play a horn." I continued. "How about a trombone. It doesn't require any fancy fingering and maybe I could use my hook and my feet."

"OK, Jeff, I'll work with you. When's your next free

• • • • • • • • • • • • • • • • • • • • • • • • • • • • • • •

period?" Just like that. Never a negative word. That was Albert Geary. He was short and solid, the very picture of the Air Force colonel that he was—positive, disciplined, always looking for a mountain to climb and willing to help a Jeff Steinberg make it to the top, too.

Mr. Geary and I decided to try the trombone. "Next to the violin," he said, "the trombone is the hardest instrument to learn because there are no preset positions. With the trumpet you push the valve down and you get the tone you want. Push two valves and you get a different tone. With the trombone you have to develop a sharp ear for tone and learn to approximate and slide to get the musical notes."

I grinned. My Dad had said I was tone deaf.

Mr. Geary helped me take off my right brace and showed me how to prop the trombone on my shoulder and support it with my right hook. I moved the slide with my right foot, and *voila!* I could do it.

By practice and patience—the patience coming from Mr. Geary, I got the knack and proved that I wasn't tone deaf. Maybe not good enough for Lawrence Welk, but good enough to prove I could play. Mr. Geary even wrote a special arrangement of Christmas music, "Joy to the Velt" (German for world), for me.

I was either a great salesman, con artist, or both. I suppose you must possess a bit of both to be good at either. I was always selling something, it seemed. One afternoon, while still in the fifth grade, just before supper, I informed Curtis about a sales contest our school was promoting. Doughnuts! Curtis believed I could sell anything, even ice cubes to the Eskimos, or maybe the Brooklyn Bridge to New York.

By buying and trading, I had built up a pretty good stock of comic books. But doughnuts? Yes, doughnuts for our school PTA, and a trophy would be presented to the winner. I was up against the entire school, including the non-handicapped "normal" kids.

"Sure," Curtis said, "you just go knock on a door, smile

big, hold out a fresh doughnut in your hook, and ask the customer how many dozen he wants delivered."

"Not exactly. I can only take pictures to show and take orders to be delivered in a few weeks," I informed him.

It sounded easy. It was easy. Going door to door in the neighborhood around Good Shepherd where a lot of people knew me, I took orders for 176 dozen in five days and won the contest, the first of many yet to come.

I recruited help from some off-duty staff at the Home and we set out to deliver the 176 dozen doughnuts (before they got stale). We were almost through when my parents drove up unannounced.

They got out to greet me. "We thought we'd surprise you," Dad said.

"Yeah, you sure did. But I have to deliver these doughnuts, or they'll get stale." I puffed out my chest a little. "I sold 176 dozen and won the sales contest at school." I showed them the plaque presented to me by the school principal.

"Very good. I always said that you would make a great salesman or attorney," Dad replied.

I added, "I did it in five days, Dad, going door to door." I thumbed my hook at my helpers. "These guys are helping me deliver them. We won't be long. Go into the TV room and I'll try to hurry."

Mom was also smiling. They told me to go ahead and they would wait. I felt bad, but the doughnuts had to be delivered.

Fortunately, the deliveries didn't take long. Some families had ordered several dozens. But when I got back my folks were restless and a bit put out.

We visited for an hour or so and I informed them that I had plans to go out with the Snyders.

They had to get back to Philadelphia. I followed after them. "When are you coming back to see me?"

"I don't know, Jeffrey. Soon as we can. We can't make any promises."

"Dad, you always say that." I caught hold of his sleeve with my hook.

"I can't make any commitments, Jeffrey. We've got to get on the road. We've got a long drive."

I stood there, now too big to cry, and watched them drive away, realizing at that point that I now had a life of my own, separate from theirs. It was as if I didn't need to fit into their world. However, I would always want their approval, since they were my parents.

Afterwards, Curtis was listening to my woe. "Look, be thankful your parents came to see you. Some of us would be glad to see a relative just once a year."

I thought about that and calmed down. "Yeah, it could be worse."

The next Sunday morning George and Erma Long had me out to spend Sunday afternoon with them and I took a ride with George on his tractor. I felt better.

Curtis and I got into handwriting analysis for awhile. We both studied together and I got to be quite proficient at it. He got a job using his skills working for a local company and at times I would help him work on a project. At the same time, I studied felt tip lettering from a social studies teacher at school. He showed me how to make old English style letters, flair them, and add little embellishments. He would use chalk and I would use felt tip pens with chiseled points.

One evening, Curtis came around with a catalog and proposed that we go into business. "This outfit will sell us imported novelties wholesale on credit. We can peddle them door to door and make a profit."

"I like it! We can have our own company. What shall we call ourselves?"

Curtis thought a minute. "How about Gemini Enterprises? Gemini means twins."

"I know that, man. But we don't look like twins."

"Doesn't matter. We are best friends and always together. People think we're brothers because we know each other so well. Twins couldn't be any closer. Besides, it's only a name for our business. You're pretty good at drawing. Make us a logo and a letterhead."

I created what looked like the top and bottom of an eye looking at the silhouette of two guys standing side by side. I etched "Gemini" in large Old English lettering across the top of the letterhead and drew "Enterprises" at the bottom.

We mailed in an order for a variety of imported novelties. I put our logo on two signs and hung them on our doors. When the shipment arrived, we were in business.

We made more than $175 that summer, then I got into Junior Achievement at William Allen High School that fall. I was elected the president of our Junior Achievement company, Jewellen Enterprises. We decided to manufacture a product and sell it. We cut little pieces of carpet into circles the size of the bottom of a drinking glass and glued them into plywood seats to make octagon-shaped coasters. Ideal for holding a glass of tea or cup of coffee. Spill anything on the coaster and the carpet would soak it right up. I sold the coasters door to door and in malls and won first place in the J. A. contest sponsored by the local Sales Marketing Executive Association. I was then entered into the regional sales contest at the Bellevue Stratford Hotel in Philadelphia. I received second prize. My picture was in the Allentown papers and our sponsoring company threw a big awards dinner in our honor.

That evening, after being told I had won the award, I called my folks. Dad wasn't there. Mom said, "That's nice, Jeffrey. Very good. I'm proud of you."

I wanted to believe that she meant it, but she always left me wondering.

CHAPTER NINE
. . . . . . . . . . .

# THE IMPOSSIBLE DREAM

William Allen High School, one of two high schools in
Allentown, was big—more than three thousand students—
and I was the only person from Good Shepherd to enroll as
a freshman in 1967. The school had to provide me with a
"Man Friday" for every class, to carry my books and turn
my key in the elevator when I needed to go from floor to
floor within the main building.

Algebra, Earth Science, and World History and Cultures
were required, leaving me only one elective to choose. I
signed up for Voice.

When my program came back from the office, Voice was
not on it. I went to see my guidance counselor, Charles
Berbarian.

"What happened?" I asked rather directly.

"I'll check it out," he promised. He reported back that
Principal Chips Bartholomew had turned down my request.

"Why?" I said incredulously. "I won an award for singing
in the junior high choir and minstrel show. I play the

trombone. I sing with the Snyder family when I go up to Lehighton. I think I'm qualified."

"It isn't that, Jeff. Voice is on the fourth floor of the annex building where there are no elevators."

"I know the music department is on the fourth floor, Mr. Berbarian. Look, I can climb stairs. I just need someone to walk with me to steady me so I don't lose my balance."

"Mr. Bartholomew doesn't think the school should take that responsibility."

"I can get volunteers," I said with rising emotion. "Voice is important to me. Music Theory is on the fourth floor also and I'll need it later. I'm thinking of a career in music."

"Jeff, I'd like to help you. Believe me, I would. But I can't go against the principal's orders."

"Let's go see him. Make an appeal."

"OK," the counselor sighed. "I'll make an appointment. Just don't get your hopes up."

Mr. Bartholomew was unyielding. Nothing would change his mind. He was going to play it "safe."

I've never lived my life playing it "safe." I always said that I would try anything once. I wonder if I was really that brave, or if I felt I needed to prove that I could make it in the outside world, like anyone else.

Looking back, I believe even more strongly that there is a tragedy that comes with playing it "safe" and not venturing out into the scary unknown. There will always be those "what if's." I might never have really known what heights I could have reached and I might have given up or settled for second best.

I felt helpless, hollow, angry. I thought of going to the newspaper. The Allentown *Morning Call* had run stories on my sales achievements. They would put Chips Bartholomew on the hot seat. Then I thought of Good Shepherd. If I raised a stink, it would create a bad impression of Good Shepherd, an institution that depended on people in Allentown for donations. With expenses mounting for the rehab Center about to open, Dr. Raker didn't need a battle between me and the school refereed by the newspapers. I swallowed hard and choked back tears of disappointment. Finally, I just said, "OK, if that's the way it has to be," and walked out with the counselor.

Someone once said, "A winner never quits and a quitter never wins." I've never been a quitter. I've never been one to take no for an answer, either. I have, on occasion however, had to accept "wait" for an answer and put my plans on hold. Though I could not take Voice or Music Theory, I did become an active part of every musical function available to me. I did sing in the high school choir. I won an award in vocal music in the Allentown Lions Club's talent contest. I kept up with pop music on radio and TV. And, I went to hear musical groups whenever I could talk someone into taking me. I continued singing with the Snyders when I went to their house for weekends. I bought albums of the Couriers, the Eastmen, the Envoys, and other gospel groups and learned their songs by heart.

My parents seldom came to visit while I was in high school—once every three or four months at most. Occasionally they would call and half of the time I was not there.

"Where did he go?" Dad would probe.

"To the Snyders."

"He goes there too much," Dad complained.

Eventually Dad took his concern to Dr. Raker who summoned me to his office. "Jeffrey, your parents called me today."

"What do they want?" I asked a bit defiantly, although I could have guessed.

"They object to your spending so much time with the Snyders."

"So . . ." My voice dripped with sarcasm. "I'm sorry, Dr. Raker, but it isn't fair. They don't want me home with them, but they don't want me with anyone else either."

"That isn't quite their objection, Jeffrey. They think you're getting too attached to the Snyders."

"The Snyders love me, Dr. Raker, and I love them. Mom and Dad Snyder treat me like I was their own son. Don't they want me to be loved, or are they afraid that the Snyders might take me away from them? If my Mom and Dad love me so much, then why don't they make me a part of their lives? Why don't they come and visit more often and take me home for weekends like the Snyders? Saying 'We love you' in a letter that I receive once in a while is not good enough."

"Jeff, I'm caught in the middle on this. I understand how you feel and I think I can see their point of view, too. I think they're afraid that the Snyders will have too much influence on you spiritually. Everything you do with them involves church services, gospel music concerts, revival meetings, and camp meetings. Jeffrey, you are Jewish and your mother and father are concerned that the Snyders are trying to 'convert' you. I'm going to restrict your visits with the Snyders. You can go to the Mennonite Sunday school and out with friends this Sunday afternoon, but overnight visits with the Snyders must be approved by me."

"But, what good will that do? They can't stop me from believing what I want, and they won't. Even if they take away all of my friends! And, what about my plans for this weekend. I made plans to spend the weekend with the Snyders, and they're counting on it."

I was angry and determined, but Dr. Raker stated firmly, "You may see the Snyders this weekend, however, from now on you may only go with them for one weekend a month. Any more than that must be approved by me. Do you understand?"

"Yes." I mumbled under my breath staring down at the floor.

"Yes, sir, young man."

"YES, SIR."

It must have been a tough decision for him to make. He was caught between my parents, me and my friends. He loved me like a father and knew my need for love and family. Perhaps he saw that the Snyders loved me and that I was happy with them. He also saw my parents' perspective and as superintendent he had a responsibility to them. He did what he thought was fair. All I knew was that I was angry at him, at "them," and at the world. It took me some time to get over my feelings. The Snyders understood and told me that they would see me as often as they were allowed. They told me to obey the rules and respect Dr. Raker's wishes and that all would work out. That wasn't easy, but I would try. Dr. Raker said that I couldn't have more than one overnight visit with Mom and Dad Snyder per month without special permission, so, we just arranged more afternoon and evening visits and special functions that got me back to the Home that same night. When the Lord closes a door, he always opens a window.

It wasn't just my parents who were complaining about me. Some of the Good Shepherd staff were weary of my comings and goings at irregular hours. They had put up with a lot because of the inspirational stories about me in the Allentown papers which reflected favorably on the Good Shepherd Home. But too often, an activity for which I got publicity conflicted with school, therapy, and other routines at the Home. Certain staff members felt too many exceptions had been made for me and that I had been too demanding.

The social service director penned in my records:

*Jeff's behavior . . . can best be described as manipulative. He has been able to achieve almost every one of his own goals simply by knowing which person to ask and in what manner to pose the question . . . After several years of more or less catering to Jeff's wishes the staff has reached a point of feeling rather resentful toward his demands. Jeff does not cooperate with the staff in trying to adhere to dressing, bath, or bedtime schedules which must be maintained due to the ratio of staff to patients in the Main Building. Jeff's attitude is one of demanding that everything be done according to his schedule.*

These complaints, piled on top of Dad's gripes about spending so much time with the Snyders, caused Dr. Raker to start cracking down. He confined me to the second floor after school for two weeks, so I would not be going out at night and after that I was to be in the building and available to the staff by 8:30 P.M.

I didn't like it. I complained to Curtis, "They get a guy who doesn't live like a handicap and they handicap him. I'm not going to live in this place for the rest of my life, no matter how hard they try to keep me down."

I was a very immature believer then. I equated discipline with being put down and treated like a "cripple." I wasn't very sensitive to the feelings of the Good Shepherd staff, either, even those who had gone far beyond the call of duty to accommodate themselves to my special needs.

Yet—and I know this sounds contradictory—it was the assurance that God loved me and had something special for me to be and do which added fuel to my demands on other people. How could I be what he wanted me to be by conforming to what people expected of a handicap? My attitude was, "I'm coming through. God wants me to be somebody. If you won't help me reach my goals, I'll find somebody who will."

A handicap must push and sometimes antagonize a person to get what he needs to survive and excel. This also tends to make him insensitive to the needs of others. He gets so accustomed to hustling people for help that he begins taking them for granted. That is the way I was. That's the way I made it. Some helped me gladly. Some thought I was presuming too much and insisting on special favors because I was handicapped. I was, sometimes. I had to have help to get where I was going. I was persistent to a fault.

I kept myself occupied in high school, doing almost everything except going out for track or suiting up for one of the ball teams. I took class notes with a pen in my mouth and used a tape recorder for more technical lectures. My profs were very understanding. Over the four years, I attained a B minus average and would have done better if I hadn't spent so much time on extracurricular activities.

The only accident happened in photography lab. I was screwing in a new flashbulb with my mouth when the bulb blew up in my face.

"You OK?" the instructor asked anxiously as he reached to pick the glass from my face.

"Yeah," I muttered. "But I burned my tongue. Taking a close-up can be dangerous."

In 1969, when the Vietnam War was raging and when I was in the tenth grade, I became old enough to register for the draft. Imagine, Jeff Steinberg in khakis! With my hook, I'd salute and give myself a concussion! I couldn't see how they could possibly want me, but I went anyway, thinking it would be amusing.

The door was open, so I walked right in, tilting my pelvis, swinging my left leg, and dragging my stiff right leg and its two feet behind. A little dumpy, gray-haired woman wearing half-lens glasses sat behind a big front desk, thumbing through a sheaf of papers.

"Our country must be desperate," I cracked. "Sign me up."

"Sign you up for what, young man?" She asked incredulously. She continued picking among the papers, barely glancing above her papers and eyeing me over the tops of her half-lens glasses.

"I'm here to help win the war!"

She pulled out a form in triplicate, placed it in the typewriter and began rattling off the questions; she didn't look at me. "Your name?"

"Jeffrey David Steinberg, ma'am!" I snapped in a military tone. I was ready to enjoy this enlistment. I was looking forward to the physical.

She kept asking questions in the same disinterested tones. Finally she asked, "Classification?"

"Four-F," I piped.

"Why do you think you should be classified 4-F?" she droned.

I replied, "Because I'm physically and medically unfit for military service." That was the way 4-F was defined in their manuals. I was beginning to get a little aggravated.

She put down her pencil and surveyed me critically over her glasses. "Do you have a doctor's statement to verify that you are physically and medically unfit for military service?"

I glanced at my hook which had been resting on the desk. "No, do I need one?"

She stood up, eyes on my hook, placed her hands on her hips and shook her head. "Oh, dear," she muttered to herself. "I'm going to have to get the supervisor for this one!"

I couldn't resist it. "Go ahead. I'm gonna be this way when she gets here, too."

She went into a back office. A moment later a tall, younger lady walked out behind her. The supervisor took one look and snapped, "Of course, he's 4-F. What else would he be?"

So much for military service. When I got back to Good Shepherd and told Curtis, he almost fell off his crutches from laughing.

What I most wanted was to get a driver's license. If I was old enough to register for the draft, I was old enough to drive a car.

For years I had pestered everybody I rode with to let me steer or apply the foot pedals, including Carl Edwards, a driver at Good Shepherd. Carl drove me back and forth to school and to various other outside functions. We became good friends. One day he asked me if I would like to take a ride in his blue 1960 Buick Electra. It had long fins like a marlin and looked like the Batmobile. It had a 450 cubic inch Wildcat engine with the last of the slush-box transmissions that shifted so smoothly that you didn't notice it.

We drove around the neighborhood with Carl letting me steer a little. It was now or never, I figured.

"Hey, Carl, would you teach me to drive?"

"Well, I'm not sure," he hesitated. Then he quickly turned and said. "Why not? How about next Saturday?"

I counted the hours and then the minutes. True to his word, Carl drove me out to the parking lot of a big office building that was closed for the weekend. He put two-by-four wood blocks on the pedals, so I could reach them with my feet, and bought a special ring from the local prosthetic supply, that would enable me to hold the steering wheel with my hook. The ring had cost him $19.50.

I got behind the wheel, started the motor, and drove round and round the big lot. I was floating when we got back.

"Hey, I drove Carl's car!" I yelled to Curtis. "But don't tell anybody yet."

In applying for a learner's permit, I had to indicate on the form my physical condition.

They turned me down flat. "In view of your disability, we feel you would not be able to keep a car under proper control in case of an emergency," the cold letter from the Pennsylvania Department of Transportation said. I reapplied and got the same answer. Then I remembered John T. Van Sant, the state senator from Lehigh County, visiting Good Shepherd.

"If I can ever help you with anything, let me know," he had told me.

I wrote Senator Van Sant and he agreed to go to bat for me. The transportation bureaucrats gave him the same answer.

I went to the driver education teacher at school, Arthur Hartman. He had lost a leg in Korea and walked with a prosthesis. "Will you let me take the driver's ed course and help me get a license?" I pleaded.

He looked me straight in the eye. "Do you think you can drive a car?"

I said, "Of course I can. Why else do you think I want a license?"

"Then prove it to me."

The school car wasn't equipped for my style, so we borrowed Carl's Buick. We went out to the parking lot where I had practiced before. I climbed in behind the wheel and Mr. Hartman sat on the passenger side. He did not appear at all nervous.

"OK, that line over there is going to be the curb. I want you to parallel park."

I did. He seemed pleased, but continued in the same tone. He pointed to the opposite side. "That line is the other curb. Pull up to it, don't touch the curb, swing your wheel all the way to the right, and back up so your rear wheel is almost to the other curb, without touching."

I performed the "K" maneuver.

"Good boy. You did that perfectly. Now do a figure eight at ten to fifteen miles an hour for me. When I tell you, turn. Don't wait a second."

Zroooom. "Turn."

When we got back to the starting point, he slapped at my hook, "Boy, you're one hell of a driver. I'm going to help you get your license."

It wasn't simple. Mr. Hartman wrote Senator Van Sant and with the assistance of Congressman Dan Flood, from the Snyders District, and Mr. Hartman, he approached the state senate majority whip, who passed the word on to the house majority whip, who put heat on the Department of Transportation. Eventually, six months after making my first application, my learner's permit came in the mail. I grabbed the envelope with my hook and ripped it open with my teeth. "I got it! I got it!" I yelled loud enough for everybody on the second floor to hear.

I called Curtis, then Carl, and the three of us went out to eat and celebrated that night in the snack shop with a "bunny and a bottle"—a chocolate Easter bunny and a Mountain Dew.

The permit stipulated that I must complete a certified driver's education course under Mr. Hartman, who had agreed to teach me if Carl would practice with me and allow me to use his car. For this, John Stolzfus, a maintenance man at Good Shepherd and an auto body mechanic by trade, built special pedals for the driver training car, a green 1970 Chevy Malibu.

I put in my six hours of required road time. Mr. Hartman sat beside me and didn't treat me any different from any other student.

"If I have to use the brakes on my side," he warned, "then you've failed your driver's test the first time. Fail three times, and you'll have to reapply for a new learner's permit and start from scratch."

He had to touch the brakes only once.

I had to open my big mouth to Dad when he called.

I heard Mom saying, "He's what? . . . . Driving a car?"

She got on the phone. "Jeffrey, you'll kill somebody. Are you crazy?"

"Mom, Mr. Hartman says I can drive as well as any student he's ever had and I have a learner's permit."

She was really steamed. "All right, go ahead, if you have an accident, we won't be responsible."

It took only about six hours of intensive road training, and then I was ready for the test. Mr. Hartman rode with me in the driver training car to the state police station. When we walked in and I announced I had come to take the test the trooper on duty turned pale. I handed him my learner's permit and certificate from driver's ed. He had just realized that he was going to have to ride with me!

He had already observed my gait. Now he looked at my hook and frowned.

He sounded grim. "OK, let's see what you can do." I executed a serpentine maneuver between the lines marked out on the course. He nodded weakly and directed me to drive past a clump of trees. I saw the hidden stop sign in time and didn't go more than two inches past the line.

"All right, let's go out on 22." U.S. 22 is the main east-west highway through Allentown. Four lanes with narrow exit ramps. "I want to see you drive in traffic," he said.

The cars were moving at sixty-five, the legal speed limit. I thought I did real well, but he wasn't convinced.

"Come back next week and try again," he said.

I was disappointed. Mr. Hartman was steamed at the trooper. He felt that the trooper had deliberately failed me because of my appearance, not because of my driving skill. I had planned on getting my license and borrowing Carl's car to drive to Philly and surprise Mom for Mother's Day the following Sunday. I wanted to prove to her and Dad that I could drive. Boy, would they have been stunned!

Mr. Hartman and I returned to the State Police barracks the next morning to retake my test. I did satisfy the trooper this time. He stamped my learner's permit and said, "You'll get your license in about six weeks. Until then, it's OK for you to drive by yourself." On the side, he had told Mr. Hartman that I was the best driver training student he had tested. He just wanted to be certain.

That night I called everybody I could think of. My folks predicted the worst. Quacky, the Snyders, and the Longs were all thrilled. "I knew you could do it," Quacky declared. "I never had any doubt."

"Neither did I," I agreed.

"All I need now is a car," I told Dad Snyder. "Know where I can buy one for a couple of bucks?"

"Not offhand," he laughed. "The Lord will provide in due time, Jeff. He always does."

I had saved a little money from selling shirts and ties to teachers at school. Curtis had a few bills, earned from his job. To mark the occasion of my getting a license, we took a bus trip to New York for a Broadway matinee of *Man of La Mancha.* I sang along with Don Quixote, holding my voice barely low enough to avoid complaints.

"To dream the impossible dream, to fight the impossible foe . . ."

I had my license! I could drive a car like anybody else!

On the way back, Curtis talked to me about the future. "Now that you've got your license, are you thinking of moving out of Good Shepherd?" Curtis had always been able to read me pretty well.

"Yeah, but I don't know where I would live. I'd like to go to college and get up a gospel singing group. The Snyders would probably let me live with them and commute to a college in this area. I think I could get help from the state."

"What would your folks think?"

"They'd scream bloody murder. They want me to stay at Good Shepherd. They don't think I can ever make it by myself."

Curtis sat up in his seat and turned his face close to mine. "Jeff, I could cook for myself and make it physically, but I couldn't break away psychologically and moved back. I guess I'll be at Good Shepherd 'til I die. You've got a better chance," he continued. "You're younger. You've got friends standing by. You have your faith in God." My friend put his arthritic right hand on my knee. "Yeah, you can make it. But you'd better leave while you can."

I hinted to Mom and Dad Snyder about the possibility of living with them and attending college. Mom Snyder curled her arm around my neck and pulled me to her. "You've got a home here whenever you want it," she said. Dad Snyder, sitting across the room, smiled his approval.

Their daughter, Betty Lou, had married a young minister, Ronald Pickett. "You can have her room," Mom Snyder said. "Move in whenever you're ready."

• • • • • • • • • • • • • • • • • • • • • • • • • • • • • •

I decided to enroll at Penn Wesleyan College, in Allentown, only a couple of miles from Good Shepherd. The Home's social worker persuaded the Pennsylvania Bureau of Vocational Rehabilitation to pledge payment for all my expenses. I would stay in the dorm during the week and live with the Snyders on weekends.

With high school graduation only four days away, I phoned my parents of my plan to move out.

"Jeffrey, that's a big move," Dad said. "Suppose it doesn't work? Suppose something goes wrong. Will the Snyders be responsible? It's a lot to think about. I don't know if it's a good idea."

He and Mom came that afternoon. "Didn't the doctors warn that your hip could give out?" Dad asked.

"Dad, my hip is OK. And I can get help, if I ever need it."

"You can't be sure. You check out of Good Shepherd and who will pay for your medical treatment? You have no assurance that you can get back in this place. You don't know how hard it was for me to get you in here."

There was no reasoning with Dad. He foresaw only the worst if I left Good Shepherd. Finally, he got to the crux of his objection: "You leave here and we might be held responsible if anything happens. We don't have that kind of money."

He stood up to go. We were both exhausted from arguing. Neither had convinced the other.

"Are you coming to my graduation?"

"We were planning on it. All of us. Now I'm not so sure."

"What is that supposed to mean, you're not so sure?"

"It depends on whether you come to your senses and decide to stay in the institution."

I was angry now. And hurt. Whatever gall I thought my father possessed before, he surely outdid himself this time. To use the biggest event in my life and their support as a lever to keep me institutionalized so they can be "secure" was the ultimate insult. Did they think I was stupid?

. . . . . . . . . . . . . . . . . . . . . . . . . . . . . . .

"So, what you're saying is that if I leave Good Shepherd, you won't come to graduation?"

"Jeffrey, if you do this, then all I can tell you is that you are on your own. We will not be responsible. Good luck, but if anything happens, don't call us. We cannot take care of you."

"Call me Saturday and let me know if you're going to stay here. If I don't hear from you, don't expect us."

I desperately wanted my family to come for the highest achievement of my life. I wanted Dad, Mom, Grandmom, and my sisters to see that I had done it. But I would not stay cooped up in a home for the handicapped like some cripple for any reason. I had a future, a potential, and no one, not even my mother and father, was going to keep me from being on top!

Over and over in my mind, I ticked off the possible consequences of the two options. Leave Good Shepherd and perhaps lose what family ties I had left, such as they were. Leave and risk becoming an invalid without any guarantee of custodial care. The Snyders were getting up in years. I couldn't expect them to be burdened with me during their old age.

And if I stayed? I saw myself living in the men's quarters with Curtis and dying in an institution. I would never have the opportunity to use my talent in music for God, as I had dreamed.

I wrestled, prayed, agonized. I talked to my closest friends.

"Whatever you decide, I'll stand with you," Quacky said.

"You'll always have a home with us," the Snyders promised.

"If the Lord's leading you, he won't let you down," the Longs assured.

Saturday morning, Dan Pearson, who had done stories before on me for the Allentown *Morning Call,* came over for an interview. I shared with him my dilemma.

"My parents want me to stay here. But I don't want to spend my entire life in an institution. I want to be an evangelist and gospel singer. I want to be independent."

"How do your parents feel about your conversion to Christianity?" Dan asked.

"Mom says that leaving the Jewish faith—it's just as if I had died at birth. You know, I almost did," I smiled.

"But how can I leave something I never had? I'm a Jew only by birth. My folks didn't raise me a Jew. I was Bar Mitzvahed, but I never went back to the synagogue after that. That doesn't mean I don't love them. I know we argue a lot, but I do love them."

I told him about college and the Snyder's invitation for me to live with them on weekends while I attended Penn Wesleyan during the week.

At Dan's request, I gave him a list of the honors I had received in high school, including serving on the student council and receiving "The Last Man Award" conferred on the senior who did the most to overcome difficulties. I showed him Dr. Raker's gift, a new cuff-link watch, which I planned to wear at the graduation exercises Sunday night. "I owe him and the Good Shepherd staff more than I can ever repay," I added. "We've had our differences, but they've taken very good care of me. If I leave, I'll always think of Good Shepherd as my home."

A dozen times that afternoon I almost called Dad. I picked at my supper that evening. I tried to watch TV, but couldn't get my mind off the decision I had to make.

I called the Snyders again. "He's your father, Jeff," Dad Snyder said. "You have to respect him."

"The Bible says, 'obey your parents in the Lord,' " I quoted.

"Yes," Dad Snyder concurred. "You have to decide if leaving Good Shepherd is in the Lord.' "

I talked to Curtis again. "Jeff, you'll soon be twenty-one years old. It's your life. Your father can't live it for you."

I went back to my room and prayed. I worried and tossed in my bed. I prayed some more. I glanced at the clock. It

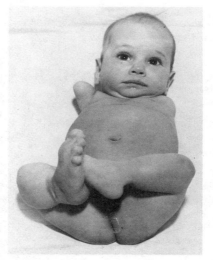

Jeff Steinberg, age two and a half.

RIGHT: Discharged from Shriners Hospital at age eight and a half.

BOTTOM: The main building of The Good Shepherd Home in Allentown, Pennsylvania.

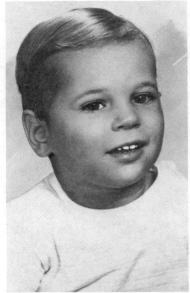

TOP: Sheryl, Harriet, Jeff (at age nine), and Linda.

LOWER LEFT: Jeff's first portrait at age three. And, yes, that is blond hair!

LOWER RIGHT: Jeff at eleven years of age.

RIGHT: Jeff's bar mitzvah when he was thirteen. With Cantor Samuel Weiss.

BELOW: The gang at Variety Club Camp, 1959.

LEFT: "R2D2, it is you!" Even *ceramics* by mouth.

BELOW: Steinberg's oil paintings by mouth, at age thirteen.

RIGHT: The Reverend Conrad Raker, superintendent of the Good Shepherd Home and rehabilitation Center.

MIDDLE: Dad, Mom, Uncle Morty, and Grandmom.

BOTTOM: "Mom and Dad" Snyder.

ABOVE: "The two shall become one flesh." Bride and groom, June 22, 1974.

RIGHT: "Look at that bow tie!" Benjamin David Steinberg, one day old.

The cover
of the album,
"The Glove."

The Wind
and Fire logo,
designed by
Jeff Steinberg.

UPPER LEFT: The Total Victory Trio: Jeffrey Rudloff, Jeff, Ronnie and Kay Fenwick.

MIDDLE LEFT: Dave Roff, Jeff, and Jeffrey Rudloff, with Wind and Fire on the PTL Club in 1977.

LOWER LEFT: The new Wind and Fire, with Alan and Joyce Witmer, 1978.

TOP: Showing off his driving skills for a TV taping.
BOTTOM: The wrecked 1966 Chrysler at Beaver Falls, Pennsylvania.
RIGHT: Masterpiece in Progress concert, a photo-portrait.

TOP: Jeff Steinberg, 1979.

BOTTOM: "Bigger-than-life advertising."

ABOVE: Co-hosting the Memphis, Tennessee, local Easter Seal Telethon, 1981.

"From one masterpiece to another . . ." Singing to Danielle Steel, the 1985 National Poster Child, on television.

TOP: Inspiring young "masterpieces" at an elementary school in Dayton, Ohio, 1977.

BOTTOM: Sharing a song and a good word at the Shriners Hospital in Houston, Texas, 1980.

ABOVE: Entertaining the troops under the beer tent in Nellingen, Germany, 1983.

LEFT: "Under the tent," Good Shepherd Day, 1984.

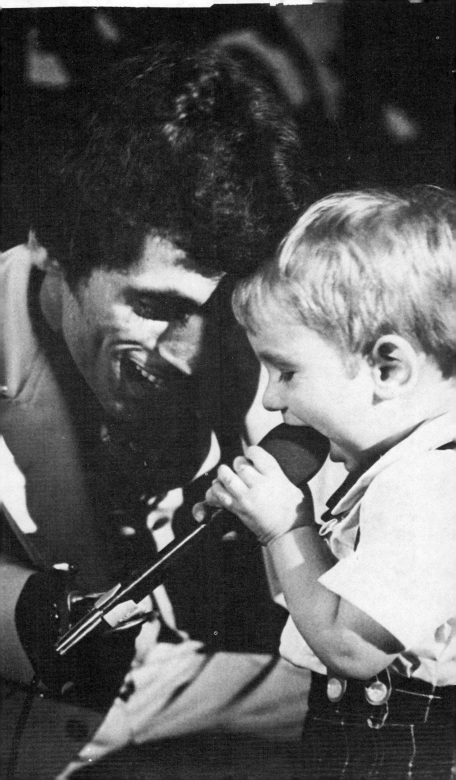

Autographing an album for Fred "Curly" Neal of the famed Harlem Globetrotters.

Good Shepherd Day, 1985, with Willie Stargell.

Jeff shares a laugh with Presidential Press Secretary Jim Brady at a Good Shepherd Day ceremony.

To Jeff Steinberg
With best wishes,
Ronald Reagan

UPPER LEFT: Harriet, Sheryl, and Linda.

RIGHT: On the winning team, Benji at age five.

"For my next number . . ." Benji's first audition, Jackson, Mississippi, age one and a half.

RIGHT: The 700 Club, with Ben Kinchlow, 1980.

BELOW: On stage with Pat Boone at the National Easter Seal Telethon, 1982.

The many faces of. . . .

was 1:00 A.M.. I had promised to be ready at 7:30 A.M. to go with friends to a church outside Allentown.

Tears flooded my eyes as I talked to God. "Lord, you've never failed me. You've never let me down. My parents have let me down lots of times. You've always been here. I truly believe you want me to leave Good Shepherd and sing and witness for you. I'm going to trust you now, Lord. I'm counting on you."

I then fell asleep.

After I got back from church, the weather turned hot and sultry. Low thunder rumbled from a distance. As time for the exercises approached, a dark cloud moved in over the city. I was sure my family would not be coming.

A staff person from Good Shepherd drove me over early in a van to the gymnasium at Muhlenberg College where the ceremonies were to be held. I went under the stands and got help putting on my blue and gold gown. Then I came back to the door where parents of the 771 graduates were streaming in.

I saw several people I knew, including Quacky, the Longs, the Snyders, and many from Good Shepherd. Curtis came swinging through the door on his crutches, smiling his congratulations.

I put on a happy face and cracked some jokes, but the pain inside could not be denied. My family had hurt me many times before. This was the ultimate.

"Hurry up, Jeff, and get to your chair," someone called.

I started in that direction.

"Yea, Jeff! You made it!" I lifted my hook to acknowledge the cheer.

I wanted Mom and Dad and my sisters and Grandmom to see me. I wanted to hear their congratulations. The lump of sadness welling in my throat felt as big as an orange.

C'mon, Steinberg, be realistic. Accept that your parents have cut out of your life. That's why they want you to stay in the institution. The voice was loud and persistent, yet I looked one more time in faint hope that I might see some member of my family.

Then I heard a little girl's voice, "Jeffrey? Jeffrey?"

There was another Jeffrey in my class. Oddly enough, Jeff Snider.

"Jeffrey Steinberg?"

She was running toward me, calling my name. My little sister, Harriet!

"Jeffrey, we came, we came." She was breathless.

I pulled her to me with my hook and squeezed. Tears of joy started to flow.

"C'mon, Steinberg, you'll be late," a boy yelled.

"OK, I'm coming."

I looked at Harriet. "Where are the rest?"

"They've all found seats. I saw you and had to come and tell you we're here. Grandmom is here, too."

I pecked her on the cheek. "Go on back to them. I'll see all of you afterwards. Run, now, and don't get lost."

I found my place amidst the rows of gowned graduates. I looked back and spotted my family in the stands. They waved. There were too many graduates for Mr. Bartholomew to hand out individual diplomas, so he made a token presentation and introduced the speaker, Arthur Zito, Manager of Advanced Space Technology for General Electric.

Outside, the air was like a steam bath. Lightning and thunder ripped across the black sky. Inside it was worse.

"I'm setting the alarm on my watch to go off in twenty minutes," the speaker said and we gave him an ovation.

He said some things that spoke to me: "No one can possibly succeed in work unless he likes it . . . All the opportunity in the world is waiting for people who get turned on by their job . . . The degree of success you achieve will be in proportion to the amount of voluntary service you perform for others."

He offered a prophecy that the United States would have

fifty to one hundred people living in space shelters on the moon by 1980.

"Ooops, there goes my little alarm," he chirped as he held his vibrating watch up to the microphone. Everybody roared. Then he said, "Just because this speech is immortal doesn't mean it has to be eternal." We roared again.

Thunder rumbled like an approaching freight train, ending in a loud clap. The speaker hurriedly closed and Mr. Bartholomew dismissed us.

I met my folks briefly outside in the hall. Mom and Dad kissed me lightly on the cheek and extended congratulations. My sisters and Grandmom hugged me.

"You didn't call," Dad reminded. "What are you going to do?"

"I'm leaving Good Shepherd."

"You're really going through with it?"

"Yes."

Dad seemed resigned to the inevitable. "If that's your choice, we wish you well. We hope it works. But if anything goes wrong," he warned, "don't call us. We can't care for you."

The Lord was telling me, "See, I'll take care of you. They said they wouldn't come, but I brought them."

The Snyders walked up. I quickly made the awkward introductions.

Dad cleared his throat. "Uh, with the weather the way it is, we'd better be going." Each member of my family kissed me good-bye and they were gone.

Mom Snyder tugged at my sleeve. "See, Jeff. I was sure they would come. God takes care of you when you trust him."

"I'll be OK, now," I murmured. "I've got peace."

"Then, let's get in the car and go get something to eat," Dad Snyder invited.

"Yeah," I said. "I'm starved."

It was raining pitchforks and hammer-handles by the time

we got to the restaurant. Several other friends joined us, including Curtis and Quacky, and we had a high old time. By the time the Snyders dropped me at Good Shepherd, it was past midnight. I went upstairs and found the nurse's aide on duty. "Help me get undressed," I asked. "I'm bushed."

CHAPTER TEN
· · · · · · · · · · ·

# LOOK OUT, WORLD, HERE I COME

Dan Pearson's "Story of a Successful AHS Graduate" covered half a page in *The Morning Call* the day after graduation—more space than the newspaper gave to the commencement exercises for both of the city's high schools. They even printed my signature under the headline with the notation that I had written it by holding a nylon-tipped pen with my teeth.

The story brought several invitations to sing in churches, but the offerings were not enough for a down payment on a car. I needed wheels if I was to attend Penn Wesleyan College during the week and commute to the Snyders on weekends. My plans were to move from Good Shepherd in July.

"Lord, I need transportation," I prayed. "I'm trusting you to provide."

One hot morning in July, I was summoned to Dr. Raker's office. I had been late getting back from a church engagement the Sunday night before and expected a reprimand. He was smiling.

"Jeff, I have a call from a Mr. Louis Koscis who owns Lehigh Valley Salvage Service. He would like you to come over right away. I'll get somebody to take you in a van."

A tall, well-built man, whom I judged to be Mr. Koscis, was waiting at the front entrance to the salvage yard. Beside him stood Dan Pearson and a photographer. What was coming off here?

When I got out of the van, the salvage man spoke to me. "I read the wonderful article about your graduation, and I would like to present you with a graduation gift." He then handed me a set of keys and pointed to a shiny blue 1961 Dodge Pioneer sedan with a white top. "It's all yours. Congratulations." He grinned.

He walked over and opened the door for me to get in. The photographer was clicking away.

I wiggled in on the front seat. A steering ring for my hook was attached to the steering wheel. The brake and gas pedals had been moved to the left and built up to where I could comfortably reach them.

It had a button starter which I could push with my hook and transmission buttons which I could touch with a small rod gripped in my teeth.

"The high-beam light switch is down under the panel," Mr. Koscis noted. "You can kick it to low beam and back with your left foot. It operates from a special electronic relay that a friend and I rigged for you."

Mr. Koscis jumped in the front seat beside me and Dan Pearson got in the back. "How about taking us for a spin?"

The car performed beautifully. "Wow!" I kept exclaiming. "This is a super car. Just super. I love it, I love it, I love it."

I pulled back into the salvage yard and got out to thank Mr. Koscis.

"Oh, don't just thank me," he said. "I had the idea, but a lot of guys helped. You wouldn't believe what this heap looked like when it was brought into my yard. But the engine was OK, and a bunch of us decided to restore it as a gift to you." He rattled off a list of auto part companies,

• • • • • • • • • • • • • • • • • • • • • • • • • • • • • • •

repair shops, and individuals, including Dopey Duncan, a local radio personality, who had installed the high-beam switch.

Dan was furiously taking notes for another story.

"Why did you do it?" I pressed.

"Well, I read Dan's story about you graduating from high school and how you want to do something with your life. I got to thinking about some people on welfare who are physically normal and sit around doing nothing for government handouts. Here you are, with all kinds of handicaps, and determined to get out and do something for yourself and other people. Dan said that you needed a car. So I called a few friends—nobody turned me down—and we went to work. We did it all ourselves. Nobody had to contribute a dime."

I was overwhelmed. I shook his hand with my hook, then drove the car back to Good Shepherd and wrote each one a thank-you note.

Curtis inspected the car, then I drove over to Quacky's and from there to the Snyder's. Dad Snyder was still at work. All Mom Snyder could say was, "Praise the Lord."

I called my parents in Philadelphia. They were flabbergasted and unhappy. "Jeff, you'll kill somebody," my mother warned. "You're not in any condition to drive."

"Mom, I don't want to argue with you. Besides, I'm over eighteen and I do not need your permission to drive a car. I just wanted to tell you that I have a car and am moving out in a couple of weeks."

When the time came, Carl and Curtis helped me pack a couple of suitcases which had been given to me. Then other staff loaded the bags, my dummies, tape recorder, a box containing my records, and other personal possessions into the car. The guys I had lived with on the second floor stood around watching. Curtis put a thin arthritic hand on my left shoulder.

"Say, when you get famous, will you come back and give us your autograph?"

"Oh, I'll be back often. How could I not?"

"Yeah, that's what we're afraid of." I turned at the sound of the familiar voice. Lucy. I was glad to see her. The feuding had long-since ended when I moved into the main building with the older guests, and now that I was leaving the Home, nothing could upset me. We had both been hard on each other because we both had our own problems to solve. But that was all behind us now. Shaking her hand proved to both of us that we were parting as friends.

I pulled away from the curb, smiled back at everybody, and turned down St. John Street. My eye caught some of the lettering from Psalm 23 stenciled around the top of the old building that adjoined the new rehab center. I whispered the words, "The Lord is my Shepherd, I shall not want."

"Yeah! Thank you, Lord."

"Mom, Dad, I'm home," I called from the car, as I drew up in front of the Snyders. Dad came out to bring my things in.

"You know where your room is," Mom Snyder said. "Go on in and I'll be there in a minute to help you put away your clothes."

I had about three weeks before college. Dad Snyder took some of his vacation and we made a number of short trips together. We sang in churches, went to a couple of concerts, took in a revival, and had a great time. Then, shortly before I was due to report for registration, the Snyders went with me to the eastern shore of Virginia where I sang at a church camp.

Driving to Penn Wesleyan College was no big deal. I had been there with the Snyders a couple of times for meetings in the chapel. I enrolled for a bachelor's degree in Theology, a course that would take five years, after which I would need only two more years to graduate from seminary. My belief that God wanted me to be a singer and an evangelist hadn't changed.

When I drove up to the dorm, a tall lanky man with

mousy blond hair came out to greet me. "I'm Ernie Ward, your roommate," he said. He carried my stuff into the dorm.

There was nothing special about the dorm. Just single beds. No bars in the bathroom or ramps instead of stairs, as had been at Good Shepherd. With a little help taking my clothes off and on, and some assistance in the bathroom, I figured I could make it.

Penn Wesleyan was the product of a recent merger of two colleges, yet it still had only 114 students when I enrolled in the fall of 1972. The grounds were level and the buildings close together. I could easily get from one class to another and there was always someone to carry my books.

I jumped into college life quickly. The freshman class of thirty-six students elected me their president. I joined the chapel singers and the radio club and took a full course load.

Penn Wesleyan was small, but hardly peaceful. Fierce arguments over dress styles, theology, and television preachers racked the campus. Some girls wore miniskirts, others granny dresses. Guys' hair ranged from below the shoulder to crewcuts.

I was conservative myself, and kept my hair a little over the ears, but I couldn't see anything wrong with bright colors. One guy I knew got "sanctified" and shucked his matching beige shoes, belt, colored shirts, splashy ties, and plaid suits for dark suits, dark ties, and black shoes. He merely went from parading his clothes to parading his piety.

"Hey, man," I said, "why not go all the way and get yourself a black hat and buggy?"

My psychology prof also taught Old Testament Bible. He presented the views of both liberal and conservative theologians, ". . . so you'll have a well-rounded view of what you'll meet in the real world." Every class turned into an opportunity for vivid discussion.

"Why do we have to listen to this liberal garbage?"

" 'Cause we need to know, that's why. How are you going inform your congregation, if you don't know what's happening in the world?"

"The Bible is enough for me."

"Then find yourself a cave and stay there for the rest of your life."

Finally I squawked, "We're never gonna learn anything if we don't stop bickering with one another."

The music classes were a washout for me in a different way.

A local lady came in and taught voice an hour a week to each of her students. She wanted me to sing like George Beverly Shea. "I respect Shea's talent and music, but he isn't my style," I said. "I want to do more contemporary stuff."

She thought my ideas on music were atrocious. She criticized my posture. "Can't you stand straight, young man?" I tried to explain my problems, but either she didn't listen or didn't care. I gave up on voice lessons after a semester.

Maybe I had a bad attitude, but music appreciation gave me less appreciation of music. The instructor babbled on and on about theories, from Bach to rock, which he assumed we knew, but which most of us didn't.

A further merger with two other Wesleyan colleges was scheduled for the next year on Penn's campus. The uncertainty of who would be president and who among the faculty would have jobs kept the teachers in a tizzy.

The squabbling, low morale, and other problems didn't offer much incentive to study. I wanted to get on with my career and put together "Jeff Steinberg and the Total Victory Trio."

Ronnie Fenwick, my drummer, was a former drug user who had played in a rock and roll band in bars and clubs. When he became a Christian, Ronnie flipped from one extreme to the other. Now he loved Jerry Falwell, the Cathedral Quartet, kept his hair an inch above the ears, and hated hard rock.

His wife, Kay, sang alto. Dark-haired and a little hefty, Kay could melt a statue with her sweet smile.

Ronnie and Kay were both students at Penn Wesleyan and planning on a pastoral ministry.

Jeff Rudloff, a merry guy with curly brown hair and mischievous eyes, was a high school senior. He played the piano by ear and could pick up any melody on a few minutes' notice—a natural talent. Jeff also sang tenor.

I met Jeff Rudloff when I attended a special service at a little Church of God in a small community called West Penn. I was asked to sing. His mother was the church pianist, but she couldn't play without sheet music and suggested Jeff.

"What key do you want this song in?" he asked.

I said, "E-flat."

He shook his head. "A-flat is a better key for you."

I looked at this kid skeptically. Four years younger than me, he was trying to tell me, the pro. But I said, "OK, I'll try it."

Perfect.

After the service, I eased up close to him. "Anybody who knows what key is best for me better than I do, I want to work with. I'm scheduled to sing at a weekend meeting in eastern Maryland next week and I was wondering if you would be interested in being my pianist. Maybe you could be my regular accompanist? Or, as regular as your schedule and your Mom permit."

"We can try it, but I can't guarantee how often I can go." That's how we got started working together.

Jeff came to the school for rehearsal and met Ron and Kay. They joined us and that evening the Total Victory Trio was born. The incident that brought him and me together developed into a little inside joke. Whenever we would start talking about the key for a song, one of us would pipe up, "Do it in A-flat," whether that was the best key or not.

The fifth member of the group—I'll call him Miles Eisenhower—was recommended to me by an evangelist friend. Miles, who was mediocre on the base guitar at best, came with long blond tresses parted in the middle and flirtatious brown eyes. He had a way with the girls. Brother, did he have a way with the girls!

We were getting set up in a little independent Baptist church one Sunday evening when the pastor came over, a questioning look in his eyes. He pointed to Miles, standing in the back holding hands with a couple of teenage girls from the church. "He's kind of familiar, isn't he?"

"Yeah," I said, "a little familiar. I'll talk to him."

I had noticed him holding hands with a girl at the last church where we sang, but decided not to make an issue of it. This time I walked over and called him aside.

"Leave the girls alone, man."

He rolled his brown eyes at me and said, "What'd I do?"

"You were too friendly. You didn't meet them until a half hour ago."

"What's wrong with that?" he snapped defensively.

"It gives a bad impression."

"OK, I won't do it again," he said grudgingly and walked away.

A couple of weeks later I caught him clutching a girl's arm. "Cut it out, man," I ordered. "You're making things hard for all of us."

"I can't help that the girls like me."

"Stay away from them. Stay close to us."

"Well, all right," he grumped.

I had put the group together, but I wanted us to be democratic. At the same time I wanted my way. We argued a lot about what songs to sing. Jeff and I preferred more rhythm.

"We can't sacrifice the message," Ronnie insisted.

Ronnie and Kay also wanted to do familiar songs such as "One Day at a Time" by Marijohn Wilkin and Bill Gaither's, "Because He Lives."

"We shouldn't walk in their shadow," I said. "Let's work up material of our own. If we can't get enough, let's do stuff nobody ever heard of. We want to make a name for our group."

Jeff Rudloff was the songwriter in the group, so we depended a lot on him for new songs and arrangements. I compromised occasionally, doing upbeat convention songs like Joel Hemphill's, "I'll Soon Be Gone," for example.

Lover Boy didn't care and Kay just smiled and said, "Whatever you guys decide is OK with me."

The Total Victory Trio wasn't terribly good. We seldom had a planned program lined up beforehand. Being the stage manager, I called the songs as we went along. We were just five young people, confident of our talents, bent on doing our thing for the Lord.

Curtis came often to our concerts, though he was no great fan of gospel or contemporary Christian music. He knew enough to catch our flubs, and there were plenty of them. He bragged about us to everybody he met and said we were better than most Christian groups and even some secular ones. Despite his wisecracking and put-downs, Curtis continued to be my most loyal friend. I always looked for him and his crutches when we made an appearance in or around Allentown.

With the college so close to Good Shepherd, I was over there every few days. I spent much of my free time with Curtis. We talked about music, the Bible, girls, anything that came to our minds. We were totally at ease with one another.

Curtis asked me one day, "You think you'll ever live here again?"

I said, "I hope not, but I keep coming back to visit, mostly because of you. There's no one else left."

One day I walked into Good Shepherd and was told, "Curtis was rushed to the hospital. His kidneys have failed."

I raced over to Allentown General. My friend had been in surgery for ten hours. I waited until they brought him out, but of course he couldn't talk. He was still under the anesthetic.

"It doesn't look good," the doctor said very grimly.

I sat at the door of his room talking to him, hoping he would hear me and respond but fearing that he might not make it. I did a lot of praying for my friend. My best friend died two days later. I took it hard. I didn't have the nightmares as when Ricky died. But the loss really tore the props from under me. Curtis had always been there when I needed him. I could come by boiling with frustrations over things at the college, or after an argument with somebody, and Curtis could calm me down.

Later, I looked back and saw that the loss of Curtis had been good for me in one respect. So long as he was still at Good Shepherd, I felt I belonged there. I needed to break further away and live my own life. With Curtis gone, this became easier. Yet, I've never ceased to mourn his passing.

"I'll see you again one day, Curtis."

During spring break of 1972, the Total Victory Trio made a tour of New Jersey, singing in a string of Assemblies of God churches. Ronnie wasn't satisfied to be just singing for the Lord; he had made a vow to talk to someone personally about Christ every day. We were on our way back to Allentown late Sunday evening after the last concert when Ronnie yelled, "Stop at the next gas station!"

We figured maybe he had an acute need to go to the bathroom. Rudloff, who was driving, pulled in at a Texaco place down the road

"Thank God, it's only five minutes to twelve," Ronnie said as he jumped out the front door and headed for an attendant. They talked for a couple of minutes, then the attendant broke away and headed back into the station.

"What was that all about?" I asked Ronnie when he got back in the car.

"Oh, I was just witnessing to him . . . and keeping my vow."

A couple of weeks before the end of the spring semester, Ronnie and I were strolling across the campus. "I'm thinking about dropping out of school for a semester," I said. "I'm not real happy with my grades. There's a lot of uncertainty around the school and dissension among the staff, and I want to be involved in ministry. That's what I came here to prepare for. I'm thinking about going full time in music."

"How are you going to make it by yourself? Who'll set up for you? Who'll play the piano?"

"Oh, I still want you guys to work with me when you can. When you can't, I'll pick up some spares. Right now, I'm having to turn down dates because of class schedules."

"Yeah, classes are a hindrance," Ronnie said dryly.

"If I drop out, will you and Kay still sing with me on weekends?"

"Sure," he said, "but I think you're making a mistake leaving school."

"Jeff thinks so, too. But I think the Lord is leading me to go full time, and I'm going to give it a stab."

The Snyders were disappointed too, but they didn't make a fuss over my decision to leave United Wesleyan as the college had been renamed after the last merger.

"You've got a home with us as long as you need it," Mom Snyder assured me.

There were others who thought I was selling myself short. I could have transferred to another college, with the state paying my expenses. But I felt I needed a break. I was twenty-two years old and not getting any younger.

I also figured it was time the Total Victory Trio cut an album. Someone recommended Casey Studios, a small four-track studio in Hampton, Virginia. I phoned Casey for a bid that seemed reasonable and we raised the money to buy a thousand copies.

Jeff Rudloff insisted we get a piano player with more experience than he had. We got Glen Kantner, a former pianist for the Eastmen Quartet. He could do some fancy licks and flourishes. The six of us drove down in June.

It took twelve hours to do the vocals, then the guys did

the accompaniment on a second set of track. We named the album for the lead song, "He Must Have Loved Me," written by Jeff Rudloff. God really must have loved us. We were raw and on the hot edge of frustration by the time Casey had a master.

That summer a local preacher rented a lot at the Allentown Fair and put up a booth for evangelism. He engaged the Total Victory Trio to do mini-concerts between the showing of Christian films.

We did a few songs, then moved among the crowd to confront people directly with the gospel. I talked to a number of people who knew me from stories in the Allentown newspaper. One guy told me later that he became a Christian "as a result of talking to you. When I saw you with all your physical problems speaking out for the Lord," he said, "I knew it had to be real."

We worked at the fair from four to ten every weekday evening for two weeks. Johnny Cash was there a couple of days and gave us a little competition from the grandstand. Two to three hundred people still showed up for each of our performances.

One warm evening we finished a concert about six. Before the next film was due to start, Ronnie and Kay moved back to talk to some teenagers. Miles headed for a row of young girls. I walked to the door of the booth to speak to people as they were leaving.

Out of the corner of my eye I saw a tall, burly guy with a walrus mustache looking at the poster showing our pictures. He reminded me of the bad guy in an old Western movie. Suddenly, Ronnie rushed up from behind and smacked him on the rear with a Bible.

"Hey, man, do you know you're going to hell if you aren't saved?"

The guy whirled around and peered down at Ronnie, who was five feet four inches and no more than eighty-five pounds soaking wet. Ronnie already had his Bible open and was poised to fire away. For a second I thought the guy was going to spit on Ronnie. All he did was shake his head and mumble, "Are you weird or something?" Then he stalked away.

I guess we were a little weird to some people. We saw ourselves as only obeying Jesus' command to "go into the highways and hedges, and compel them to come in . . ." (Luke 15:23).

Jeff Rudloff went to Houghton College, a Wesleyan school in upstate New York, in the fall. Ronnie and Kay continued their studies at the college in Allentown. Miles stayed in the area, earning a few bucks from odd jobs and working with Total Victory as we needed him. I was so fed up with his flirting that I would have told him to get lost if we could have found another bass player.

Jeff Rudloff came home on occasional weekends. When Ronnie was filling a pulpit somewhere, Rudloff and I worked together. He played the piano and we did a few duet numbers, but I was the star act, singing solos and giving my testimony. We were a sensational duo. Many times we were told by other singers that the two of us sounded like a group, probably because of the chord patterns he played behind us that gave us a fuller sound.

Jeff and I argued about theatrics.

"What's wrong with doing things in a professional way?" I asked him.

He looked up at me from the piano where he was running through a melody in preparation for the night's concert.

"Nothing," he said, "so long as your heart is in it. I just don't see how you can say the lines every time and stay sincere."

"Don't worry about me, I can do it," I insisted.

I found that an audience really listened when I straightforwardly described my handicap and related my struggles to get where I was.

I also told stories between songs about Ricky, Curtis, and others I had known in the Good Shepherd Home. I used show business techniques, pauses, facial contortions, gestures with my hook, smiles, frowns. I made cracks about myself that broke people up with laughter. I made people feel better when I poked fun at myself. I was merely following Curtis' advice not to take myself too seriously. I felt that if I could get across my feeling that God loved me and had a greater purpose for my life, then they could more easily apply God's love to themselves.

Early in October of 1972, on a Saturday night, I drove to Pottstown, Pennsylvania, to attend a rally for Jerry Falwell's "Old Time Gospel Hour" TV program. I was impressed and moved by the music and story of a 327-pound soloist, Doug Oldham. He spotted me sitting near the front, glowing, soaking in every word and enjoying the music enthusiastically. In front of twelve hundred people, he paused between songs, looked in my direction and asked me, "What is your name?"

I was startled. "Jeff Steinberg," I replied with pride.

Doug turned to the audience. "This young man is breaking me up." He continued with a grin, and a tear trickling down his face. "He praises the Lord even with a hook, and most of us don't appreciate what we have. God has been good to me." He broke into a song, "Through It All," written by Andre Crouch. I was impressed. I wanted to meet this man. Following the service, I did just that.

I approached someone in the hall who told me that Doug Oldham wanted to meet me. I walked over to introduce myself.

We talked for a bit. He told me that I inspired him.

I shared with him a bit of my story and my desire to sing and minister. He asked me to sing a song. I sang "Follow Me," written by Ira Stamphill. He then joined me and we sang a duet on a chorus of "Through It All." Jerry Falwell and his entourage reentered the auditorium during our duet and were so moved that Jerry approached me afterward.

"That was great, Jeff. Would you consider coming to Lynchburg, Virginia, to share at Thomas Road Baptist Church this Sunday?"

"Would I? I would love to." It was a dream come true. I had been discovered.

It seemed almost miraculous the way it all fit together—juggling my schedule, flying down instead of driving, and then singing and sharing my story and song before 3,000 people in the auditorium as well as to thousands on national television.

Doug Oldham and I walked up to the platform and sat down near the pulpit. Doug leaned over and whispered, "You'll be singing over 200 TV stations and several radio outlets in the delayed broadcast of the "Old Time Gospel Hour." I looked across the balcony and saw the TV cameras beamed at us.

Unbelievable! Sixteen months before, I had left the institution. I had driven more than 300 miles in my own car and would soon be singing to probably over a million people. "If only Mom and Dad could see me now," I said. "Hey, maybe they can, if I can find out when the program is telecast in Philadelphia."

Doug introduced me very informally before Dr. Falwell spoke. "Folks, when I met this fellow, I didn't see how he could walk, but he does. Most important, he walks with the Lord. Will you welcome Jeff Steinberg, a full-blooded Hebrew who has accepted Jesus Christ as his Messiah."

I took the cord mike with my hook and stood up, shifting my weight until I was balanced on my crooked left leg and my artificial foot on my right side. Doug had promised that I could give my testimony in the evening service, so I launched right into the song I had chosen, "Follow Me." I finished to a chorus of amens. Then I sat on Doug's lap and we sang a duet. They loved us.

In the evening service I described briefly the "multiple congenital anomalies" with which I had been born and how my parents had put me in the institution, where they wanted me to remain.

After the announcements, I came back and told how I became a Christian through the love and witness of friends. As I sang "Tears Are a Language That God Understands," I saw people wiping their faces with handkerchiefs.

Later, I checked the station listings and found the "Old

Time Gospel Hour" wasn't on TV in Allentown. Mom and Dad Snyder would be disappointed, but it was aired on channel 17 in Philadelphia. I called my parents and said, "Hey, you can see me sing on TV in two weeks." I gave them the time and station.

"I hope you're proud of me," I said hopefully.

They didn't seem thrilled at all. They didn't even promise to watch. I hung up the phone.

When I got back to Allentown, I didn't have much time to brood over Dad's indifference. Calls started coming from pastors after the program aired on the first stations. I phoned Jeff Rudloff at Houghton College. "Hey, man, my date book is filling up," I said. "When can you come and help me?"

# CHAPTER ELEVEN

· · · · · · · · · · · · ·

# DATING AND WAITING

I hadn't seen my family in Philadelphia since my high school graduation. I had called them several times to keep in touch and they phoned me once or twice, only if they had some important reason. They never called just to say "hello" or just to talk. Just a "hello, how are you doing?" would have been welcomed. When we did speak, the conversations were brief, casual on the surface, with obvious tension crackling underneath.

My album was an example of my accomplishments to show them that I was making it. And I was making it on my own. Not that I didn't have or need help, but nobody can make it for me. Here I was, with my first solo album, standing at her door. Jeff Rudloff went with me. My family had moved from Placid Street further northeast to a two-story plain red brick duplex on Jeannes Street.

I rapped on the door with my hook. Mom opened it, and stood surprised at the sight of her handicapped son holding a splashy record album with his name emblazoned in bold letters on it. There were the usual hugs and kisses.

"Well, aren't you going to invite us in?" I asked.

She did. Dad was at work. Linda was now married and had moved to California, Sheryl was in college, and Harriet was at a girlfriend's house.

The inside of the house was a mirror image of the house on Placid Street with the same aquamarine couch covered in plastic, same spinet piano, and the same wrought-iron trimmed dining room furniture. The only changes were the surroundings.

"You're looking well, Mom," I said.

I handed her the album. "This is for you."

"Oh yeah?" She looked at the cover, turned it over, and put it down.

"Very nice, Jeffrey. Thank you." She invited us to sit down and offered us something to drink.

"No thanks. We can't stay, Mom. I just wanted to bring you my first solo album, and say 'hello.' This is Jeffrey Rudloff, and he plays piano and sings with me. He also writes some of my songs."

She was very cordial, but cool. We were there no more than ten minutes. It was tense.

"Well," I said, a bit awkwardly, "we'd better be moving on. 'Bye, Mom."

She shook hands with Rudloff, kissed me fast on the cheek, and said, "I'll tell your father you came."

End of visit.

I walked to the car in a fog. Jeff opened the door on the driver's side for me. I drove along for several miles without saying anything.

Jeff tried to cheer me up. "You've got a lot going for you, Steinberg. Talent. Opportunities for service. Friends, like me."

"Yeah," I said. "It's times like these I need friends like you." We didn't say much about my family for a while. I knew he understood. Jeffrey Rudloff and I had gotten to know each other pretty well. He had replaced Curtis in my life.

We drove on toward Allentown, taking the same road my parents had when they took me to Good Shepherd. Rudloff fell silent, not knowing anything to say. Finally, my thoughts burst out of my head, hot and bitter.

"She could at least have said, 'I'm proud of you.'"

I glanced over and saw my buddy's lower lip quivering. He hurt for me.

"Thanks," I said.

"For what?"

"For coming with me, although I'm sorry she didn't throw a party."

Crazy guys that we were, we both broke up laughing.

My first solo engagement after Thomas Road was December 2 with the Hanes Baptist Church in Winston-Salem, North Carolina. Clyde Phillips, one of the laymen in the church, had been in the services when I sang at Thomas Road. He persuaded Harold Perry, the pastor in Winston-Salem, to invite me to sing for the Sunday morning service and sing and give my testimony that night. The church paid for me to fly down. Clyde and his wife, Dot, were there when I landed. "You're going to stay with us," they said.

We started walking toward the baggage claim area. "You've got a good pianist, one who can play by ear, I hope. I couldn't pack mine in a bag," I said with a smile.

"Oh, we've got the perfect one for you," Clyde laughed and winked at Dot. "She'll be at the church to rehearse with you on Saturday morning." I figured something was up, but I didn't say anything.

On Saturday morning, we went over to the church. "Hey, Debbie, he's here," Clyde called. A 4-foot-10-inch tall, bouncy little hazel-eyed blonde, whom I judged to be just a few inches taller than me, came over to me.

"This is Jeff Steinberg, the fellow I've been telling you about," Clyde said. "Jeff, meet Debbie Poplin, your pianist."

Though she might be the first to admit that she was not a candidate for a beauty pageant, she had an inner beauty that seemed to shine through her smile, a beauty that transcends hairstyles and the latest fads and fashions, and conveys a definite contentment with herself. I saw someone more beautiful than eyes could behold.

"I'm the church pianist. Clyde has told me a lot about you."

"Yeah, he said you were perfect for me."

She said, "We saw you on TV, sitting on Doug Oldham's lap. You were very good."

Clyde stepped in. "Well, why don't we get started?" It was then that I noticed a group of teenage girls who were there at the church for the regular Saturday morning live radio broadcast from the church. They were all giggling.

Debbie got down to business. The minute she hit the first note I knew she was good. The rehearsal went off without a hitch. After a short rehearsal, I sang a couple of songs and spoke on the church's live radio broadcast.

We chatted a little more before the Phillips took me home with them. Debbie told me she was a junior in high school, planned to be a teacher, and had a younger brother and sister. She had attended Hanes Baptist Church most of her life. Her father was an air-conditioning and heating engineer, a deacon, and a Sunday school teacher in the church, and her mother also taught Sunday school.

The Phillips had both me and Debbie at their house for Sunday dinner. I complimented Dot Phillips for the delicious food and dominated the conversation with stories and escapades about my life on the road. Debbie hardly said a word, but just sat quietly and smiled demurely.

Debbie and I got to talk some more before the evening service. I mentioned to her that another church in Winston-Salem had booked me for Monday night. "Do you think your parents would let you come and play the piano for me?" I ventured.

"Oh, I'm sure they'll let me come."

I stole a glance at Debbie. *She's really a good-looking girl;*

*she's sweet, not at all like some of the groupies that hang around Christian singers' record tables,* I thought. *What a shame she's only sixteen.*

To this point, I hadn't given girls much thought. I did like one girl named Ea at William Allen High School. We played chess and worked on a couple of assignments together. Once she invited me over to her house, and we took in a couple of gospel concerts together. I thought we had a date for a third. She was to meet me at Good Shepherd and we were to go with another couple in their car. Then she waltzed in with another guy. We never dated again, but we remained friends.

I never expected not to get married. I just figured that the Lord would send the right girl at the right time, one whom I could love and who would love me and share my ministry without pity. Debbie interested me. She was different from the rest. She was quiet and seemed very genuine. Not at all dazzled by the glitter. She was so young, but so mature!

Debbie's folks proved to be as strict as I figured they would be. They did consent to her playing the piano for me at the other church in Winston-Salem, with some hesitation.

I explained to her the complications of having a group who had other things to do besides singing with me. "Jeff Rudloff can help me only a few weekends this spring," I noted. "If I had a regular pianist, I believe I could make it on my own."

"I can see where you need someone, Jeff," Debbie said. She didn't volunteer for the job, nor did I think it realistic to consider her as my pianist at this time.

On Monday, Clyde Phillips took me over to the Christian radio station in Winston-Salem. I called Debbie from there. "You're never going to believe this. I was telling them here at the station about how I needed a piano player and a young lady about twenty-two, my age, applied for the job. She's really interested. What do you think?"

Debbie knew I was baiting her. She paused, while I hung

on in suspense. "Well," she finally said, "you have your life to live, Jeff. But I don't think it would look very good for a single man to be traveling around with a single woman and singing in churches. Do you?"

She had said what I wanted her to say. "Yeah, I guess you're right," I said with a grin that she couldn't see through the phone. "I don't think it would look right either."

Our team concert went off beautifully, and we got better acquainted. Mostly I talked and she listened.

Much later I learned that when she saw me on TV, she thought I was conceited, arrogant, and egotistical. Needless to say, she didn't like me at first. I didn't know it then, and Debbie would never have told me, but she had already decided that I was the man God had picked out for her future.

Something else I didn't learn until much later. Debbie had this decision confirmed at a revival a few days after my first trip to Winston-Salem. She and her best girlfriend, Lisa Childress, went to hear a man named Bill Stafford. These girls didn't go to dances or shows—about the most "worldly" thing Debbie did was serve on the high school pep squad. Going to revivals was their social outlet.

Stafford preached from John 14:13, 14, and 15:7, that if you stay in close fellowship with the Lord, you can ask what you will and be sure your prayer will be answered. Debbie's conclusion was: "Lord, I'm abiding in the center of your will for my life. I don't ask foolishly, for my desires are centered in you. Therefore, I ask, believing, that you will give me Jeff Steinberg for a husband."

She confided to Lisa after the service, "I believe that Jeff Steinberg and I will be married, but don't you dare tell a soul."

Debbie's parents sensed her feelings for me and tried to apply the brakes. "I hope you aren't thinking about him just because you feel sorry for him, handicapped as he is. Dating out of pity is not a good reason. And you shouldn't put your hopes on him just because he's a gospel singer. That kind of life isn't as glamorous as you think," her mother warned.

Whatever their motives, they didn't have much effect on Debbie. She imagined us traveling together, performing before big crowds, seeing hundreds of people receive Jesus as Lord and Savior. She didn't think much beyond that.

Clyde hustled me into his car on Tuesday morning and got me to my plane on time. All the rest of the month, even during Christmas with the Snyders, I kept thinking of Debbie and cute things I intended to say to her when I went back to North Carolina.

Meanwhile, I was having some second thoughts. Debbie was a beautiful girl, quiet and somewhat withdrawn. I liked her a lot. But she was so young and we didn't know each other very well. We had only been together a couple of times, and then with a bunch of other people around. And with the offerings I was receiving, I wasn't half certain I could support a wife. The prospect of marriage on such limited income scared the fire out of me. I liked Debbie a lot, though I wasn't sure that I loved her enough to marry her. I don't know if I was infatuated by her caring for me or if I really loved her.

Perhaps I was afraid that the price tag of real love was too steep for someone like me to pay. Not that I had given up my dream of marrying the right girl, but I was afraid because I was handicapped and she would have more to do for both of us. I lived on love offerings and that didn't guarantee a large or even sufficient paycheck, which can make an insecure marriage even more insecure. And I traveled a lot and lived like a nomad, from place to place. That was a tall order for a guy only 4 feet 6 inches tall, and a scary proposition for even the bravest of souls.

I stayed in touch with Debbie by calling her every week, sometimes more than that, a fact I'm sure Ma Bell appreciated a lot. I saw Debbie also several times between January and April while on tour in the area and, whenever possible, I would drive to Winston-Salem to see her and spend a couple of days with her. Perhaps I cared more for her than even I was willing to admit.

There was another consideration. In March, I met Lynn. It started out simply enough. We were guests of Ivan and Nancy Ollis and their children, Lynn and Randy, while Jeff Rudloff and I sang in a Baptist church in Holland, Michigan. Lynn was taller than Debbie, about 5 feet 7 or 8 inches tall with long, full, thick, shiny black hair and cool brown eyes. She was of Greek and Hawaiian ancestry and quite beautiful.

There was nothing shy or reserved about Lynn. She was a Northerner and matched me quip for quip, all in good fun. People could feel the sparks flying between us. Her mother liked me and egged Lynn on.

As we began to sing more often in that part of Michigan, we were invited to use the Ollis house as headquarters, and we became like adopted members of the family. Lynn and I were just good friends. As we got to know each other better and spent more time together, we became very fond of each other. We began to date and grew to love each other. Lynn also enjoyed singing and performed a few concerts with me and Jeffrey in the area.

We dated through the summer whenever we were in Michigan and between concerts. But I couldn't forget Debbie. I did not call or write her all summer even though she continued writing to me at least one letter a week.

At the end of the summer, and after spending a lot of time with Lynn, I had an engagement in Goldsboro, North Carolina, about 150 miles from Winston-Salem. I phoned Debbie and asked if she could play the piano again for me. She planned to bring Lisa along.

Debbie's antenna detected a slight distance in my voice. She suspected something had happened but wasn't sure until she and Lisa came over to the house where I was staying. When I stepped out of the living room, Debbie glimpsed a letter I had inadvertently left open on the coffee table. She caught the first few lines in a delicate feminine handwriting, "Dear Jeff . . . it was great fun having you at our house. . . . When are you coming back?" That, for Debbie, explained my cooled ardor.

She had masked the hurt by the time I got back in the room and said nothing about the letter. I didn't know whether she had seen it or not. Nor did I know that she was crushed and cried on Lisa's shoulder all the way home.

Her faith had weakened that I would ever pick up the torch. It was only her friend Lisa that kept her from giving up. On the way back from Goldsboro, where Debbie had been devastated by seeing the letter from Lynn, Lisa kept telling her, "It doesn't matter if he has fifty girlfriends. You are the one he's going to marry."

Bill Stafford came back for another revival in Winston-Salem in August 1973, and Debbie and Lisa went to hear him again. Debbie felt he was speaking directly to her when he said, "If the Lord has given you assurance about something, the Devil will make you doubt and want to give it up. What you must do is step out on faith and tell somebody else that it is going to happen."

Debbie marched up to him after the service and announced, "Bill, Jeff Steinberg and I are getting married next June."

Bill remembered her from the last time and looked at her curiously. "Has he proposed?"

"No, and I haven't heard from him in two months. But I believe the Lord has given him to me and we will be married next June."

Summer broiled along. I stayed busy and didn't call. I thought about her pretty often, but the urge wasn't strong enough to get in touch.

I managed to swing by Holland again. This time Lynn and I got into a hot argument over my singing in Pentecostal churches.

Lynn was an independent Baptist, like Debbie. But unlike

Debbie, who never criticized anybody, Lynn had some peculiar ideas about my singing for Holiness and charismatic churches.

"I don't see how you can be true to the Lord and the Word and sing in those churches," she said.

"I don't feel threatened by anybody," I shot back. "I know what I believe. I go to minister, not to pledge allegiance to every doctrine which a church teaches, including yours."

We both backed off a little while, then I said something favorable about a church of another denomination, which she didn't approve of. The alarm bells were ringing in my head. Though we cared very much for each other, there were obvious areas we did not agree on, and yet those disagreements never changed our feelings for each other. I knew then that we were not right for each other for marriage.

I wasn't too unhappy when we left Holland.

The old blue '61 Dodge was now a thing of the past.

Jeffrey Rudloff and I, along with a short-term helper, Steve Frankenberry, a high school junior on summer vacation, left on a trip to Texas to sing for Evangelist Freddie Gage's "Pulpit in the Shadows" in Houston. I had just purchased my first brand new car, a 1973 Chrysler Town and Country Station Wagon, only five weeks before.

I was speeding along I-20 in eastern Texas at a seventy-mile-per-hour clip (then the speed limit) when the right tire blew and peeled off and the rear axle locked. The wagon skidded into the median, jumped a little bump, bounced over a hill, and rolled over several times onto the wide median strip.

Immediately a couple of men stopped to help us. I kicked the cracked front windshield out as the one gentlemen reached in to help when the other man, observing from the other side, saw no arms and suddenly cried out, "Don't touch him. Don't move him. He may be hurt!!"

"Shut up!" I yelled, and I turned to the first man and continued, "Don't pay any attention to him. Get us out of here. We're all right."

We sat and lay on the soft grass of the median in the warm sun beside my new wrecked car waiting for the ambulance, singing: "I have decided to follow Jesus. No turning back, no turning back." A black Baptist minister stopped to help, heard our singing, and said, "You boys are either saved or you are crazy."

The rescue squad from Tyler, Texas, was there in minutes. A couple of paramedics jumped out to find four banged-up guys sitting beside their bottom-side-up wagon. They slid backboards under Jeffrey, who had banged his head and twisted his back, and Steve, who looked the worst but had only a few bruises and scratches, and then turned to assist me into the ambulance. Suddenly, I remembered my hook had come off at the elbow joint in the melee.

They could see I had no arms. "Pardon me," I said to the guy at my side, "would you mind getting my arm out of the car?"

"Your arm!" he shrieked.

"Yeah, it's in the front seat. I was driving," I added.

"You were driving this vehicle?"

"Yeah."

"Ya gotta be kidding!"

"Do you want to see my license?"

"Forget it, I believe you. Get in the ambulance, and let's have you guys checked out."

We had only bruises. When we described the wreck to the intern at the hospital in Tyler, he shook his head in amazement. "Somebody must have been watching over you guys."

"Somebody was," I told him.

The doctor helped us gather our salvaged sound system and albums and tapes from the wagon, loading them into his clean car. We turned it over to the insurance company and called more than twenty-five local churches for assistance getting to Houston, with no success. We finally hitched a ride to Houston with a local gospel singing group recommended to us by a clerk at the drugstore near the motel, across the street from the medical center. Jeffrey

Rudloff later made up a little card that he suggested I keep in the glove compartment of any vehicle I was driving:

*IN CASE OF ACCIDENT, FIND SPARE ARM IN TRUNK AND SPARE LEG UNDER SEAT*

Jeff also went to Nashville with me where I was invited to sing at the National Quartet Convention where we sang to more than 10,000 people in the huge Municipal Auditorium. We sang a song written by Jeffrey called "He Died," that was arranged as a medley with a chorus written by Bill Gaither called "Because He Lives." We received a standing ovation.

Dottie Rambo, a well known southern country-gospel songwriter whom I had long admired, and her husband, Buck, were waiting in the wings when I went out to do my song with a sound track. Jeffrey Rudloff stood near them. According to him, Dottie fastened her eyes on me and said to Buck, "Look at that boy. I'll never complain a day in my life again. That young man's out there singing with no arms and I get upset when I have a headache."

J. D. Sumner, the famed bass singer for the Blackwood Brothers Quartet, walked up to me as I left the stage, with tears in his eyes, and handed me a $50 bill and simply said, "God bless you. You blessed me."

Jeff was the only one who remained with me following the breakup of the Total Victory Trio. Ronnie took a pastorate in Maryland. Lover Boy, Miles, drifted away and I didn't see him for eleven years. By then he was married and had a couple of kids. I also noticed that he was balding. Poetic justice, I suppose.

Lynn was past tense, but I didn't get in any hurry about Debbie. Though I didn't talk to her for a two-month stretch, she hung in the back of my mind.

September came and Debbie's Uncle Andy and Aunt Norma came for a visit to Winston-Salem from their home in Maumee, Ohio. Debbie played the Total Victory Trio album and showed them my picture. "Jeff and I are going to be married," she declared.

Uncle Andy knew I hadn't called in months. "Debbie, you're just infatuated with the idea of getting married," he said. "Forget this gospel singer and get on with your life." That made her angry.

The next day he tried a different tack. "Debbie, suppose he does marry you. Do you know what you're in for? This won't be fun and games. He isn't your ordinary man. You'll have to care for him. If you're fortunate enough to have children, they'll be screaming while you're trying to care for a handicapped husband." That didn't work, either.

He tried teasing. "How long has it been since he called you? Three months? He's got another girlfriend, I'll bet."

The telephone rang. Debbie's mother answered. Debbie ran to pick it up in the bedroom.

"Hi, remember me?" I said.

Debbie almost dropped the phone.

"Hello." She tried not to sound too thrilled. But I could tell she was glad to hear from me.

"We need to talk," I continued.

She agreed.

"I'm coming to Winston-Salem in a few weeks to sing and would like for you to play for me." I told her about the concerts in the area, we set up a date to meet, and said good-bye.

She hung up the phone and ran back into the kitchen where her parents and aunt and uncle were playing Rook.

"Uncle Andy, he called! He called!" She danced back to the bedroom phone and called Lisa.

I called every few days after returning to the Snyders. I guess Debbie's folks decided the situation was hopeless, for they let her fly up to meet my "family," the Snyders, and other friends. I arranged for her to stay with a nurse friend I knew at Good Shepherd.

Mom and Dad Snyder loved my southern belle. "She's a winner," Mom Snyder said. "Don't let her get away."

Quacky was equally high on Debbie, as were the Longs. I was afraid to take her to Philadelphia, fearful that Mom and Dad would talk her out of marrying me.

We were driving around Allentown one day and talking about upcoming events. Debbie would be finishing high school the next June. "My schedule's clear then," I said without thinking. I don't know who mentioned it first, we just came to a conclusion: "June's the best time. Let's get married."

I saw her off with a kiss at the Allentown airport and called her that night to ask about her flight home. "Wonderful," she said. "Please thank everybody for helping me have such a good time."

"Let me talk to your dad," I requested. She called him to the phone, figuring I had something important on my mind. "Hey Mr. Poplin, how are you?" I asked, and then got right down to business. "I want your permission to marry your daughter." Debbie was hovering around the phone, making sweet eyes at her father.

"You sure you want her?"

"Of course, I'm sure, why else would I ask?"

"You can have her then." Debbie let out a shriek of delight.

The next month I went to sing in the Bahamas. Where else do gospel singers from the cold, frozen northland go during midwinter? It's a nice place from which to send romantic picture cards. I announced to the people in the church where I was singing that I was engaged to be married in June. They were amazed—so much so that they invited me to return with my bride and honeymoon there and sing a few nights for the church. One couple offered us free use of half their house if we would honeymoon there.

I flew back to Allentown and left the Snyders in plenty of time to get to Debbie's the evening I said I would arrive. Unfortunately, I didn't look at the gas gauge until I was in southern Virginia, on I-81, still several hours from Winston-Salem. The little needle was parked on empty. I pulled over at a truck stop to fill up.

• • • • • • • • • • • • • • • • • • • • • • • • • • • • • • •

"Let's see your license," the attendant asked. Then I remembered that gas rationing was on and gasoline could be bought only on odd or even days of the week, depending on the car's license number. "Sorry, this is the wrong day for you," the attendant said.

"But I'm from Pennsylvania and going to see my girl in Winston-Salem. I can't make it there tonight without gas."

He shook his head. "I'm sorry, but it's the law. I'll be in trouble if I sell you some. Now you wouldn't want that, would ya?"

I wanted to crown his head with a bucket, but he was larger than I. He also had arms.

"There's a motel down the pike a ways," he noted. "You've probably got enough to get there."

I spun angrily out of that truck stop and back onto the Interstate. Five miles down the road, my 1969 Pontiac began burping. I coasted over to the shoulder and stopped to wait for a policeman. The sun was sinking behind the trees and a cold wind was sweeping over the mountain plateau. There's never a policeman on the highway when you really need one.

I thought I would freeze to death. Debbie and her folks stayed up until nearly midnight. "He ain't comin'," her daddy said. "Let's go to bed."

"He'll be here," Debbie said confidently. "Something happened. Oh, I hope he hasn't been in a wreck. Ohhhh."

At 7:00 A.M., I got out and hiked a mile to the next exit where there was a Shell station. A cop pulled up behind me on the exit ramp. "Where were you, when I needed you last night?" I asked.

When I explained what had happened, he took me on over to the station where I borrowed a can and filled it with gas. Then he drove me back to my car. I rolled into Debbie's driveway a little after breakfast, eyes bloodshot, hair askew, looking like a convict that had just crawled out from under a rock.

"You're a little late aren't you, son?" Mr. Poplin drawled, a good old country boy type, with short hair slicked down and cut above the ears. "A day late and a dollar short, that's what you are." His sheepish grin suggested that I ought to have a good story.

"You know, I discovered something," I said as I flopped into a chair at the kitchen table. "The cops on I-81 all go home at night." Then I told them about the man's refusal to sell me gas, and I think they believed me. At least Debbie did. That's when I realized I cared for her more than any other girl in the world.

Debbie drove me to a jeweler—the Poplin's second car wasn't equipped for a handicap—and we picked out her engagement ring. I paid the clerk and put the ring in my pocket. We walked back to the car and Debbie opened the passenger door for me. Then she went around and got in on the driver's side. That's when I reached over and pushed the ring on her finger with my hook. "Now," I said, "will you marry me?"

"Let me think about it for a minute. . . . Yes, guess I will." She laughed, we kissed, and then she started the car.

After having our engagement pictures made, and before I left for the Bahamas, I checked on requirements for getting a marriage license in North Carolina and found I had to have a birth certificate, something I didn't have immediately available.

I was told the quickest way was to send a dollar to the Bureau of Vital Statistics in Philadelphia. They would need the date of birth, the name of the hospital, and the doctor who delivered me. I called my folks for the doctor and hospital and announced that I was getting married.

Mom made a kind of choking sound. "Say that again?"

"I'm getting married, Mom. June 22, Winston-Salem, North Carolina, to a beautiful southern belle named Debra Jean Poplin. Are you coming to the wedding?"

"Is she Jewish?"

"No, she happens to be Baptist. We're getting married in her church, but it's OK for you and the family to come. Can you be there? You've got five months to make plans."

"Uh, well, I don't know. Your father may not be able to get off work."

"Mom, it isn't very far. It's on a Saturday afternoon. You can drive down easily and drive back that same evening if you don't want to stay over."

"Jeffrey, we'll see."

I could hear her talking to Dad in the background. "Mom, are you there?"

"I'm here. What do her parents think about their daughter marrying a young man in your condition? Do they realize what she's getting into?"

"They think it's great."

Mom was telling Dad, "I think her parents are crazy. I wouldn't let one of my daughters marry someone like Jeff."

"Mom, are you coming?"

"We'll see. I doubt it, Jeffrey, because it's in a church, and you know how your father feels. We can't make any promises now."

"Please talk to him and try to come. Now, can you give me the name of the doctor who delivered me? And the hospital."

"It's Einstein Northern. It was Philadelphia Jewish Hospital. And the obstetrician was Dr. Androsciere. Is that enough?"

"Yes, I'm sure that's enough. Thank you." And I hung up.

The old hurt feeling welled up in me again. I knew they wouldn't be coming. There was no need including them in the arrangements.

I asked Mom and Dad Snyder if they would stand in as my parents. They said yes and I had their names put on the wedding invitations.

CHAPTER TWELVE
. . . . . . . . . . . . .

# A NEW WIFE . . .
# A NEW DIRECTION

"Jerry Falwell brought us together. Let's ask him to officiate at our wedding."

"Do you think he would?" Debbie wondered.

"No harm in trying."

Dr. Falwell said yes on condition that we come to Lynchburg for premarital counseling. I drove down from Pennsylvania and Debbie drove up from Winston-Salem. We met with him in his office at the Thomas Road Baptist Church. He could not get to the Friday night rehearsal, but would fly up in his private plane for the 2:00 P.M. Saturday afternoon wedding.

"I'll be cutting it close, but I'll be there," he promised.

I asked Jeffrey Rudloff to be my best man and Debbie asked her sister, Phyllis, to be her maid of honor. We had decided to buy a mobile home and live in the Allentown area after our marriage so I could be close to the people who worked with me. We also decided to live away from either set of parents in order to begin our own lives without depending on them for help. Debbie's folks weren't too happy about that, but they accepted it. I wanted to be prepared, so about a month before the wedding I picked out a trailer and had it staked down on a rented lot in Highland Estates, a mobile home community about fifteen minutes from Allentown.

Jeff Rudloff drove down from Houghton College to ride with me and our friend Steve Frankenberry in my Pontiac to Winston-Salem.

"Man, with your long hair, they may not let you in the church," I jested. Actually his straight brown hair was shoulder length in the back and did not come below the ears on the sides. "They're strict, very strict. You certainly would give them some good sermon material."

"I'm not coming to join their church. I'm best man in your wedding. They'll have to accept me as I am, or take their best shot. They couldn't have anyone better to shoot at."

"I'm serious. You'd better do something with it."

Jeffrey decided that he was not going to get a haircut just to please one pastor or church, but he would compromise and tuck as much as possible behind his ears and use a lot of hair-spray. I was still a little worried, though.

I had told all my friends around Allentown that I was getting married. Most cheered me on, but there were a few skeptics. Someone who knew me very well said it would be a miracle if the marriage lasted five years.

Shortly after Jeffrey and I arrived, Mr. Poplin called him aside. You see, he was having some worries about my potential for fathering children.

"You know Jeff pretty well, don't you?"

"Probably better than anyone," Rudloff joked.

"Is he . . . ? Can he . . . ? Will he be able to . . . ?" Debbie's father couldn't quite bring himself to spell it all out.

But Jeffrey got the idea. "I'm sure you have nothing to worry about."

• • • • • • • • • • • • • • • • • • • • • • • • • • • • • •

When Jeffrey told me about the interrogation afterwards, I almost split my sides laughing. But I guess the father of the bride does have the right to know if he can expect to be a grandfather.

The air at the Friday night rehearsal at the Hanes Baptist Church was tense. Part of the confusion came because Debbie and I had planned some variations from the standard wedding ceremony. Debbie's Mom, a quiet little brunette lady, was not saying much at all, walking about as if she married off a daughter every day. Her dad shuffled about as if he were getting ready for a funeral. The pastor, Rev. Harold Perry, a tall stately man who was filling in for Dr. Falwell for the rehearsal, kept frowning at Rudloff's hair. Debbie was talking to her bridesmaids who were fluttering around nervously.

In order to accommodate our honeymoon plans, we decided to have a "cake cutting" reception after the rehearsal dinner, so we could leave immediately following the ceremony to catch our plane.

By 1:30 P.M. Saturday the church was pretty full. The Snyders had driven in for the reception, and the Longs arrived in time for the ceremony. After putting Mom and Dad Snyder as my parents on the wedding invitation, I had written the Steinbergs off. I hadn't talked to my folks in Philadelphia since January.

Pastor Perry had gone to the airport to meet Dr. Falwell. At five minutes before Debbie was to walk down the aisle, they weren't back. Suddenly, the side door opened and there they were!

In a breathless two minutes I filled him in on our special music and the candlelighting ceremony and he told me his order of service. The rest was up to him. He was a pro. I should never have worried. Wearing white tux, Jeffrey Rudloff and I quickly got in line behind Dr. Falwell and walked to the platform. The bridesmaids entered, escorted by the groomsmen, and took their places.

Debbie waited behind the big double doors at the back of

the church. When the officiant, my best man, and I were in place, I turned toward the audience and began to sing to her:

*It is springtime, here in glory.*
*There is beauty beyond compare.*
*But we were meant to sing together*
*And our greatest thrills we always shared.*

*Come away my love, I'm waiting,*
*Sever earth's hold, take wing.*
*The winter is past and over,*
*And the time is come to sing."*

Debbie responded from behind the closed doors, through a special sound system we had rigged for the occasion, with a recitation from the Song of Solomon over a microphone that we had set up in the back from behind the closed doors:

*My beloved spake, and said unto me, Rise up, my love, my fair one, and come away; For, lo, the winter is past, the rain is over and gone; The flowers appear on the earth; and the time of singing . . . is come. . . . Arise my love, my fair one, and come away. . . in the secret places of the stairs, let me see thy countenance, let me hear thy voice; for sweet is thy voice. . . . My beloved is mine and I am his. . . . Arise my love, my fair one and come away.*

The organist, Linda Mathis (Debbie's former piano teacher), sounded the wedding march on the organ and the doors opened and Debbie appeared.

Mrs. Jeff Steinberg, my bride. She was beautiful. She stood waiting to make her grand entrance and take her place at my side. She wore a gown of white satin overlaid with Chantilly lace. The empire bodice, embroidered with seed pearls, had a Victorian neckline and long lace sleeves.

Ruffles of lace accented the hemline, and a lace-bordered chapel length veil fell from a lace headpiece. She carried white carnations with miniature orange carnations, white daisies, and baby's breath. She was escorted by her father.

Words can't describe the emotions I felt: joy, pride, elation, even a sense of accomplishment. This was my moment, our moment. A hundred thoughts raced through my mind as I surveyed my bride.

I remembered the counsel of my family and "friends," advising me not to get married. "After all," my mother told me, "you're handicapped. I wouldn't want my daughter to marry you." Debbie Poplin apparently did, and her parents didn't seem to mind, and I knew I was the most fortunate short guy with a hook that ever lived. To all of my friends who predicted doom and gloom for us, I only wished for them, in our moment of happiness, a wife as wonderful as Debbie.

When they reached the front, Dr. Falwell began the ceremony. During a prayer, and before the pronouncement, we walked to the side of the platform to a table with three candles, two of which were lit. We each picked two unlit candles and lit them from the two that were burning. Debbie and I lit the center candle together, symbolizing that we were to become one flesh. While we were doing this, Jeffrey Rudloff sang "This My Prayer."

At Dr. Falwell's instruction, we exchanged our vows and then I took the wedding ring from Jeffrey with my hook and pushed it on Debbie's finger. I could sense that people were asking: will she put a ring on his hook? She didn't.

Dr. Falwell declared, "I now pronounce you man and wife." Debbie bent down slightly to kiss me. We lifted our faces in smiles and turned toward the congregation.

"Ladies and gentlemen, may I present to you Mr. and Mrs. Jeff Steinberg." After millions of pictures, or so it seemed, Debbie and I hurried back to her parents' house to change clothes for our honeymoon trip. Jeffrey Rudloff drove my car back to Allentown with our friend Steve

Frankenberry, and left it at our trailer. The Poplins had given us a maroon '66 Chrysler for a wedding present—they were looking out for Debbie when I was traveling. Boyd and Bobbie Poplin, my new in-laws, ferried that vehicle along with our wedding gifts and many of Debbie's personal things back for us.

Our honeymoon plans were to fly from Winston-Salem to Miami, spend the night in the honeymoon suite at the King's Inn, and hop over the next day to Spanish Wells, a small island in the Bahamas, where the hosts on my previous trip there had offered us an apartment. Our first meal together at King Arthur's Court, the hotel restaurant, couldn't have been more romantic.

Knights in armor were stationed around the room. Violinists strolled among the tables playing dreamy music. After awhile a big fellow with a thick beard waltzed over to our table and asked, "Do you folks have a favorite?" I whispered proudly, "Uh, we just got married."

"Congratulations," he said with a grin. "What'll it be?"

Debbie shrugged and looked to me. "The Shadow of Your Smile," I said, our song while we were dating.

The violinist and his friends gathered around our table. I reached across the white linen with my hook and grasped Debbie's delicate white hand. How sweet it was! Violins, candlelight, prime rib (we were starved!), and a whole life of love before us.

We had arrived late and it was ten o'clock before we got settled into our room.

No, Debbie didn't carry me—I walked across the threshold with all three feet. The bellman had already delivered our bags to the room. And what a suite this was! It had a large sitting room for entertaining, an even larger luxurious bedroom almost too beautiful to imagine, and a huge bathroom with a giant sunken bathtub that looked more like a small swimming pool. This was every honeymooner's dream come true.

Everything else was easy after that.

We had a tremendous week in the Bahamas. The members of The Peoples' Church held a small reception for us when we arrived and filmed the part where Debbie and I fed each other cake. It was messy, but great fun. We had long talks, baked on the beach, sang a little for our hosts at the Peoples' Church, and mostly kept to ourselves, which is what honeymoons are for.

Our hosts, Newman and Sylvia Sweeting, who lived in the other half of the house where we stayed, had promised to leave us alone. They were as good as their word. They fed us well, introducing us to various forms of seafood including crawfish and conch, treating us like royalty. We learned, unfortunately, that Debbie was allergic to shellfish.

The warm days, gentle breezes, and soft nights passed all too quickly. As we stood on the dock to leave, a large group from the church came to see us off and to wish us well. Willie Pinder, a leader in the church, told us that we were invited to return for our first anniversary, to sing and celebrate with them. It was hard to say good-bye, we had made so many new friends.

Jeff Rudloff met us at the airport in Allentown and drove us to our new mobile home. After I showed Debbie around—it was the first time she had seen the trailer—we had a toast to our future with Cokes.

Saturday evening, after we returned from the Bahamas, the Snyders and my friends from the Lehighton Wesleyan Church gave a wedding reception for us. Debbie's family and best friend, Lisa Childress, were there also. The next morning at the morning worship service, I introduced one of my favorite groups, the Envoys, who did a concert as part of the wedding celebration. Tuesday, Debbie, Jeff Rudloff, and I went to the Hymntone Recording Studio in Harrisburg to work on my solo album, "Something Special from Jeff." Hymntone studios, a sixteen-track studio owned by a former Courier member, Don Baldwin, also had its own musicians, art department, and print shop to print the album jacket slicks. Jeffrey Rudloff sat at the piano and worked out our arrangements with Nick Bruno, the studio's keyboard player and producer, while Debbie watched from the control room. It was our first time in a studio of this size and caliber.

"Something Special from Jeff," my album, was a milestone for me because it featured some of the most requested and most enduring songs, like "The Army of the Lord," that I opened every concert with for more than five years, "The Little Boy from the Carpenter Shop," "Through It All," "Follow Me," and "Tears Are a Language (God Understands)."

This album was special also because it featured a backliner recommendation from the big man from Lynchburg, Doug Oldham. He wrote: "Jeff Steinberg sings well and communicates even better. Of all the people I've worked with over the years on radio and television, I received more comments and mail over the one appearance with Jeff than any of the others."

I took Debbie to Philadelphia to meet my parents. They had not been enthusiastic about me marrying. How would they receive my wife?

I needn't have worried. Mom and Dad met us at the door. It was love at first sight. Mom hugged Debbie tightly and exclaimed, "You have to be a saint!"

"Why, why do you say that?" Debbie asked.

"Anybody who can live with Jeff has to be a saint," Mom continued. "I couldn't do it. I always felt that anybody who married him would have to be nurse, mother, wife, and mistress."

"He isn't so much trouble."

Dad was just as taken with Debbie. He was friendlier to me than I could remember since I had left Good Shepherd. They wanted to know everything about Debbie. Where was she from, her hopes, dreams, expectations. Why she married me. We stayed much longer than I had anticipated and when we got up to go, I couldn't help but wonder if they didn't love and admire her more than me.

• • • • • • • • • • • • • • • • • • • • • • • • • • • • • • •

"When are you coming to see us?" I asked.

Mom shrugged and looked at Dad.

"I don't know, Jeffrey." There was that familiar tone of voice. "We'll have to let you know."

"Well, you're welcome when you do come," I added, not pressing the invitation further. I felt progress had been made.

For the rest of the summer Debbie, Jeffrey, and I traveled together, with Jeffrey setting up the sound equipment and playing piano. I took Debbie's acquiescence on the piano to mean that she felt Rudloff was a better pianist for me.

Glenn Kantner replaced Jeffrey when he went back to college in September. Glenn, a pastor's son, was from Hamburg, Pennsylvania. He was very personable and practical, and highly skilled at playing those fancy licks on the piano. Glenn became a favorite part of the program, playing his elaborate arrangement of "What a Friend We Have in Jesus" for the offertory. His knowledge gained from traveling with the Eastmen Quartet and from his dad's church became invaluable. So many stories come to mind when I think of Glenn, but two stand out as the most memorable.

We did a full week of high school assemblies in the Cincinnati, Ohio, and northern Kentucky area, where we received overwhelming ovations. Most of our assemblies, arranged through local pastors, opened up opportunities for communication between students and faculty. Our program was designed to use the songs, upbeat anecdotes about school life, poking fun at principals and faculty, and telling a part of my story, to encourage and help them realize that they are special. I wanted them to know that God created them with potential. I wanted them to know that the God who created them loves them. Without sounding too evangelical in my approach, I tried to tell them, "If Jeff Steinberg can make it, you can, too." The results were gratifying, because I had the chance after the programs to talk to several kids about their hurts, grades, and ambitions.

During those months, we had been hauling the sound equipment, record albums, and other paraphernalia in a little silver 4' by 6' utility trailer, hitched to my Chrysler. One rainy day, on our way to a meeting in Ohio, at Beaver Falls, on the Pennsylvania Turnpike, a low flatbed trailer-truck jackknifed in front of us. We were unable to swerve around him, nor could we stop in time, so we collided, our right front bumper smashing into the right rear corner of the trailer. No one was seriously injured, but our car and trailer were completely destroyed. I remember the sick feeling at seeing our speaker cabinets protruding through the front wall of our trailer. Our equipment still intact, we made our engagement, a bit shaken though, and continued our tour by renting a U-Haul trailer and pulling it with our 1969 Pontiac for a while.

I made a deal in Delaware for a green '67 Ford van. I exercised my artistic talents by painting in bright red script letters "Jeff Steinberg," and using an overhead projector, I was able to paint a black line drawing of me singing.

Glenn and I stayed busy doing performances mostly along the east coast, as far north as Maine, as far west as Michigan and Texas, and as far south as Ft. Lauderdale, Florida. Debbie went along for most of these engagements, sold albums, and waited around until Glenn and I were ready to go.

The year passed quickly. Jeffrey Rudloff came back the following May. We took mostly short trips, one of the longest being to Holland, Michigan, where Debbie met Lynn for the first time. I was nervous about the meeting for obvious reasons, but was relieved to see them quickly become friends.

Rudloff and I were excited about a long-planned six-week tour to the west. I looked forward to meeting my Uncle Morty for the first time and seeing my sisters Linda and Sheryl again, for both lived in the Los Angeles area near Uncle Morty.

I talked up the tour to Debbie. "This will be like a second

• • • • • • • • • • • • • • • • • • • • • • • • • • • • • • •

honeymoon for us," I promised. This would be the first time I would see my Uncle Morty in more than fourteen years. I would also get to spend time with my oldest sister, Linda, and her family, and Sheryl. It was probably twelve years or more since I had seen Linda. We had never really got to know each other. We would make this tour a reunion tour, and they would meet my wife. I wondered how they would respond to her. I was certain they would like her as much as Mom and Dad did. Debbie liked the idea, though she was a bit nervous about the meeting. Jeff Rudloff would drive, and a new man named Doug Buter from Lynn's church in Holland, Michigan, went along to help out.

We were ready on schedule. I piled into the bucket seat across from Jeffrey (the van wasn't equipped for me to drive). Doug reclined on a cushion behind the driver. Debbie perched on the engine cover behind and between the two Jeffs up front.

For the next several hours the four of us talked music and traded cracks and quips and generally had a good time. Then Doug snoozed in his corner, Jeff and I talked serious music and future plans, and Debbie sat in silence, feeling like a newcomer or an outsider. Jeff and I were also planning an album.

After a while, I looked back and saw Debbie squirming. "How are you doing on that thing?" I asked.

"Fine, I guess. It's just that this seat is getting a little warm."

"The engine is hot. I should have thought of that," Rudloff said.

"Come up and sit with me," I invited.

The seat was small and she almost sat in my lap. I liked the close communion, but Jeff and I had business to discuss. Rudloff and I picked up where we had left off.

"We've got to have some songs that people recognize," Rudloff countered.

"Naah, let's get all new material." I started humming a melody.

Debbie wanted to neck. "You love me?" she asked as she kissed my cheek. "How much do you love me?"

"A bushel and a peck and a hug around the neck." I leaned over and gently kissed her on the lips.

"Let's include the song you like, Jeff," I said. "Maybe we could use it for the lead."

Debbie sat up and shot me a hurt look. How could I keep my mind on business at a time like this?

Rudloff sensed what was happening. "Let's take a rest stop. Have a Coke and stretch our legs." Doug perked up in his corner at that idea and Rudloff pulled off at the next oasis.

We sat around long enough for the engine to cool down. When we got back in, Debbie took her place on the engine cover. Rudloff and I resumed our shop talk. The engine heated up again, giving Debbie a good reason to get back in the front seat with me and pick up where she had left off. This time I was more receptive.

I could tell Jeff was embarrassed by our romancing, so from time to time I shot a remark at him, just to let him know he was still a friend. Debbie ignored him as if he wasn't there. Doug slept through it all.

This went on for the rest of the morning, Debbie sitting on the engine cover until it got hot, then moving up to cuddle with her husband. It was tricky trying to keep up my love life and plan an album with Rudloff.

Rudloff began getting down to specifics on the songs. "What'll we do that one in?" I asked.

"A-flat. What else?" He laughed at his own attempt to be funny.

After hearing the A-flat routine several times, Debbie looked at me puzzled. She didn't have the faintest idea of what was going on. When I realized this, I said, "Oh, it's just a little inside joke between Jeffrey and me." I then proceeded to tell her the story. She smiled, though she didn't say a word, and slid back to her old place on the engine cover.

Our first engagement was in a huge Nazarene church in

Denver. Doug didn't sing with us until we got to California. He sang baritone, I took the lead, and Rudloff did a second tenor and accompanied on the piano. Debbie sat in the audience most of the program, though she played piano on some songs. I was too obtuse to recognize how she felt. When we were dating, she had thought she would be my piano player and share the spotlight with me. She now knew that when Jeff was on tour with me, this was not in my plans. Now as Rudloff rippled the keyboard, and we three guys harmonized, the truth of the situation really began to sink in with her.

They gave us a small reception. Afterwards Doug, Jeffrey, and Debbie sold records, and I stood around greeting people as they came by. Young girls crowded around me asking for my autograph and told me what a good singer I was and how much I inspired them. Some even wanted to kiss me. Debbie didn't appear to mind as though she understood that it was part of the territory. I'm sure there were moments of doubts, when she wondered if I didn't belong more to them than to her, but when we got to the motel, she never said a word to indicate any disappointment.

We motored south to Phoenix and found a couple of churches on our itinerary had cancelled. We were counting on the offerings in Phoenix to keep us eating to L.A. Now we had to skimp, eating at McDonald's and staying at flea bag motels. Debbie still didn't complain. Jeffrey and I had seen it all before, so it was no big deal.

Uncle Morty, my Mom's brother, received us with open arms and invited us to stay with him in his one bedroom apartment, just off Hollywood Boulevard, and to use it as our headquarters while in Los Angeles. Sixty and going on thirty, a bachelor, Uncle Morty was young at heart and always busy with the Shriners, his weekly card games, and singing and performing for cruises and local civic and social groups. At five feet tall, with wavy graying hair, he was always the life of the party and quick with a joke or an encouraging word.

Perhaps my talent for singing and entertaining came from

him. Mom did tell me on several occasions that I had hair like his. He threw a party for us at a posh restaurant in Santa Monica, which my sisters, Linda and Sheryl, and Uncle Morty's friend, Shirley, attended. He treated me as a celebrity and invited me to sing for friends in his lodge. I felt as if I had known him all my life, when actually we were just beginning to get acquainted. I felt comfortable asking him questions about my past, Mom and Dad, and anything he knew about those years. He answered openly and honestly. The closer I came to my family, the more I needed to know about myself. And it was easy to see that he loved me, that I was special as a child, and that he was proud of my accomplishments. He fell in love with Debbie instantly and she with him. I was thrilled beyond words. He beamed when I gave him an old Total Victory Trio album.

"Boy, you're marvelous. I'm proud of you, real proud." I didn't try to change Uncle Morty's life-style, and he didn't alter mine, but I left L.A. with a soft spot in my heart for my favorite uncle.

We were booked for a string of Assemblies of God churches along the coast from L.A. to Oregon. At every stop we were greeted by large crowds, loud ovations, shouts of "Praise the Lord," and people making decisions for Christ. After we hit L.A., Debbie seemed to perk up. She enjoyed meeting and getting to know my relatives. She got caught up in the excitement of the concerts and rejoiced in the spiritual victories. I noticed only one dampening feature. She said as little as she had to Jeff Rudloff. My wife and my best friend were just not hitting it off.

Five weeks into the tour we turned east from Albany, Oregon, for an engagement in Billings, Montana. Rudloff warned me that Billings and our next stop in Austin, Minnesota, shouldn't have been scheduled only a day apart as they were so far apart. I told him I felt we could make the distance by driving from Billings into the night, spending the night in a motel after midnight, and zipping on the next day into Austin, Minnesota.

A man in the Billings church gave us two golden Labrador puppies, one for us and one for Jeffrey. Jeffrey decided to call his pup Aenobarbus, after a Roman soldier in Shakespeare's *Julius Caesar.* We named ours Augie Doggie, after an equally famous TV cartoon dog. Debbie cuddled one on her lap and the other slept at Doug's feet. It turned out that the distance was 850 miles. We drove all night and most of the day to get there. Rudloff, Doug, and Debbie were zonked from taking turns driving. They were also exhausted from wrestling with the puppies. I had grabbed a few winks in the front seat and didn't feel so bad.

Jeffrey was boiling by the time we got there. "Next time take my advice, or look at a map."

"OK, OK," I yelled, too stubborn to admit making a mistake. "Let's get set up."

"Sure, sure, it's OK when you don't have to drive." Rudloff was really steamed.

"All right, it was my fault. Now will you shut up?"

But he didn't shut up and neither did I. Debbie and Doug stood there, gaping at these two "great" Christian musicians, yelling at each other in front of the church.

Jeffrey Rudloff and Doug Buter went back to school in the fall. Jeff continued to help me on some weekends while at other times I picked up piano players wherever I could or had Debbie play. I could tell Debbie wasn't happy being used as a second-string musician, but there were some songs with rhythm styles and chord patterns that she was not able to play, limiting me to taped music or to finding a keyboard player who could. Working with me, obviously, wasn't turning out to be what she had expected. I sensed her disappointment, yet I couldn't find the words to perk her up. I was really puzzled. I was enjoying married life and my ministry in music. Why wasn't she?

Her parents urged us to move to Winston-Salem. They would sell us their home and move into a mobile home on an adjoining lot.

"Why don't we do it, Jeff?" Debbie kept pleading.

• • • • • • • • • • • • • • • • • • • • • • • • • • • •

It seemed logical. She didn't care to make long trips with me and a couple of other guys. Being close to her parents, she wouldn't be so lonesome.

"Yeah, why not." I agreed.

I had made one solo album, "Something Special," and was planning another which we called, "No Turning Back." That album was recorded and released in spring of 1975. It had a southern gospel sound, and included some of Jeffrey's songs, such as, "All He Asked for Was Love," "Alive and Living," and "Have a Nice Eternity." It featured also our first "stacked duet," Jeffrey and me singing together on several tracks. This album had a song just for kids called "I Came Here to Stay," with Bible stories that encouraged persistence. It became a favorite. Jeff and I sang together on one of the most popular songs on this album, "I'm Never Goin' Back Again."

Don Baldwin, owner of the recording studio in Harrisburg, Pennsylvania, where we recorded my albums, heard me talking about moving to North Carolina and offered to trade his equity in a twenty-five-foot Superior motor home for our stake in the mobile home.

"This is providential," I told Jeffrey. "The engine in the van is about shot. And a car isn't big enough to haul a bunch of people with instruments and equipment. A motor home is just what we need."

We made the deal and moved to Winston-Salem, North Carolina, behind Debbie's parents.

Debbie and I had never had an argument. We always backed away when we saw one coming. But moving at the time we did might have saved our marriage.

I didn't have the most secure and stable life to offer a wife. I insisted that we not make a flat charge for a concert, but that churches take up a love offering. The trouble was, these offerings were very irregular, $40 from one concert, $400 dollars at the next, a "gold strike" of $1,000 every six months or so. The number of the audience was no determinant. We sang to 500 people and received less than

• • • • • • • • • • • • • • • • • • • • • • • • • • • • • • • • • •

$200 and before 150 who gave us more than $400.

From these offerings I had to pay travel, including lodging and meals on the road, plus salaries for the fellows who worked with me. More than once I came home to Debbie from a two-week road trip with only $25.

The personnel changed from tour to tour. Jeffrey Rudloff, with all our squabbling, was my best friend and the brother I never had. He was the guy I could always count on for special occasions and important concerts, but he was bent on finishing college. Glenn Kantner worked with me off and on.

Bobby Pires, a big tall strapping athletic type, whom I met at a church in New Bedford, Massachusetts, did first a three-month stint and then a six-month tour as sound technician, driver, and personal assistant. Bobby was the off-season training partner for the pro football player Franco Harris of the Pittsburgh Steelers.

Besides their going to college, there were a variety of reasons why I couldn't keep musicians and assistants. The uncertain pay was one, the grueling road trips another, the lack of appreciation from some of the churches still another. We came away from some churches feeling used. We would get there and find the preacher wanted only a couple of songs and a brief testimony from me before his sermon. The offering would come at the end of his sermon, the second collection of the service. Sometimes we got only part of the "Love" offering. After driving half a day to get there, I told one pastor, "You didn't want Jeff Steinberg, the person. You wanted Jeff Steinberg, the sideshow." I never went there again. I had determined that I was not going to be used as a gimmick to draw a Sunday morning crowd.

Another factor was their difficult boss, who had to be helped in the bathroom, disassembled at night, and reassembled in the morning. I don't think, however, that the fellows minded helping me with my physical needs as much as they resented my insensitivity. I didn't recognize it then, but now I can see the kind of person I was. I made it out of the institution by pushing and shoving and manipulating people. These same characteristics were later hurting me in my relationships with people in the music business, my associates and, more important, with my wife. There is a very delicate balance between perseverance and pushiness, and more often than not I tipped the scales in the wrong direction.

By this time, early 1976, we were releasing my third solo album, "Thinking of Love," a more spiritually inspirational album that took me steps further in musical production and a more contemporary, though still not a rock and roll, sound.

The year 1976 was America's bicentennial and a year of much patriotic celebration, so we decided to feature a song written by my friend, Neil Enloe, of the Couriers, called, "The Statue of Liberty," depicting the freedom we have as Americans and the freedom we have as Christians. I had an arranger compose a fully orchestrated score using horns, strings, tympany, and the whole shooting match. It definitely was a hit.

When Jeffrey Rudloff was tied up in college, I would call him a couple of times a week. We would talk for a half hour about schedules and songs, what other gospel music groups were doing, and anything else that came to mind. He and I understood each other pretty well. We knew how to fight and when to back away. Debbie and I still hadn't had our first argument yet.

Debbie and I seemed to have a good relationship, though she was beginning to tire of travel. After all, we were together twenty-four hours a day for two years. She did what I said, not always with a smile, but she did it. She was raised to be meek and submissive and she played that role. I took that to mean she was satisfied with our marriage. I felt sure we had a good relationship. Maybe I'd disappointed her on occasions, but her love for me, I believed, was always strong enough to lift her spirits.

I took marriage as an accomplished fact. The doubters

were silenced. I had achieved. It hardly crossed my mind during our first years together that a good marriage isn't born, but developed through hard work and emotional giving and receiving. I saw us as having only one real problem—money. That I believed would be taken care of in due time. One year, two at most, and I would be a big-name artist, pulling in enough income to make us comfortable. Debbie had worked part-time as a secretary during her senior year in high school. She volunteered to take short-time jobs as a Kelly Girl to help us stay afloat until my ship came in.

The end of 1976 saw us working on album number four, "Beautiful," a lighter, more melodic album, that even featured a hint of country. Jeffrey wrote the title cut, "Beautiful," "He Must Have Loved Me," "I Ain't Stoppin'," "God of the Little Things," and "I'm Yours." This album had a fold-over jacket with pictures of me and Debbie and various candid shots, and a reproduction of one of my oil paintings on the back cover. It was one of my more popular albums.

At the recommendation of Jeffrey, Dave Roff, a former classmate from Houghton College, appeared at my door at 4:00 A.M. on January 28, 1976, to begin traveling with us as a driver and as my assistant. Roff, with his orange hair and a neatly trimmed beard to match, looked like a redheaded leprechaun. He had a cheery supportive disposition that seemed to make you want to smile whenever he was in your presence. He reminded us of "the Christian answer to Elton John."

Jeffrey had told me that Dave played a "little bit" of piano, so he sat down at my piano to show me what he could do, and he stayed seated at the piano for the next two years. In fact, he played a lot of piano! Dave had a strong background in contemporary light-rock music. Having traveled in a college group, and being familiar with my ministry, he played an important role in changing the direction of my music, to better suit the message he felt I had to share. He believed that I should expand the range of my music, and encouraged me to try new vocal styles. He was always telling me, "I know you can do better. Try it."

Dave was also a songwriter and opened up for me some of the songs he had written, many of which I used in my fifth album, "Son of Abraham." Some of those songs included, "Mountain Song," "He Calmed the Sea," "Great Is the Lord," and "Walk in the Power of God."

Dave had perfect pitch and aimed his talents and skills toward musical arrangements. He was a better than average arranger, and was especially good with Jeffrey's songs. I also included four more of Jeffrey's tunes on this album, including, "Brand New," "We're Gonna Have a Good Time," "That's Not the Way for You," and "When You Know for Sure." I attempted to use as much of their music as possible in my programs and on my albums, rather than singing the same songs other groups sang, because I knew that if I sang new songs, people would pay closer attention, and we could develop a reputation for having a unique ministry.

Dave and I traveled for six months in the Superior motor home with my name and screen print picture on both sides. Once, after a concert on a Sunday morning in DuBois, Pennsylvania, on our way to Alliquippa, Pennsylvania, we pulled into a McDonald's for lunch while on our way to another engagement that evening. As Dave opened the door, two kids about twelve years old walked by and noticed my name and picture on the side of the motor home. We heard the one say to the other, "Jeff Steinberg, who's he?"

"I don't know," the other replied. Just then, Dave jumped from the vehicle. "There he is! That must be him!" the second boy shouted. "But, what does he do? And why does he have his name on the van? But he doesn't look like the picture." They were really curious by now. Dave turned and placed his left arm around my back and his right arm under my legs and lifted me out of the the vehicle and turned toward the restaurant with me still in his arms.

"I know!" screamed the first kid. "He's a ventriloquist!!"

Dave immediately put me down, and I walked toward the restaurant with the stares of both kids following me all the way.

"Wow!" they both exclaimed together, rather dumbfounded.

Until March 1976, Debbie had been playing the piano for most of the concert program, and Dave was driver and assistant. In March, Dave took over as pianist, and Debbie spent more time at home. Dave's musical talents then began to reshape the direction of my ministry.

At this time, because we were traveling without Debbie, he recommended that I get a bass player. He suggested a young man from Bath, New York, Denny Siegrist. We picked Denny up in Harrisonburg, Virginia, in May 1976. Denny was a tall and very slender, quiet fellow with dark brown hair and a thick closely cropped beard. With Denny on board, Dave began to craft our arrangements. They worked well as a team. I bought matching dress blue denim suits for Dave and Denny and I dressed in a pale red suit with cream stitching along the lapel and a matching cream shirt with a colorful tie.

We did a revival in Lewiston, Maine, with an evangelist friend, and Dave had to meet us up there because he was attending his sister's graduation. On our way up to Maine, we planned a practical joke on Dave. When Dave arrived, we told him that a certain girl (a groupie) that he knew liked him (though the feeling was not returned) was planning to fly up to Maine and spend the week with him. We had called the airlines and made reservations just in case he called to check our story, and we arranged for the pastor to give him a note with the details. Dave immediately went upstairs (in midafternoon), undressed, and hopped into bed and announced emphatically that he was staying there until she left, and then he was going home to his mother. We laughed hysterically at him, told him the whole thing was a joke and waited for a smile to appear. It did, though it was short-lived. He didn't think it was very funny for a while.

We put a lot of miles on, tramping out West twice, going

to Ontario, Canada, and down into Texas and up to Pennsylvania. I was determined to have a bus. Friends in the music business warned me that a full-sized travel bus would eat up our income.

"You don't know what you're getting into," Dottie Rambo said.

I wouldn't listen. I visualized Jeff Steinberg with Wind and Fire rolling down the Interstate in a big show bus, our names and logo painted on the side. People would say, "They've made it in gospel music." It would raise our image, increase our album sales.

In September 1976, I financed a 1960, 4104 GMC three-bedroom coach with plush velvet carpet for $14,000 from Hosanna Ministries in Maine. Hosanna had picked it up from a transit company in Boston and customized the interior. It had more than a million miles on it when we got it, but with a new balance wheel it was supposed to be in tiptop shape. We bought the bus in September and almost immediately, it seemed, our troubles began.

As I said, many professional singers, from the famous Blackwood Brothers to the Couriers, advised me not to buy a bus, but I would not heed their guidance. Perhaps it was because I thought that they were convinced that I couldn't make it in their game. I was determined that we were ready for a bus and no matter what others thought, I was going to learn the hard way, and I did.

The bus arrived with a broken balance wheel on the engine. A short time after we fixed it we needed to repair the engine, and then the clutch, and then the transmission. In August, we broke down in Phoenix, and Denny was forced to stay in Phoenix with a local pastor for two months while the bus was being repaired.

October 1976 saw the return of Jeff Rudloff. He joined Dave and me, and later Denny, and we formed Jeff Steinberg with Wind And Fire. Denny left the group shortly after Jeff returned.

I look back on those times now and I realize that these were times for great and sometimes rapid changes in my message, music, and presentation. I felt trapped in a wilderness of isolated situations, not all good, that attacked me from all sides. It was hard to know what I wanted to wear, much less where I wanted my ministry to be in five, ten, or more years. But I was slowly being refined and polished through the people that became a vital part of my life.

Very rarely on our tours did we get set back by adults. They were too polite. Kids were not so predictable. We were getting ready for a concert at a Baptist church in Lewiston, Maine, when a little girl, about ten or eleven, came up, swishing her pony tail and squinting at my hook. "What's that?"

I looked at her very seriously. "All of us are special in different ways. This is one of the ways the Lord lets me be special." I flexed the hook and showed her how I picked up a hymn book.

She didn't say what I wanted her to. "Ah, you're not special," she declared. "You, you're a shrimp!"

Her mother, who had been nervously watching from a pew, came running. "Ann, you apologize to Mr. Steinberg for saying that."

"No, I won't," she piped. "He is a shrimp."

The mother could have died right there, but it didn't bother me. I almost doubled up laughing. I told the story at the next church and it brought the house down.

Rudloff went along with the fun-and-games, but he kept nagging me about repeating my testimony with the same lines, night after night. We had had this hassle before. "You ought to allow for spontaneity," he said. "How can God lead you if you go up there and do it the same old way."

"I know what turns the audience on. If I find something isn't working, I'll change it."

"I still don't buy it. You can get too professional."

"Just because we're Christians doesn't mean we shouldn't be professionals. There's no virtue in shooting off your mouth from the top of your head."

Rudloff was losing and he knew it. "Well, I'll have to

admit, you can say something the hundreth time and come off as fresh as if it's the first. I could never do that."

"We each have our gifts, yours is music and mine is communication and audience rapport. To each his own," I responded.

Since my days in Shriners, I had watched professionals perform on television. After I became a Christian, while at Good Shepherd, I began sizing up Christian singers and speakers. Most, in my mind, left a lot to be desired.

To me, being professional meant more than having something to say and saying it well. The sound system had to be as near to perfect as the building would allow. The mix of instrumentals and vocals had to be exactly right. A sound track had to sound as though the instruments and background singers were live and had to be started on cue, not five seconds late. If I was using a sound track and my guy wasn't right on the second, I'd tell him afterwards, and he'd be on cue the next time.

Of course, we had an occasional accident. I liked to take a cord mike and go into the audience for at least one song. One night I went too far and jerked the plug out of the socket. Rudloff, in his blue denims, came running after me, reeling in the cord, while I kept singing.

Another evening, Rudloff, Dave, and I were performing in New Brunswick, Canada, in a church which had a platform about four feet above the floor with a metal railing along the front. The deacons moved the pulpit to give us more room but forgot to take away the little rug the pastor stood on to keep from wearing a hole in the carpet.

With Dave at the piano, the three of us were doing the chorus, "I keep falling in love with him, over and over and over again . . ." I was leaning toward the audience, holding my mike in my hook. Just as we hit "falling," I tripped over the rug and wound up hanging upside down by my leg brace over the railing, still singing, never missing a word or beat.

Dave was singing from the piano, which blocked his view

of me. He had no idea why the crowd was going bananas and kept on playing as I hung there, still singing, "I keep falling . . . in love with Him over and over again . . ."

Rudloff, who was close to bursting a gut, finally reached out and retrieved me like a sack of potatoes and put me down. We went right on with the song as if nothing had happened.

Debbie and I hadn't seen much of each other that summer. I came in and out of her life, a week here, a couple of days there. When I came home, I was bone tired. We got along because we didn't talk too much. I was too worn out and she had her job, her parents, and her friends.

One evening, after I'd had time to rest up, she fried a skillet of chicken. As I was wiping my lips in satisfaction, she popped the question, "Was this the best chicken you ever ate?"

Ordinarily, I would have said "yes." This time I forgot and said, "It's good, but to be perfectly honest, Dear, Margaret Ann's is better."

Her face widened in astonishment, tightened in a frown, and exploded in tears.

Grasping the table, I pulled myself to my feet and lurched to where she was sitting. "Dear, you asked me if it was the best I ever ate, and to be truthful, Margaret Ann's is better." Margaret Ann was a good friend and we had frequently eaten at her house. But to see Debbie's face, you'd have thought I'd been unfaithful.

Still crying, she got up and began clearing the table. I stood around awhile, making small talk, trying to brighten her up without success. Finally I went into the living room like a whipped cur.

After awhile she came in to be with me. We talked, but neither of us brought up the chicken. Try as I would that evening, I couldn't melt the coldness between us. If it would have helped, I would have said the sky is green. I vowed from that time on never to say anything to Debbie that would hurt her feelings.

CHAPTER THIRTEEN
· · · · · · · · · · · · · ·

# "WE'RE IN THE BUSHES!!"

Debbie's parents, I felt, accepted me. Mom Snyder let us know they would welcome a grandchild, but the joke in the family was, "He's never home long enough . . ."

Debbie's parents didn't seem alarmed about the possibility of us having a baby with defects, but then we never discussed it with them. I didn't lose any sleep about the prospect either, although a question always lurked in the back of my mind. I still didn't know about the medication given my mother when she was carrying me. I figured my stunted development had been a fluke, considering I had three normal sisters. Anyway, that was what my mother and father told me whenever I had asked.

When Debbie did discover that she was pregnant, we called Dr. Moore at Shriners Hospital to ask him about the possibility of our baby being born handicapped. By then he had long since retired and was unavailable for help. We were referred to a specialist at Bowman Gray School of Medicine in Winston-Salem for examination. I wanted to know so that we could get extra medical assistance if necessary, and to prepare ourselves emotionally for what lay ahead.

I was singing with Wind and Fire at Fort Mitchell, Kentucky, when the doctor did a sonic scan on Debbie. "The baby appears normal," he reported, "but it has a lot of development ahead." He looked at Debbie thoughtfully. "What if the child should be born like your husband?"

Debbie didn't hesitate in replying, "If that's the case, then I guess we'll teach him to be like his father. He couldn't have a better example. We would love him no less because of his handicap."

When I came home I wanted to see for myself. "Bring her back in," the doctor said. He put the scanner over her stomach and pushed the button as I peered at the little screen. "That's my son," I marvelled as I stared at the screen. "I can see his arms and his legs appear to be normal. That's all I need to see. My son is normal."

"Uh, we don't know the sex," the doctor cautioned.

"Oh, I know it's a boy." I remarked proudly, "I told my wife I wanted a son and she always does what she's told." They laughed.

"What are the chances of a serious abnormality?" I asked the specialist.

"Based on Debbie's good health and what we've researched about your situation, I'd say very slim. No more than one in eight hundred." Those were pretty good odds. They were the same as most pregnancies.

For the rest of the pregnancy I kept in very close touch with Debbie. I held the tours down to two and three weeks. Debbie had a list of phone numbers where I could be reached, and every day she didn't call me, I phoned her.

We were hoping our son would be born June 22, 1977, on our third wedding anniversary. The call I'd been waiting for came on June 19. Jeff Rudloff, Dave Roff, and I were eating a midnight snack at Shoney's in Anderson, South Carolina, with the pastor and his wife from the church where we had sung earlier in the evening. Fortunately, their

• • • • • • • • • • • • • • • • • • • • • • • • • • • • • •

daughter had stayed home and told Debbie where to reach us.

Debbie had been going to natural childbirth classes and urging me not to worry. "I know what to do when the time comes," she assured. "Mother and Daddy are here if there's any problem."

Now she was calling me on the phone. "My water broke, what do I do?"

"What do you mean, what do I do?" I said. "You go to the hospital."

"But I have a regular doctor's appointment tomorrow morning. I'm not having any labor pains."

"You know how serious water breaking can be. Get yourself to the hospital. Don't wait around."

"But, I'm not ready to go. The baby wasn't due for another three or four weeks. I'm not even packed."

I don't know why she asked me at all. She didn't go until about one o'clock in the morning. She had to call her boss, and she promised to call Lisa and who knows who else before leaving. She then stopped by her parents' house on the way to the hospital to tell them she was going.

Meanwhile, we left at midnight, right after she called, and drove straight through to Winston-Salem, five hours away. We parked in the hospital lot as the new day was dawning. The night receptionist saw me coming and said, "You're Mr. Steinberg? Go down the hall, take the elevator to the third floor, walk towards maternity and push the button at the door."

I bumped the button with my mouth. "Yesssss," a voice answered.

"I'm Jeff Steinberg, Debbie Steinberg's husband."

"Oh bless your heart, we thought you'd never get here."

A few moments later, out came an orderly with cap and gown with pants. He took one look at the two shoes on my right leg and threw the pants across the floor. "We don't need these. We'll slip on this gown and get you in there with your wife. I must say, you had us all worried that you

• • • • • • • • • • • • • • • • • • • • • • • • • • • • • • • •

wouldn't make it in time." I followed him into the labor room and to my wife's bedside.

Debbie was getting ready to be wheeled to the delivery room. An intern had been helping her with her natural childbirth breathing exercises.

"You did this to me," she grimaced as she took hold of my cold hook.

I didn't deny it. I said, "I'm here. We're going through this together."

She held on to my hook as the contractions increased. I talked and told her I didn't want my son to be wrinkled. Debbie didn't want him to be fat.

They wheeled her into the delivery room. Dr. Pollack, her obstetrician, entered with a cheerful greeting, "How are you doing, Mr. Steinberg?" and conferred with the intern. He saw me craning my neck to see what he was doing in the mirror over his shoulder on the wall near the ceiling. "You can't see anything from there. You're not squeamish, are you?"

"No," I replied.

"Then, why don't you come down here. You can help deliver your baby. You're not going to faint, are you?"

"No, not after all of the years I've spent in hospitals and all the surgeries I've gone through."

Debbie did fantastically.

"It's coming now," the doctor said, and got down to business.

I stood beside the doctor and saw it all. My son was born at 5:52 A.M., June 20, 1977. My beautiful, beautiful son! Who would have dreamed Jeff Steinberg has a son! Two good arms and two good legs. Not red or wrinkled, or fat. My gorgeous son. Praise God!

We had already picked out a name: Benjamin, for the youngest son of the Hebrew patriarch, Jacob, meaning, "Son of my right hand." David, for my Lithuanian namesake, his great-great grandfather.

Benjamin David. I curled the words around on my

• • • • • • • • • • • • • • • • • • • • • • • • • • • • •

tongue. I liked the sounds, but we called him "Benji" for short.

They wheeled Debbie into the recovery room and whisked Benji to the nursery for a scrub down. I bounced into the waiting room where Jeff Rudloff and Dave Roff were sleeping. "Get up, you lazy bums!" I shouted. "I've got a son."

Rudloff opened one bleary eye. "So, sons are born every day in this hospital."

I jerked the cushion from under his head with my hook. "Get up! This is my son! I don't have a son born here every day!"

Rudloff and Roff came alive and congratulated me.

I called a string of people, including my parents. *"Mazel Tov!"*

"Well, what's he like?" Mom quizzed impatiently.

"He's beautiful, and normal," I crowed. "Two good arms and two good legs, he has a thick crop of dark brown hair and he looks like a little old man."

"Thank God! Thank God! Is Debbie OK?"

"She's fine."

"Well, congratulations and much happiness."

"Thanks. Now that you've got a grandson, you have no excuse for not coming to see us," I added hopefully.

"We'll see," was all she said.

When they put Benji on display, I pressed my face against the glass and spotted him easily among the lot. The one with no wrinkles. The best looking one in the bunch. "Hey, hey," I chirped to no one in particular, "That's my son."

We left on tour for Virginia Beach two days later. We had several concerts, back to back, in the area. I wanted to get done and get back to Debbie and Benji, but the show must go on. On Thursday, Debbie and Benji were ready to leave the hospital. A friend from the immediate area where we were singing paid for me to fly back. I was there to check them out and take them home. That was another great day.

The Fourth of July weekend we had important company

coming to visit. My Mom and Dad! The first time they had ever been to visit us.

"We've come to see our grandson," Dad announced.

Benji was asleep in his crib in our bedroom. Debbie and I took them back. Mom stood on one side, Dad on the other, peering down at their first grandson, the only grandson to carry on the Steinberg name. Debbie and I were deeply moved just watching them adore little Benji.

Finally they turned and followed us back to the living room. "Take a seat and relax awhile," Debbie invited.

Dad nodded and he and Mom sat down on the living room sofa across from us. "Does Benji eat well?" Mom asked Debbie.

"He eats a little and falls asleep, then he wakes up hungry and falls back asleep. He doesn't sleep long enough for me to get too much rest," Debbie complained.

"Oh, I can tell you how to fix that," Mom said knowingly. "Keep him awake until he's finished all his food and give him a couple of teaspoons of baby cereal. Don't let him go to sleep until he's done. Then he'll sleep all night."

When Benji woke up they played with him and tickled his tiny ribs.

Dad glanced at his watch. "We'd better get back to the motel."

They stayed until Monday. When they came to the house, the center of attention was the baby, with Mom giving Debbie more grandmotherly advice.

When they were ready to leave, my parents gave me the usual perfunctory kisses on the cheek. Mom hugged Debbie and remarked, "You do have to be a saint to care for both Jeff and the baby."

I, too, thought Debbie was something special.

Jeff Rudloff had graduated cum laude from Houghton College in May before Benji was born, with a major in psychology and Bible. He had gotten married two weeks before Benji was born. He married Joan Hall from Corning, New York, a fellow choir member at Houghton College.

Joan was a product of the "Jesus People" era, and as she put it, "came to know the Lord in the living room of someone's house." I recall that everytime we met, she referred to me as "Brother Man." I kind of liked it and her. She had a wonderful mezzo-soprano voice and, in fact, in 1976, she was a guest soloist for the Rochester Philharmonic Orchestra.

"I'm applying to Penn State's graduate school," he said. "I hope to become a school counselor. You know, a steady job."

"Yeah, I get the hint. Working with me isn't very remunerative."

"Now that you bring it up, it isn't. It also keeps me away from home a lot. There's another little matter," he continued. "You and I don't complement each other very well."

"Whatta ya mean, don't complement each other. We make a great team, Wind and Fire. You're the wind and I'm the fire." I laughed at my own attempt to be funny. Rudloff didn't.

"Steinberg, you know me and I know you. We're too much alike. We both want to be the star. I can sing as well as you, but I don't have your appeal as an overcomer."

"We've had our differences," I admitted. "But we always iron them out, don't we? You haven't been accepted for grad school yet, have you?"

"No, but if I don't get in at Penn State, I'll try somewhere else."

"Well, then, what's keeping you from continuing to work with me and Dave? Minister to people? Keep a little bread on the table?"

"I'm married, man, that's what."

"What's the big deal," I said. "Look, I know Joan has a good voice. She can sing some with us. We'll put you two in a private room when we're on the road."

"OK, I'll talk to Joan," he relented.

Penn State turned him down. He tried at another state

school and was not accepted there either. I figured it was his Christian commitment. Rudloff never was any good at soft-pedaling his faith.

He had been writing songs for me all along. We had made one Wind and Fire album. When the third university said no, he began wondering. One day, while praying in the chapel at Houghton, he told God how angry he was at the way his life and plans were being messed up. He rose from the front of the chapel and while he walked to the student lounge, a distance of approximately 100 yards, a new song came to him. The song practically wrote itself.

It was as if God was giving him his reply to Jeff's prayer. Jeffrey quickly picked up a tablet and pen and wrote furiously:

*There've been many days, I thought I knew my way;*
*I thought that I knew just which way to go.*
*Just when all seemed bright, things were going right,*
*God stretched out his hand, he told me "No."*
*That's not the way for you,*
*I'll show you a brighter star to reach for,*
*Give you a higher mountain you can climb;*
*That's not the way for you,*
*I'll give you a sweeter song to sing,*
*If you'll give up your will and follow mine.*
*So when your plans fall through, you don't know what to do,*
*Remember, it's God who holds the key.*
*His way is always good, things go as they should,*
*When we obey at his call, "Follow Me."*

It became one of the ones in our repertoire. It also confirmed something for Jeff.

"I'm coming back with you," Rudloff said. "Joan and I think this is the way for us for the immediate future."

Jeffrey and I were an unusual duo in that we were so much alike and such good friends that we could be brutally honest and fight like cats and dogs at one point and clown together the next. We understood each other and loved each other, and I guess that is what friends are for. No matter what decision he made, my life was distinctively better because of him.

Debbie had stopped work as a Kelly Girl when Benji was born. Before going back to work, she brought Benji along with us in the bus for an all-night sing at Hallem, Pennsylvania. Everybody who was anybody in gospel and contemporary Christian music was there. This was a very special concert for me. We were singing to an audience of more than 13,000 people, in our home state, and my son was two weeks old. I recalled a concert several years back when Neil Enloe, lead singer for the Couriers, brought out a giant poster to announce the birth of his son Tim. At the right moment in our stand, I had Debbie carry out our new son for everyone to meet and greet personally. He smiled at the audience and, in general, his stage presence was perfect. He received a standing ovation, though he never sang a note.

After the concert, we were humming along I-83, headed toward Damascus, Maryland. Jeff and Joan were sleeping in the back bedroom; Debbie, Benji, and I in the middle bedroom; and Dave Roff was driving. Our room had two bunks. Debbie and I slept on the lower one with Benji wrapped in a blanket between our feet and a closet. We had thrown our suitcases, books, and other paraphernalia on the top bunk.

All of a sudden, along about 6:30 A.M., the bus started bouncing up and down and rocking from side to side. At the same time we heard a terrible scratching on the outside. Then we jolted to a sudden stop and the stuff on the top bunk in our room came crashing to the floor.

Debbie grabbed the baby. "Benji! Benji!" she cried with growing alarm. I sat up and immediately looked to the foot of the bed. With my arm off, I was immobilized. The awful thought hit.

"Is Benji all right?"

"Oh, thank God, thank God!" Debbie exclaimed. "He's breathing! Benji's alive, and I think he's OK!"

We looked out the window on our side and saw the dark outline of bushes. The window across the hall showed the same picture, bushes.

Rudloff was in the hall, walking toward David, who had fallen asleep at the wheel, and was now sitting at and pounding his fist on the steering wheel, and muttering to himself, "Darn! darn! darn!"

"Where in the world are we?" Jeff asked Dave.

"We're in the bushes."

"I can see that, you clod. Where are the bushes?"

"We're on the median, somewhere in the Baltimore area."

Dave and Jeffrey stepped out of the bus and took a couple of steps ahead and suddenly fell back.

"My Lord! There's an overpass. We stopped just short of going over the edge. If we had, we'd probably all been killed. Thank God, we're just in the bushes," Rudloff said.

Debbie helped me get my arm, leg brace, and my pants on. By that time Joan was outside with her husband and Roff surveyed the damage. There were some ugly gashes in the paint on the sides, a dent in the radiator cover, and our large engine batteries were lying out on the grass. There didn't appear to be too much body damage. It was too early to tell how extensive the damage was.

Rudloff walked down to a telephone and called the police. A couple of cops looked the situation over.

"You guys really went in the bushes," one said.

The police were extra nice when they learned we were a Christian group. We couldn't drive the bus, so they gave us the name of a mechanic. Rudloff walked down the highway and called the man. He got out of bed and came right away. He towed the bus to his shop where we got in touch with the pastor at our next engagement which was only two hours down the road.

The repairs were finished the next day and we were grateful for God's protection. We also laughed a lot about the experience. Anytime we got into trouble after that and someone asked what was wrong, we said, "We're in the bushes!"

The problem was that we were getting "in the bushes" with the bus too often. The transmission went out—$2,400. We lost the clutch—$500.

All the while, our ministry kept enlarging. We went into a high school in downtown Pittsburgh, in an area that looked like a war zone from race riots. We could hear the boos and catcalls while we were getting ready backstage.

"We're gonna get a nice welcome," I told Rudloff. "Got your flak helmet on?"

They pulled back the curtain and I walked out first, gripping the mike cord in my hook. Dave Roff was playing the piano. I started singing:

*Where do you go when you come to the end of the road?*
*Who really cares when your song is sung?*
*When you've seen all you wanted to see,*
*And you've become all you wanted to be;*
*And you still don't really know where you belong.*
*You go to the place where life begins,*
*To a love that never ends;*
*To the One whose arms are open wide,*
*"Come on inside, you should have come sooner."*

*Where do you fly when all your dreams have kissed you*
    *good-bye?*
*Who really cares when your song is sung?*
*When there's no place for you to hide,*
*And no one to take your side;*
*And you feel like the only one out on your own.*
*You go to the place where life begins,*
*To a love that never ends;*
*To the One whose arms are open wide,*
*"Come on inside, You should have come sooner."*

When I finished you could have heard a toothpick drop. We sang another, an upbeat song made popular by Barry Manilow, called "Daybreak."

I then attempted to identify with them by telling corny

stories about my school days and cracking jokes about
school and their principal: "When I entered today, I was
taken immediately to the principal's office. The door was
closed, so, like the good student I've always been—I listened
at the door. I heard the principal say, 'I'll teach you to kiss a
girl in this school!' I heard another voice say, 'You don't
have to, I already know how to do that!' " It was a love
affair from the very beginning. I think they knew that I
cared about them and that I was on their side. I then
announced the "best male and female lovers" from names
given to me prior to the assembly, usually an upper
classman. I would have them come up on stage and read
some goofy poetry as if written by the guy to the girl.
Everyone went crazy, cheering them on. I then sang a more
serious song, "My Walk with God," and proceeded to share
with them my story.

"My name is Jeff Steinberg," I began. "I was born in
Philadelphia without arms and with feet turned in, scissored.
The doctors called my condition Phocomelia, multiple
congenital defects."

They were in the palm of my hand as I described my
years at Shriners and Good Shepherd. "Is life really worth
living? Some of you may think I'm supposed to be
handicapped," I concluded, "but I have a wife and son and
travel a hundred thousand miles a year, singing and speaking
all over the country. I have my own home. God made
something beautiful out of me. If you'll let him, he can
make something beautiful out of your life."

We did another song, a finale, then I thanked them for
being such a good audience, bowed, and walked off the
stage to a standing ovation. Afterwards, they flocked around,
asking questions, requesting my autograph. Not an unkind
word.

The principal stood by amazed and thrilled. "I can't
believe these are the same kids I have in this school," he
said. "Thank you for coming."

We appeared in a juvenile detention center in Arizona

• • • • • • • • • • • • • • • • • • • • • • • • • • • • • • •

and saw a "tough" fifteen-year-old boy cry as I shared my story. I was honest with them. "When I'm finished, I will go home and you will stay. But you can make a new start and see God make something beautiful out of your shattered dreams. If he can do it in me, he can do it for you, if you want him to." Again, we got a standing ovation.

After the concert, a Puerto Rican boy, about sixteen, asked me to come to his room. He handed me a pencil drawing of the way he thought Jesus looked. "I want you to have it," he said. "You really touched me. If you can do it, man, I can do it."

A prison chaplain invited us to Pennsylvania's Western State Penitentiary. I gave a full concert program and shared my testimony. About midway through the concert, a whistle blew indicating that those who wanted to could leave the auditorium and return to their cells. Almost three-fourths of the audience stayed for the finish of the program. Again, I said, "There isn't a one of you guys who wouldn't want to be where I am right now. I can leave when I finish. So let's not kid ourselves. Why am I here? Because I want you to know that where you are, right now, you can put one foot in front of another and come to realize there's someone who cares about you and even loves you, in spite of how rotten or ugly you think your life may be. I care about you, and God loves you, just as you are. If you can turn to him and let him forgive you and love you, he can give you a chance to make right all the wrongs you were responsible for in society. I did it and you can do it, too."

Another standing ovation. As we were packing our equipment to leave, the activity director said, "I really didn't think you guys could make it here. They booed another singer off the stage here after three songs."

A couple of days after the concert at the prison, we were driving to a church in Virginia. Debbie and Joan were in the middle bedroom with Benji. Dave Roff was sleeping in the front bedroom. I sat beside Rudloff, the driver, in the jump seat, peering into a blackening sky.

"Nobody else could have gotten the respect those cons gave you," Rudloff said.

"You think so?"

"I know so. You showed them what God can do with a guy who has two strikes against him. They could relate. You gave them some hope. I could see it in their eyes."

"Yeah. They're like those kids back in the Pittsburgh school. Many of them grew up in broken homes and low income housing. I'll bet most never knew what it was to have a family, just as I never knew. I want them to have hope so they can look to the Lord and fight and survive."

"That's been both your strength and weakness," Rudloff said.

"I know. I've thought of it many times. If I hadn't been so headstrong, I'd never have made it out of the institution."

"You're still that way," Rudloff said. "If you can't get where you're going the ordinary way, you just bull your way through. You had to have this bus and it's breaking us. You insisted that Joan and I stay with you and it's putting a terrible strain on our marriage. I don't know how long we can continue. I'm not saying God doesn't want us with you, but sometimes I'm not sure."

"Thanks, but no thanks," I muttered.

"You've got a ways to go, in my opinion. For one thing, you can't seem to decide what you want to be. You want to be Jeff Steinberg, the unique handicapped singer telling people, 'If I can make it, you can make it.' You also want to have a group and a bus and be like the rest."

I blinked. Sometimes, this guy knew me better than I knew myself. I did want to be unique, but I couldn't break away from the pattern set by others. Perhaps I didn't believe I was good enough by myself to sing solo. Or, maybe I was still convinced that if I had to have assistants, they should be musically inclined.

"You know we don't always agree, Steinberg, but . . ."

"So what else is new?"

"Will you let me finish? What I'm trying to say and you

• • • • • • • • • • • • • • • • • • • • • • • • • • • • • •

won't let me, is that I think you are somebody special, very special. You have a ministry and an appeal like nobody else. We were talking about those cons and the kids in that Pittsburgh school. But you do it in churches, too. Here's a guy who comes in depressed. Maybe his wife is about to divorce him. Maybe his kid is on drugs. Maybe he is about to lose his job. Whatever. He sees you stagger on stage, grab a mike with your hook, and start talking about how good God is to you. He begins to think, 'My troubles are nothing compared to his. If he can believe God is good to him, maybe I can believe God loves me.' "

Rudloff put a hand on my crooked left leg. "Steinberg, God has made you special for his own special reason. Don't you ever forget that."

"Thanks, pal," I said, my voice choking a bit. "I won't."

There were people, however, who thought I could be improved on physically. Not by doctors, but by the Lord, if only I had enough faith. Some suggested that I must not be walking with the Lord or else he would grow me two arms and straighten out my legs. One woman sent me a package of emery boards, "to trim your fingernails when my prayers are answered."

Several times I was told, "Just think how much more effective your ministry would be if you were healed." Some asked permission to pray for me to be healed.

"What for?" I asked. "I'm not sick."

"But you don't have arms and your legs are crippled."

"Suppose I came into your church, 6 feet 4 inches tall, with arms and legs like a weight lifter's. Suppose I got up and said there was a time when I was 4 foot 4 and had no arms and my legs were all fouled up. Would you have believed me?"

"I don't know, I guess I would."

"You know you wouldn't. You'd think I was a screwball. I appreciate your wanting to pray for me. I do need prayer for a lot of failings in my life. But not for what the world calls handicaps. God made me this way to be special. Because

I'm this way, I can go places with no arms and bum legs and say things you could never say. God can use me to pick people up and cause them to quit comparing themselves with others who the world calls normal."

Sometimes this satisfied these dear folks. Sometimes it didn't. But it satisfied me.

CHAPTER FOURTEEN
· · · · · · · · · · · · · · ·

# MASTERPIECE
# IN PROGRESS

The response at every concert indicated that Jeffrey Rudloff
was right.

"Tonight, you really inspired me," a redheaded college
student said in Miami. I realized God's love in a new way;
now I know that he loves me.

An army private told me at Fort Monmouth, New Jersey,
"I was ready to can it all. You made me feel like going on."

The comments I overheard were just as pleasing. "Jeff
Steinberg's the greatest thing that ever happened to our
church."

And yet, in spite of the encouragement from those to
whom we sang, that year I was convinced that my ministry
was about to fall apart. Perhaps that is what I needed to feel
to force me to get to where I was supposed to be.

In November 1977, Dave Roff announced that he was
leaving at the end of the year. He didn't feel that we were an
effective team. In fact, he wasn't sure that we were a team at
all. Perhaps it was more accurate to say that we were three

singers, each doing his own thing in the same group. To compound my problems, Jeffrey also announced his resignation, effective at the same time.

"Hang on a little longer," I pleaded. "We'll get somebody to replace Dave. We'll find someone to set up the sound system and help with the driving."

Jeff stared hard at me. "You forget, I'm a married man with a wife who doesn't want to live on the road."

"Neither does mine," I interjected.

"Debbie is accustomed to a husband being gone all the time. Mine isn't. I'm totally ignoring her needs. Maybe you and Debbie can hack it this way, but we can't.

"Something else," he continued. "You and I have a hold on each other. You think you can't make it without me. I've assumed I can only have a ministry through you. We've got to get apart and give each other breathing room. Understand?"

"Yeah, I think I do," I said. "But I still don't like it. You and I have been through too much to split like this."

"Steinberg, can't you get it through your thick head that you are the show? You're the one who gets through to the people. I've heard you say a thousand times, 'God made me special.' Well, if he did, get out there and act like it and start making it on your own."

For some unexplainable reason, I didn't believe that I was a good enough vocalist to make it on my own. I reasoned that since I enjoyed singing harmonies and since I needed someone to travel with me to help me, I might just as well find someone musical and share them with my audience.

There was no changing Jeff's mind. Deep down, I knew he was right. Yet I clung to the security of having a group. I wanted to appear as the guy who had it all together. Yet, with all the self-assurance I portrayed to others, I was scared inside when I came on stage, feeling I needed somebody to lean on.

The Total Victory Trio had gone down the drain, now Wind and Fire looked to be gone. But, I wouldn't allow it. I found a new couple, Alan and Joyce Whitmer. Alan, a tenor, was magic on the piano. He had perfect pitch and was a good arranger. Joyce sang alto, played the synthesizer, clarinet, and flute.

I never changed the logo. It was still Wind and Fire, but with new members.

The new Wind and Fire had problems working together. We argued about songs, style, arrangements—almost everything. I wasn't happy and told them so. Ditto for them with me.

The bus was a big part of the problem. We were really "in the bushes" when it broke down in Milton, Florida, and had to be towed to a garage.

"Your engine is gone—shot," the service manager reported.

A sinking feeling swept over me. The last few offerings had been slim, barely enough to pay for gas with a few bucks left over for Alan and Joyce Witmer, and Bob Thompkins, a bass guitarist we had hired. Debbie was back in Winston-Salem, doing her thing as a Kelly Girl to keep us out of bankruptcy and taking care of Benji.

The three of us trailed the garageman into his office. He made several telephone calls to check on the costs of a new engine. We anxiously watched him punch the figures into his adding machine. Finally, I dared to ask, "How much is it going to cost us to get out of here?"

"You boys have a pretty expensive set of wheels out there. A new engine doesn't come cheap. Even after subtracting a discount, the best I can come up with is $6,000."

Alan coughed nervously. Joyce turned green. I was getting there fast. "We don't have it," I declared gloomily.

"Well, you guys won't be going anywhere."

We stepped back and held a conference. We couldn't abandon the bus. Finally I said, "I'll have to try and borrow the money."

Finally, after a lot of calling, praying, and working together, Alan's father agreed to finance the repairs to the bus by borrowing the money for us. At this, I figured I would be owing more than it was worth, but at least we would have wheels.

The paperwork for the loan and installation of the new engine took a week. We lost three concerts and with aid of a local pastor who came to check us out and help us where possible, we had the opportunity of sharing in two area churches, which helped make up the loss of engagements. At one point we found it necessary to fly to one engagement in Washington, D.C., where I was introduced to Mary Crowley, president of a major sales corporation based in Texas. We sang for her company's sales representatives' awards banquet, using a borrowed sound system.

But, we made it out of Milton. That wasn't much consolation in the face of the trip to Maine we were about to make. The bus began to blow black smoke, and we started consuming oil at the rate of one quart for every ten to fifteen miles. P. T. Barnum once said, "There's a sucker born every minute." I wonder who gave him my name. I called the garage and they told me that it would use more oil until the rings seat, whatever that meant. I brought it, all the way to Bangor, Maine. Somehow I guess I hoped it would improve.

"Lord, I'm between the rock and the hard place," I prayed, "and I think I'm about to get crushed."

A couple of days later, in Maine, I was spilling my woes to Dallas Henry, a pastor. Dallas, a former baritone and piano player for the Envoys, one of my favorite groups, is a man I greatly respect and one of my dearest friends. I knew that he truly loved and believed in my ministry. He understood also the pitfalls of Christian music. Dallas took me to a verse in Proverbs, "In a multitude of counselors there is safety" (24:6). He also told me that I shouldn't make all of the decisions myself, but that I should have "wise and godly" counsel.

"Get yourself a board of business and professional people who love the Lord and believe in your ministry," he urged.

"Let them incorporate you into a nonprofit ministry, give you spiritual counsel, and help you put your financial affairs in order. Do what they say."

"Do I have any other alternative?" I asked.

"Yes, disaster. A loss of credibility because you are not keeping your commitments."

I left his office feeling low. I had always been my own boss, calling the shots. That had been my problem in working with creative, talented musicians, who also tended to be self-willed and assertive. Could I work under a board? Did I have any other choice in continuing the ministry? No.

We left Maine, nursing the bus (as we did on the way up from Florida), and got as far as Baltimore. The bus broke down again and would go no farther. We took it to a Detroit Diesel/Allison garage in the area just off U.S. 40. They examined the engine and informed me that the repairs in Florida were not done exactly according to specs. The ring gaps were not in proper alignment, causing a large consumption of oil, and the sleeves were oversized. They then gave us the bottom line. It would cost more than $9,000 to re-repair the engine. There was no way that we could manage that.

I was still reeling from a $6,000 repair job in Florida just two weeks prior. When I tried to contact them to make good, they refused unless I returned the bus to them. I even contacted an attorney in Florida, and I soon learned that there was little or nothing that I could do. You can run a garage in the state of Florida as long as you own a screwdriver and a hammer. There are no laws about qualifications. The Department of Consumer Affairs informed me that they could do nothing to stop them from operating a garage because they were not a chain.

Things smoothed out for awhile, and we were temporarily traveling in a car, pulling a trailer. We received notice from the garage that our bus had been placed in mechanics lien. The bus would be sold at auction and any monies raised above the amount of the repair bill would go toward paying the bank for our loan. However, the bank would only release title for payment of $2,300 plus the commitment that the garage would begin bidding themselves at $10,000 to satisfy the note.

At the auction, I was informed that the bidding opened and closed at $10,000. No one else bid on our "poor old bus." Johnson & Towers became the "proud" owners of a 1960 GMC 4104 Coach. The inevitable came. Alan gave me notice that at the end of the year they were leaving. They were having marital problems and our precarious situation with all of the tensions wasn't helping them gain solutions.

"Lord, lead me to people who can help me," I pleaded.

A few nights later I was singing in Memphis for a sales banquet, at which Mary Crowley, the president of Home Interiors, was to speak. Afterward, an attractive woman came up and introduced herself as Mary Martin.

"I'm from Central Church—have you heard of us?"

I was told that Central, an evangelical congregation, had an auditorium that seats about 2,000. They later relocated and built a beautiful building to seat 4,500.

Mary continued, "I can have Don Johnson, the associate pastor, call you about possibly scheduling a date. Could he call you tonight if he is able to?"

"Sure."

Central's vast sanctuary took my breath away. I had sung in such large auditoriums, but not often. I went over the next day and sang for Don Johnson to introduce him to our ministry and to schedule a date in February 1979.

It was a snowy day in Tennessee, and my morning concert in Madison had cancelled, so I arrived at Central Church to set up in the early afternoon. The snow had pretty well melted away by mid afternoon. Alan and Joyce had left December 31, 1978, and now Bob Pires was doing the driving of a Winnebago motor home, a gift to us from Mary Crowley and her company, Home Interiors and Gifts in Dallas, Texas. The concert went well, they gave us a standing ovation, and we received our largest offering to date and sold a record number of albums and tapes. They appreciated our ministry. I was getting the message. I could be good and effective without hiding behind a group. But there were still problems to be solved.

The next day, Bill and Mary took me to lunch. Bill was one of the most successful home builders in Memphis.

"What kind of organization do you have?" he asked.

"You're looking at it." I shared my financial problems and fears of trying to make it on my own.

They took an interest in me, my family, and my difficulties. "OK, I think I can help you," Bill said. "I have some friends who will also help if I asked them. But it would be easier if you lived here in Memphis."

After more conversation with Bill and some other men in Central Church, I went back to Winston-Salem and talked to Debbie.

"What do you think about moving to Memphis?" I asked.

"Wherever you go, Benji and I will go." I don't think she was prepared for that question, though we had considered moving before.

Debbie and I flew to Memphis on Friday, March 29, 1979, two days after her twenty-third birthday. That evening we celebrated her birthday and our new future by going out to eat with Bill and Mary and some of their friends. The next morning, the Martins took us to see a house in Collierville, a suburb of Memphis, that Bill had been building. We loved the house and Bill told us that he would give a very substantial discount and arrange the financing. Debbie found a job as a word processor at St. Jude Children's Research Hospital. All in one weekend!

We went home and told her family, who had kept Benji while we were gone. We struck a deal with her sister and brother-in-law to buy the house that we had purchased from her parents. Debbie had to give two week's notice at her job in Winston-Salem. She worked out her time, and then, on April 20, she and Benji drove to Memphis to set up housekeeping in our new home. I was on the road.

It was as if the Lord had taken his foot and kicked us out, all in less than four weeks. Bill spent quite a lot of time meeting with me, sometimes late into the evenings and then early in the next morning, reorganizing, helping me get things in order, correcting me in areas of business, getting the ministry into a sound financial posture and looking ahead to future plans and dreams.

Sometimes even he would get frustrated. It was apparent that my gift was singing and sharing, and not finance. But I tried. And he knew it.

I then contacted Jim Buchanan, a lawyer, to prepare and file the papers for Jeff Steinberg Handicapped Ministries to be incorporated. We established a small working board of directors to include Bill Martin chairman, Jim Buchanan, Wayne Drake, a CPA, Debbie and me. On one occasion, Bill took time off from his business to accompany me on a week-long tour to western Arkansas and Oklahoma. He tried running the sound system, playing the sound-track tapes, setting up and tearing down the system, and helping me get dressed and undressed. He came home with the hives. Bill, while on that tour, helped us purchase some new speakers for our sound system. They were smaller, lighter in weight than the ones we were carrying, and they sounded just as good. In June 1979, he also arranged for us to sell our motor-home. The money helped us pay most of our bills and helped us to make the down payment on a brand new 1979 Ford van. A special friend in Florida later customized the interior, and another friend in Indiana did a custom paint job on it. We would put more than 300,000 miles on that van in five years.

Several months had passed and, feeling that he had accomplished his goals and had brought us as far as he could, Bill Martin decided to step down and Jim Buchanan became our new chairman. Much later, near the end of

1981, we sought to expand the board and moved the office into a building near the Memphis International Airport.

Bob Pires left almost as suddenly as he had come. He stayed only three months this time. Bob was one of the most gentle men I've ever known. Having grown up in the streets and ghettos, he always wanted to be a professional football player, and wanted to work with youth, to help them to know God's love, to get off the streets and away from a life of stealing and drugs. Bob left me to pursue his dream.

I was certain that everything that happened had a purpose, no matter how difficult it was to see. I was equally certain that God would send just the right people for this ministry at just the right time. Though the "right" person didn't mean "musician," it would have to be someone who was strong and could handle heavy sound equipment, and someone committed and caring enough to help me in my ministry and help me with my personal needs when Debbie couldn't travel.

May 1981, one of the saddest occasions for me was to sing in Harrisburg, Pennsylvania, at the farewell concert of my friends, the Couriers, who were disbanding as a group. I had known Dave Kyllonen, Duane Nicholson, and Neil Enloe for many years and had sung in many of their concerts. In fact, the Couriers gave me some of the wisest counsel, "Don't buy a bus!" If I had only heeded their advice! I might have saved myself a lot of heartache and struggle. I've had the privilege of singing and recording several of Neil Enloe's songs, including, "The Statue Of Liberty." And I recall the night, while still living at the Good Shepherd Home, that I took a taxi to Rockaway, New Jersey, for the dedication service for the Envoys' new Silver Eagle Bus. The Couriers were the special guests, and they invited me to ride back to Allentown in their bus. I was thrilled! And I felt important showing off my Home.

One of the brighter sides of that farewell concert for the Couriers was meeting tall, bearded, dark headed Kevin O'Connell. He seemed perfectly suited physically to provide the help I would need for someone to travel with me. When I asked him if he was interested, he seemed eager. Kevin, from Corning, New York, had had electronics training in school and experience with another group.

Much more was involved in setting up than plunking down a couple of microphones, lugging in a tape recorder for the sound tracks, hanging up a couple of speakers, and plugging in a cord.

I had learned the hard way that every auditorium has its own shape. If the inside walls are brick or hard plasterboard, sound will bounce off and feed back into any microphone that happens to be in the way. We both learned to use a graphic equalizer to handle this problem. I didn't realize that when I became a singer, I would also have to become sound tech, booking agent, road manager, public relations man, and marketing expert all rolled up in one.

Kevin didn't know everything there was to know about electronics, and I wasn't much of an expert either. We almost came to blows a couple of times before he got the knack of eliminating the feedback. After that, Kevin and I worked well together.

I started to realize that my message was changing. I had always been evangelistic, urging people to receive Jesus the Messiah as their Savior and Lord. What I was learning, from the ragged-edge experiences of my life and from confidences shared by other believers, moved me to focus more on the here and now and the things that God can do through me that I couldn't do for myself. I discovered that he not only loves us, he wants to use us—like a carpenter uses a pair of gloves—to build a house. A very important song, which became the title song of an album I recorded during the summer of 1981, is entitled, "The Glove":

*Just an empty glove lying on the table,*
*Was my life without the Master's hand.*
*Nothing on my own, so useless, alone;*
*Lord, fill this willing glove with your hand.*

*A tool, nothing more, is the glove that is worn*
*On a carpenter's or on a surgeon's hand.*
*And no credit belongs to the one He has on*
*When God touches lives with His hand.*
*Lord, let me be the Glove you wear, today.*
*Use me, Lord, to show someone you care, today.*
*This is all I ask as you perform your task,*
*Lord, let me be the glove you wear.*

*- Gordon Jensen*

It was also time for changes within the organization.

A little later that year, 1981, I convinced the board that I needed help with the booking. I wanted someone with experience, yet I needed someone who knew the ministry inside out and who believed in it thoroughly. I called Jeff Rudloff and asked him to come back to work for me.

"It'll be different this time," I assured. "I have a Board to keep me straight. You and I won't be on the road together competing for the limelight. You always did want to schedule me, so now's your chance. You and Joan will be living in Memphis and have a regular salary. Joan can keep Debbie company while Kevin and I are on the road."

"I should know better, but let us pray about it for a few days, and we'll let you know," Rudloff said.

They came. Debbie was delighted to have a close friend in the neighborhood. Being away from her parents in North Carolina, with me gone four-fifths of the time, had been tough on her and Benji.

Jeff Rudloff knew my direction was changing, for he and I had remained in contact. I phoned him two or three times every month. He and Joan came to my concerts when I was in the Allentown area. His song, "That's Not the Way for You," remained one of my favorites.

Jeffrey did well as a booking agent. He kept us busy and spaced the engagements within one day's driving distance.

We continued the policy of taking churches regardless of size with only the promise of a love offering. One night I

• • • • • • • • • • • • • • • • • • • • • • • • • • • • • •

sang to a thousand, the next to fifty. The smallest crowd was in Hooker, Oklahoma. Eight unsmiling elderly people sat on the back pew in a little church, daring me to entertain them. I gave them all I had.

My father called me one day to tell me that the Philadelphia Variety Club was going to have their annual fund-raising telethon and he knew a gentleman who could arrange for an appearance if I was interested. I accepted with great pleasure.

"The Variety Club sent me to camp when I was seven years old," I said before my song. "You can't imagine how much that meant to a boy who had spent almost all his life in the Welfare Shelter and in Shriners Hospital. I've come back to say thanks from the bottom of my heart."

The show was telecast live from the stage of the Channel Six studios, in the Bellevue Stratford Hotel in Philadelphia. Both Mom and Dad came. They heard me sing in person for the first time. We greeted each other warmly.

"How'd I do?" I asked.

"Very good, Jeffrey," Dad said.

"I remember you once told me that if I ever decided to sing for a living, not to do it around you." We all smiled.

"You've improved." Mom was speaking proudly, "You were very good. How's Debbie and the baby?" She changed the subject.

"He'll soon be four years old and smarter than his old man, he thinks. He's a Steinberg."

Dad laughed.

Not long after the Variety Club telethon, I was on tour in Houston. I received an emergency call from my wife. My sister Sheryl had called to say Dad was in the hospital. They were running tests because of pain in his back and sides. They were afraid he might have lymphoma, cancer of the lymph glands. She promised that she would call me as soon as they had the results.

She was as good as her word. She called the next day to

tell me that the results were not good. But, they were not sure how extensive the cancer was. "A form of lymphoma," she called it.

I called Mom at the hospital. "I don't know what to say, Jeffrey." She continued, "The doctor is still running tests."

I spoke to Dad. "How are you feeling?"

"I have a lot of pain in my lower back and side. They're still running some tests, so, we'll know in a day or two. How are Debbie and Benji?"

"They're fine." I made small talk about Benji and school and my tour schedule.

There were so many things I wanted to ask him about my birth and early years.

"Jeffrey, when will you be in the area? I want to talk to you," he said directly. "I want to talk about why we made some of the decisions we did about you. We may not have made all the right ones, but we wanted what was best for you. I know you have questions and I think it is time for us to talk. What does your schedule look like?"

"I'm planning to be in Philadelphia the last weekend in August. Let's plan to spend the entire day together August 29, OK?"

"OK," he said. "So long."

Mom came on the phone. "You don't need to be in any hurry, Jeffrey. Your father is not in any danger."

"Mom, I want to come. Dad has something to tell me that's important."

"Let it wait awhile. You've got your work and Dad needs to rest."

"Mom, I travel all the time. I have business in Philadelphia the last of August. Why can't I see Dad?"

She wouldn't hear of it. I can only guess from what was said, that she wanted to protect him from the pain of the truth. She worried that if we came and my sisters came in, then Dad would suspect something. Not that he didn't know that something was wrong. Maybe he was still protecting her. Perhaps he felt she would worry if she knew how much of the truth he knew, and for how long. The fair maiden now watching out for her gallant knight.

Every couple of days I called to see how Dad was doing. After a week of tests, the doctors decided to operate. They would go in and, they hoped, be able to remove the cancer. If it was a lymphoma, then it would not be a difficult operation. "If wishes were horses . . ." The doctors opened my father up and found fifteen pounds of pancreatic cancer, and closed him back up. They told Mom there was nothing to do but wait. The end could be anytime from two weeks to six months. The doctor advised her to get things in order, and whatever things they were going to do, they should go ahead and enjoy the remaining time left. What a shock! All their hopes and dreams jammed into an unknown allotment of time. Everything you ever wanted to say, and now there seemed to be no words.

He remained in the hospital for another week and started to show some signs of improvement. But, I was afraid, and would have used any excuse to go to Philadelphia, but Mom didn't want Dad to think it was serious. If the family came home, then he would know. Or, did he already know and just kept it to himself? I was afraid . . . What if he didn't . . . Suppose August 29, comes too late???

"There's no point in your coming. Dad is still too weak."

Dad did show signs of improvement even at home, though, to those of us who knew him even a little bit, he didn't sound good. Once again, I called everyone I loved and trusted, only this time prayer on his behalf and not about anything he did. I hoped for a miracle, believing we were as close as we would ever get, and as close to finding out who I am, what happened, and why. And those were just for starters. I had within me emotions I had never known or would acknowledge.

"Jeffrey, wait a few days and give him a chance to regain his strength," Mom begged.

I kept calling and Mom kept me somewhat informed.

After that week at home Dad started to go downhill. He had a lot more pain and they were back at the doctor's office trying to ease Dad's suffering. Before I realized what was going on, Sheryl called to tell me that the doctor had admitted Dad into the Philadelphia Oncologic Hospital, and that the situation did not look good. He would stabilize for a day or even a few hours, but then he would decline, being in excruciating pain. And when I would call, he was either too weak or too heavily sedated to talk. My father was dying!

On the evening of August 12, 1981, my sister Sheryl called again from California. "Jeff, you'd better come right away. If you want to see Dad alive. I'm catching a plane tonight. Mom is not guaranteeing that he will be coherent. He drifts in and out. She says sometimes he doesn't acknowledge or recognize her. We just don't know how long . . ." Her voice trailed off. I could hear her sobbing, trying to pull herself together.

I hung up and yelled, "Debbie, get packed. We're going to Philadelphia."

We couldn't afford the airfare so we decided to drive straight through to Winston-Salem, leave Benji with Debbie's parents, shower if time allowed, and go straight to Philadelphia.

We left within an hour of Sheryl's call. The wheels of our car hardly touched the ground. We arrived in Winston-Salem about eleven hours later, took a shower, shaved, got something to eat, and started for Philadelphia that same afternoon. We had already called a friend in the area for help—Bobbie Richter, one of the managers of Home Interiors and Gifts, Inc. She would call Mom or the nurses' station and get information on a regular basis and we would stop every hundred miles and get a report from her.

I drove through the night up Interstate 95 through Virginia, stopping once for gas and a couple of times to pay tolls and to call Bobbie. The last time, I said, "What's the latest?"

"Your Dad's sinking fast," she said.

We pulled into the hospital parking lot at exactly 5:55 on Friday morning, August 14, 1981. As I turned into a parking space I felt strange, a deep sense of loss and futility. I got out of the car and ran in as fast as my legs would carry me and asked for the ward where they had Dad. By the time I got there it was straight up six.

The family was standing in the dingy hallway, sobbing aloud just outside of the room when I arrived. The only member not present was Grandmom. There was a hush and despair that permeated the floor. Sheryl and Linda came over and hugged us. Harriet stayed with Mom. We walked toward them.

"When?" I asked.

"Five minutes to six. Jeffrey you missed him by five minutes." By now Sheryl was sobbing uncontrollably. I turned pale at the remembrance. My father had passed away just as I was parking the car. Sheryl and I embraced for about three minutes.

"I want to see him." I cried. Linda, Sheryl, Debbie, and I walked to my Dad's bedside. Mom was crying at his feet.

Mom stood crying, watching Dad's lifeless form.

"Did he know that he had cancer?" I asked.

"I'm sure that he's known for several days." Linda had managed to pull herself together enough to tell me what happened. "He had to know. He kept saying, 'I want to see Jeff. I've got something to tell him.'"

Linda left soon after to go pick up Grandmom.

Debbie and I stayed for the funeral. Dad was buried as he willed, in a plain pine box, dressed in a shroud. The funeral was a traditional service at the downtown funeral home. The attendance was massive, thirty-three cars in the procession to the grave site in northeast Philadelphia. We cancelled all engagements for the week and stayed with the family to observe the customary Jewish mourning rituals. During this week, all mirrors are draped in black, a special candle is lit and not extinguished, perhaps symbolizing that our love for him is as a light that will live in our hearts and never be dimmed. The family receives guests who come by to offer their condolences throughout the week.

The Ruthe Steinberg I saw was a survivor. Now there was no one to protect and shield her, and she would have to cope.

After the funeral we returned to Memphis. Some things got back to normal again. Kevin remained with me for fifteen months. Then he went to upstate New York to visit a girlfriend. He flew back to Memphis and announced that he was leaving in six weeks to get married. I was dumbfounded and more than a little put out.

"Where am I going to find somebody to take your place and train them in six weeks?" I demanded. "Can't you postpone your wedding a couple of months longer?"

He wouldn't. Despite all my fears, the Lord provided a talented and dependable successor. I was singing in a large church in Pittsburgh, Pennsylvania, and mentioned that my assistant, Kevin, was leaving to get married. A tall, skinny kid with glasses, whom I judged to be about seventeen, introduced himself as John Bugay, and asked to be considered for the job.

I eyed him skeptically. "How old are you?" He appeared as an unlikely choice.

"Twenty-one." He had just graduated from the University of Pittsburgh with a degree in English, and he was carrying with him a thick volume from the works of Wesley.

I warned him about the low pay and the tedium of traveling for weeks at a time. Going to a different place every night. Hearing the same songs and stories from me.

"Why would you want this job?" I inquired.

"You really touched me," he continued. "I looked at all I had accomplished and decided that I wanted to use what I have to be a blessing to others. I want to help you get your message out there where others can hear it and be inspired." He seemed to have a beautiful servant's spirit.

Could he do Kevin's job, running sound, driving the van across the country and help me with my personal needs?

"I can learn," he said.

"Well, you've got three weeks before he leaves. I'm going to take a chance and see what you can do."

I turned John over to Kevin. They made a perfect teacher and pupil.

There were other changes in the works. New members to add to the board of directors for new leadership into the future. We added: Claude Koch and Richard "Rusty" Walton, both businessmen; T. Tarry Beasley III and Jerry Taylor, both attorneys, and Rev. Don Johnson, associate pastor at Central Church. Bill Martin had resigned to go back to his business, knowing that we were in good hands, as did Jim Buchanan, though I would always appreciate their help and personal involvement. T. Tarry Beasley was then named chairman. Also, we later added an advisory board to call on for special counsel: Mary C. Crowley, president of Home Interiors and Gifts, Inc., Dallas, Texas; Pearl Burns, area manager of Home Interiors and Gifts, Bethlehem, Pennsylvania; Pat Boone; Dr. Robert Albee, a physician from Atlanta, Georgia; Tom Gregory, an architect from Valdosta, Georgia; Dick Hatch, a radio broadcaster from Pittsburgh; the Rev. Jimmy Latimer, pastor of Central Church in Memphis; the Rev. Jess Moody, the pastor of First Baptist Church in Van Nuys, California; and my friend, the Rev. Dallas Henry, pastor of Hosanna New Testament Ministries in Oxford, Maine.

One evening Jeff Rudloff called to say he had written a new song. He told me, "I was turning and tossing last night in frustration over my inability to deal with certain problems in my life," he said. "Suddenly it was as if the Lord took my hand and wrote the lyrics."

"What are they? Give them to me," I said impatiently.

He sang the first stanza of the song he had entitled "In Your Image."

*When I see you working in my life,*
*That the job is yours and not my own*
*For, I see the mess I've made of all my yesterdays,*

*And I'd do the same tomorrow, left alone.*
*But, I'm slowly learning how to let you do the work,*
*Not struggle, but, to rest in faith in you,*
*Knowing that in spite of all my imperfections*
*I will be just what you want when you get through.*
*In your Image, that's my goal and my desire,*
*In your Image, though it takes me through the fire;*
*In your Image, make me, Lord, as you promised in your*
  *Word,*
*That your presence may be stored, In your Image.*

I broke in, "I love it! It describes what I see as happening in my life perfectly. Send it down and let me try it out."

"But that's not all," he announced. There was an air of excitement in his voice, as if he had caught the goose with the golden eggs.

"Listen, I'm working on your song. This song is definitely for you."

He sang the first stanza:

*When an artist starts painting on a blank piece of canvas*
*It doesn't always look very good.*
*You're wond'rin' what it's gonna be like when it's done,*
*If it's ever gonna look like it should.*
*But when the colors start blending,*
*And shapes begin forming,*
*You begin to see the master design.*
*When the stroke is painted, and the brush is placed*
*It's exactly what he had in mind.*

I got even more excited, and said, "This sounds like God gave you this song for me. Sing some more."

He sang the second verse:

*When you look at me,*
*You see a half finished picture,*
*Pieces of what I'm going to be,*

*'Cause God is still working real hard in my life*
*Painting things that only he can see;*
*Sometimes the colors are bright ones,*
*Sometimes they're dark ones,*
*But they're all a part of what he has planned.*
*He'll complete what he started in his own perfect time,*
*If I'll submit to the brush in his hand.*

The first time I sang Jeffrey's song the audience response confirmed that it was God-given. They broke out in thunderous applause.

When he heard me singing it and saw the reaction, he felt the same. "That's the experience of every believer, but it fits you best of all," he said.

"Yeah, the world is so hung up on appearances. People think a masterpiece is a blond, blue-eyed, 6-foot-2-inch model for a television commercial. God has a different idea."

When we were ready to record "Masterpiece" on a new album, I knew just who I wanted to produce and arrange it. I contacted Randy Hammel, who had produced my album, "The Glove" and Don Hart, who had arranged three of the songs from that album. Randy said, "I like it. It's message is different. I especially like the chorus:

*I'm a masterpiece in progress,*
*God is still working on me;*
*I may not look like it, yet,*
*But, you better bet I'm becoming what he wants me to be.*
*I'm a masterpiece in progress*
*And, it won't be too long till I'm done;*
*A few more strokes of the brush and the Master's touch,*
*And I'll be in the image of his Son.*

"Aren't we already in his image?" he asked.

"Yes," I said, "in position we are. But for me to say the way I am, live, and act now is identical with Jesus Christ would be absolute heresy. I'm only in the process of becoming like him, and there are still many areas where I come short."

Randy Hammel and Don Hart did a dynamite job on the album and "Masterpiece in Progress" became the keynote of my concerts. I frequently followed this song with Gordon Jensen's "The Glove."

"Even when you see that you're a 'masterpiece in progress,' you need to know and accept your limitations," I said. "This is not giving up. It's coming to where you can say, 'OK, Lord, you do through me what I cannot do for myself. Lord, let me be the glove you wear. Lord, touch someone through me.' "

## CHAPTER FIFTEEN

· · · · · · · · · · · · ·

# "I DO"— AND I'D DO IT AGAIN!

"My son!" Every time I said that word I got a warm feeling. And looking at Benji, I marveled. Who would have ever thought that such a beautiful child could be my son! Benjamin David, "Son of my right hand." Looking at his soft features, with straight and sturdy limbs, and blond hair, most people commented that he looked like Debbie's side of the family. She was quick to tell them he had my personality.

"Her beauty and my brains," I added.

When he was four years of age, I found him hard to keep up with, knowing also he would soon be taller than his father. Now that was disconcerting! It's not so bad being shorter than your offspring, unless your offspring is under ten years old!

I regretted that my father never had the relationship of grandfather with Benji. I hoped I would have a richer relationship with my son than I had had with my father. "God help me," I prayed.

One day his friend, Eddie Stafford, our next door neighbor, came over to our house to visit. I was home from tour, and Benji, now four years old, ran to get the door. Eddie looked at me in astonishment. Benji very calmly and casually said, "Eddie, this is my Dad. He doesn't have any arms. He has a tickle hand," and promptly proceeded to attempt to remove my shirt to show off how we wrestle (tickle) all over the floor. Most of the time I stopped him before he got to the first button. If I hadn't, every kid in the neighborhood would be wanting demonstrations.

Everyone in our house was "handicapped." We all had needs and had to help each other. Once, a toy broke and Mom was busy, so Benji came to me. "Fix it," he cried.

Unfortunately, I couldn't and he had to wait for Mom. Often he told his friends how I wrote with my mouth. He wanted me to show off and then they tried with little success the first time. At least they tried, I thought, and perhaps they will not be afraid of the next unusual personality they meet.

Jeff Rudloff had engagements lined up for me more than six months ahead. Three weeks out, one at home, then hit the road again, just John and me. It left very little time with my wife and son.

Debbie seldom complained about my long tours when we lived in Winston-Salem. Now she did. "Sometimes, I wish we had never left Winston-Salem. At least I had my family and friends there."

"But you have Jeff and Joan, Central Church, and our new friends, Saul and Carol," I reasoned.

"Jeff and Joan try hard and they mean well, but Joan has Jeff at home and now with a new baby, they have plenty to do without coming over every day to keep me company. At church I feel like a fifth wheel." She continued. "And I'm just getting acquainted with the Karesh's. I'm anxious for you to meet them. They really have been blessed by your ministry, and they are looking forward to meeting you. They are Jewish, you know."

One Sunday afternoon I called Debbie from Columbus, Ohio. "How was the service at Central?"

"I didn't hear much of Pastor Latimer's sermon. I sat there watching the couple in front of me and feeling sorry for myself. Oh, why can't we move back to North Carolina?"

"Debbie, we've been over that a hundred times. You know why we moved to Memphis."

"Yes," she moaned, "I know, but I'm lonesome."

When I came home there was always a pile of mail to answer and a long list of phone calls to return. I worked in the home office until late at night, leaving Debbie to curl up with a book. We didn't seem to be communicating as well as during the first two or three years of our marriage. She didn't snap to as she once did when I asked her to do something, partly because she had her own routine. When I came home, I interrupted that routine, and then I buried myself in the office. Sometimes, we attributed these incidents to physical problems, but, I don't think either of us really believed that these excuses weren't just that—excuses for not dealing with the real problem.

On one of the occasional trips she took with me, I sang for a Messianic Jewish congregation in Maryland. Debbie fell in love with the people and their style of worship.

"I can just picture what it was like in Bible times," she glowed. "This is wonderful."

Back in Memphis, Carol and Saul Karesh invited the both of us to their house for supper. They wanted their twelve-year-old son, Robbie, to be Bar Mitzvah as a Messianic Jew—as one who believes that Jesus is his Messiah. I contacted my friend, Dan Juster, pastor of Beth Messiah Congregation, in Maryland. He arranged for someone from their congregation to come down and officiate the Bar Mitzvah. I had the privilege of being part of the music for the ceremony, which was held in the chapel at Central Church. From that beginning sprang a desire for more fellowship with other Jews who had met the Messiah,

Jesus. This was the simple start of a Messianic congregation in Memphis.

Debbie was delighted. "This is wonderful. We can have something in Memphis like they have in Maryland."

I was interested, but not as gung-ho as Debbie, perhaps because I had so many other things to do, perhaps also because I had been pressured by Messianic Jewish people in other parts of the country to accept that the only valid ministry for me, because I am Jewish, was a Messianic ministry. They thought I should drop everything, throw away my songs and unique message, and sing only Messianic Jewish songs.

I left for another tour and was not there for the start up of the small congregation. When I came home I went with Debbie and Benji for Friday evening services. The men wore yarmulkes and prayed to the God of Abraham, Isaac, and Jacob, in the name of Yeshua, the Messiah. They sang some traditional Jewish songs and some newer praise choruses in both Hebrew and in English. Saul would invite a guest speaker to come and give a short sermon showing how Yeshua (Hebrew for Jesus) had fulfilled the Old Covenant prophecies to be the Messiah, and tie them into the New Covenant Scriptures. Once a lady came with a scale model of the Tabernacle and did a study with us about worship in the Tabernacle.

Debbie sat enraptured, her face shining. She looked at Benji, playing with the other children there.

"We must bring our son up to appreciate his Jewish heritage."

Debbie jumped into the Messianic work with both feet. She helped the Kareshes in any way she could with the growing needs of this work. She learned to cook many Jewish foods and exchanged recipes with other Messianic Jews. She went on Messianic retreats. She almost became more Jewish than I, not that that would be hard.

When I came home, she told me things about my heritage that I didn't know. I learned more about Judaism and being a Jew from my "Goy" (Gentile) wife than I ever learned from my Jewish father. I wonder about all of the arguments about my religious beliefs he led me into when I visited him, if they weren't a sort of self-recrimination for his lack of involvement in my spiritual growth. I wanted to know more, but I was tired from cross-country travel, motels, restaurant meals, and entertaining people. She wanted me to go places with her, and I would rather not. I would go sometimes just to please her. Then there were times when I wouldn't go, not knowing or considering the importance she placed on it.

"OK, Benjamin and I are going," she said one night. I looked at her in amazement as she bustled around to get Benji ready, then jumped in the car, and was off to do her thing. With Debbie occupied, I figured my troubles were over. At last she was standing on her own and not begging to go home to mama and daddy.

There was no stopping this new wife of mine.

I sat impressed as Benji recited Scripture passages and Jewish songs. "Debbie," I said, "he's only five years old and knows more than I did at thirteen when I was made Bar Mitzvah."

Every time I came home, Debbie had something going with the Messianic group. She'd want to talk about it and I'd say, "Dear, I'm tired. Can't we discuss this another time?"

"Why aren't you interested? You're Jewish. I'd think you would want to know about your people and the Bible."

"I'm interested, dear, but I'm also very tired."

After I got rested, I wanted to go out with the Rudloffs, only to find she had something planned on her own. It was worse when I arrived home unexpectedly. "Oh, I wasn't expecting you and I've got this week scheduled."

I came to resent her activities that didn't include me. I sulked and moped around the house. She just kept on going, ignoring and neglecting her husband, I felt. When I did catch her on the run and voiced my objection, she said,

"You ought to be pleased that I'm keeping myself busy. Weren't you the one who was sick of me complaining of being lonesome?"

When I walked in from a trip, she didn't greet me as the conquering hero. Instead it was, "Will you get a plumber. I've been trying to get a toilet unstopped for a week." This is a familiar syndrome, I've discovered, among many performers and evangelists, who expect that because the rest of the world treats them as stars, their wives and children should welcome them in adoration: "Yea, verily, Father and husband is home. Glory to God. Bless you, O returning king."

Debbie was a little that way early in our marriage. But she soon got over it.

When I hinted that she ought to show more respect, she yelled, "Come down off your throne, Buster!"

I spent as much time with Jeff Rudloff as Joan would allow. We were the same old pair, talking shop, music, shooting the breeze, planning upcoming tours.

"You're killing me with work," I told him. "Give me a day or two off now and then."

He eyed me curiously. "Look, your board hired me to get you engagements. The more concerts you give, the more money you bring in to keep us out of the red. Right now we're right on the edge."

"OK, OK, I get the message. So, what else is new?"

He laughed and we went on to the next item.

Jeff Rudloff hadn't been on the road in months. "You've booked me far enough ahead to deserve a trip," I told him. "C'mon and let's do this California tour together. You can help drive out and help me with the orchestra for the Easter Seal Telethon. It'll be like old times." Joan wasn't too happy, but he went.

The highlight of the trip was singing for Pat Boone's annual National Easter Seal Telethon in Los Angeles. This was my third year, and I would be performing live on national TV with a live orchestra! I was thrilled beyond belief. Pat did the show at the Sunset Tower Studios, just off Sunset Boulevard. The producer sat a handicapped child on each side of me, a boy and a girl, in wheelchairs. The orchestra struck up Rudloff's "Masterpiece in Progress" and I sang the song to each of them, turning to one child, then to the other.

When I finished, the producer leaned over to Jeffrey and whispered, "This is the most powerful thing we've ever done in the history of the telethon."

Rudloff smiled and said, "I only wrote it. It's his song. Nobody else can sing it with such effect."

Sometime later, Sue Farr, the wife of an army sergeant in Germany heard me sing at a Baptist church in New Hampshire. She told her husband, Jim, about me, and he recommended me to a chaplain in West Germany. This resulted in an invitation to do a series of concerts for an Air Artillery group in Pattonville, near Stuttgart.

"Come with me," I urged Debbie. I thought the trip might improve our relationship. I had a growing realization that our marriage was becoming much less than a masterpiece.

She didn't light up as I had hoped, but agreed to go if her folks could keep Benji.

This was in October 1981, and we were to go overseas in early January and be there for three weeks. John would go along to set up and run the sound system.

In November, Debbie astounded me with the news that she was pregnant. When she began having problems she asked her doctor to rule on the trip.

"Stay home," he said bluntly. "You get over there, something happens, and you won't know where to get help."

Her first pregnancy had been almost perfect. Could something be wrong with this child? I really didn't have time to worry, for John and I were booked for a tour from which we wouldn't return until December. There would be just a few days left until we were due to depart for Germany.

Debbie's curtness and unwillingness to discuss her

problems with me made the uncertainty worse. I called from Phoenix and asked, "How are you doing?"

"All right, I guess. I've been spotting a lot today."

"Have you called the doctor?"

"Jeff, I'm OK. You don't have to worry about me. I was just at the doctor last week and I mentioned the spotting and he doesn't think it's anything to worry about. Go on and do your thing."

"Your thing is my thing. I want to know what's happening. I'm your husband."

Long silence.

"Debbie, are you there?"

"Jeff, I don't feel like talking any more."

Debbie prayed for "a normal, healthy child, and if anything goes wrong, Lord, you know what I can handle. If I can't, then You'll take the child."

I had to find this out later. Debbie was talking to God, but not to me.

I still held out hope that her condition would stabilize and the doctor would let her make the trip. I felt we desperately needed to do something together.

The very last day arrived on which we could apply for passports in time for the tour.

"You guys go ahead and I'll stay home," Debbie declared with a certain resignation. It was as if she was relieved.

"Yes, the tour is planned. I guess John and I will have to go without you."

The day after John and I turned in the passport applications to the post office, Jeff and Joan Rudloff invited me to go Christmas shopping with them.

"Do you mind?" I asked Debbie.

"No, I'll stay home with Benji."

"Will you be OK?"

"Go on, I won't need you."

Shortly after I left she called her doctor and told him everything. She was miscarrying.

"Get somebody to bring you down to the emergency room," he ordered. "I'll meet you there."

She called a baby-sitter and had a neighbor take her to the hospital. The doctor treated her and allowed her to return home with the neighbor. I called home from the mall and she answered sounding somewhat sleepy.

Finally, she told me she had had a miscarriage.

"Why didn't I know about this?"

"You were shopping. How could I have found you?"

She was up and walking around that day getting things ready for a Christmas party that night.

"I can't get over you, Debbie," I chided. "You act as if you were glad to lose the child."

"No, I'm not, Jeff. There was obviously something seriously wrong with our baby, and the miscarriage was God's way of ending the pregnancy. That's the way I prayed."

"Then why aren't you upset?"

"What good would it do?" she said in resignation. "God was in control and he knew what was best."

"Did you ask the doctor if he could tell what was wrong, or even if was a boy or girl?"

"No, I just wanted it to be healthy and it wasn't. I was the one having the problems, Jeffrey, while you were traveling around the country." When I continued to fret, she exploded—something that was, up to this point, very uncharacteristic of Debbie.

"Jeff, there's nothing to be upset about, I told you. You're acting as if you're the one who had the miscarriage."

"It was my baby, too."

She turned to face the wall. "Go away. I don't want to talk if you're going to be like this."

We didn't say much to each other for the next two weeks. We went through the motions of Christmas, with both of us trying to cover up the strain between us.

Shortly after New Year's, Debbie and Benji, Jeff and Joan,

and several other friends went to the airport to see John and me off. With the special assistance from Delta Airlines, our sound system was checked as baggage. Jim Farr, who had returned to Germany, said we couldn't count on the Army for such technical assistance.

Debbie walked with the others to the security check and gave me a good-bye kiss as if all was rosy between us. I put on a happy face that turned to a scowl as I followed John down the corridor to our gate. This was a trip I had looked forward to when the invitation came. Now I would just as soon have stayed home.

After we left Debbie talked to a Christian marriage counselor. They discussed the alternatives before her: stay with me and try to rebuild our relationship; separate for awhile and then make another stab at the marriage; file for divorce.

"Divorce is wrong for me," Debbie declared. "My parents ingrained in me that 'you make your bed and lie in it.' If I should get divorced, I could never remarry."

I called her from Germany. "How are you? How's Benji?"

"We're OK." Her voice sounded cold and distant. I sensed that more than an ocean separated us.

"Is anything wrong?"

"No. How are your meetings going?" She was very cordial and controlled.

"Tremendous. The soldiers are really turning out. The chaplain in charge says I'm an answer to his prayers. More than a hundred have come to him for counsel after hearing me. Most of the men here are away from their wives. They're lonesome and easy prey for drug dealers and alcoholism. The military is such a bureaucracy that the ordinary guys can't see where they count for anything. Poor self-esteem is a real problem, and the chaplain says I'm a big help on that."

I rattled on with Debbie asking only an occasional question or making a brief comment. "We spend most of our off hours with Jim and Sue. John has to carry me around Germany because of the snow and ice, and then carry me me up and down four flights of stairs a couple of times a day. I miss you."

Debbie had fallen silent on me. "You sure everything's OK?" I probed.

"I'm sure."

"Well, we'll see you in a couple of days. Give everybody our love . . . Bye." I didn't want to sign off, but on an overseas call you can't talk forever. I lay awake a long time that night, probing into memories of our marriage, asking, "Where did we start drifting apart? Where did I go wrong? Where do we go when I get back?"

I called Jeff Rudloff when we landed in Atlanta. "What's happening? How's Debbie?" Jeffrey had always been frank with me.

"You and Debbie have problems. She needs to talk to you more than I do about them."

For the first time in our marriage, I was afraid Debbie wouldn't be there when I got home.

We landed in Memphis on schedule. John carried our hand baggage and I lurched behind him, eyes peeled in hopes of seeing Debbie in the welcoming party at the security check.

"Dad! Dad!" There was Benji on Jeff Rudloff's shoulder. Where was Debbie?

"Lord, let her be there!"

A woman near Rudloff moved and I caught a glimpse of blonde hair. Debbie! Thank God, thank God! She hadn't left me yet.

Benji grabbed me around the neck and almost lifted me off the floor. Debbie brushed my lips with a kiss and with a frozen smile stepped back so the others could say, "Welcome home."

Debbie drove home with me in the front seat beside her with Benji leaning up from the back. "Dad, did you fly over the ocean? Did you visit a castle? Did you bring me back a surprise from Germany?" John Bugay sat beside Benji quietly, as my son chattered. Debbie gazed frostily at the traffic in front.

We reached the house. John carried in our bags and took Benji into his room to show him some souvenirs, leaving us to be alone in the den.

We exhausted the small talk. I glanced at Debbie. She sat stonily on her end of the couch, staring at the wall. Finally, I said, "Are you leaving me?"

"I have no plans for that."

"Where do we go from here?"

"I don't know. I'm doing a lot of praying."

"Debbie, I didn't know it was serious until you lost the baby."

"Of course, you didn't; you were busy with your ministry." She spat out the words as if she were emptying her mouth of poison. "You couldn't have known," she continued. "You were never here."

"I was here," I protested. "You were busy with your people."

"Jeff, I had to do something. I was sitting home crying my eyes out, praying you'd move back to Winston-Salem. Then I realized this wasn't going to happen. So one day I said, 'Debbie, you can't change your husband, so get up and do something for yourself.' That's when I got involved with the Messianic group. They saved my sanity. You liked that for awhile. You thought it was great for me to have friends and go places when you weren't here. You thought I wouldn't complain so much when you did come home. But you found and I found that I didn't need you as much as I once did."

"Debbie, why didn't you tell me this before?"

"I was brought up to be meek and submissive to my husband, and all that jazz. A wife is supposed to be quiet and suffer in silence. I suffered until I couldn't take it any longer. Now and then I tried to reach out, but you were too engaged in more important things to catch on."

"Debbie!"

• • • • • • • • • • • • • • • • • • • • • • • • • • • • • • • •

"You know it's true. It's how I felt, and how you were."

My head ached. My senses reeled. What was happening to us?

"Jeff, you assumed that because we didn't quarrel that things were wonderful. You took me for granted because I let you take me for granted. When we lived in Winston-Salem, I could always go to my parents or to Lisa, but when we moved here, I didn't have anyone for a long time with whom I felt I could confide. Somewhere along the line I became an independent woman. I found people to talk to. I learned to get by on my own. For the first time in my life, I quit playing a role to myself. I became assertive and more honest with people, with everyone except you. I just couldn't tell you flat out how I felt. I figured you ought to be smart enough to catch on. Apparently, you weren't."

"Debbie, let's start over. We can. I'll try to be different. I'll listen to you. I'll do what you want. I'll . . ."

"No, Jeff, maybe you'll change for awhile, but you'll go right back to putting everything ahead of me."

"My ministry?"

"Yes, your precious ministry and all that's associated with it."

"God put me in this ministry."

"Jeff, you don't get my point. Your ministry has become your everything. Benji and I are just little appendages, necessities when you come off the road."

We talked far into the night and finally fell asleep from physical and emotional exhaustion. We talked most of the next day. We decided that the Lord had put us together to serve him, and that the Lord had worked miracles in keeping us together. Where we would go from here, we were not sure.

I saw that the wounds could not be healed over in a week or so. There had to be a basic change in my will. I had to say to her and mean it, "Hey, our marriage is too important for any ministry to ruin it. If it means that I will never sing again and keep you, then I will never go on another stage."

We agreed that we had too much invested in our marriage to let it fall by the wayside. It would be hard, but we would try, with God's help, to make a go of it.

One of the things that helped Debbie was a women's course by Diane Lewis at Central Church on emotions. They talked about the woman being in control of her feelings, without letting her feelings control her. Debbie shared some of the things she was learning: "You choose to be angry when you get angry. You choose to be hurt when you get hurt. You choose whether or not you're going to react in a negative or positive way. Love is an emotion, but also something you do, both an action and a reaction. You love because you are loved and choose to love because you are loved." It made sense. We began to understand that if our marriage fell apart, there would be nobody to blame but us.

It was then that we actually said, "We're going to slow down. We're in this thing together. Jeff Steinberg is going to spend less time on the road, do fewer concerts, and if the money doesn't come in, then God will provide some other way or show us something else to do."

We shared this with our board and they concurred that I had been gone from Debbie too much. But fewer concerts would mean a drop in income. We couldn't afford a booking agent.

One of our pledges was to be more honest in our personal relationships and with others. Debbie then admitted to Jeff Rudloff how jealous she had been of him. They actually became good friends before he and Joan moved back to Pennsylvania. Debbie understood that he would always probably be my best male friend, but that I would never again let him come between us. Debbie quit her full-time office job and went back to being a Kelly Girl. She could turn down assignments and devote more time to Benji and manage the office when I hit the road. During the last couple of years she had virtually opted out of helping in the ministry.

We also decided that she would teach Benji at home

during the 1982-83 school term. She enrolled him in an accredited Christian correspondence school. Our home school worked so well and Benji made such excellent grades that she decided to teach him again the next year.

Still another decision was that Debbie and Benji would join our traveling road team on a somewhat regular basis. "This is what I dreamed of doing when we were dating," Debbie recalled. "I soon found out that my ideas were more fantasy than reality. But I think it will work now."

We made our first long tour together in several years. One engagement was for a men's fellowship dinner at a camp in New Jersey. Before we arrived, Benji, now in the second grade, surprised us by asking if he could introduce his Dad.

I said, "Yeah, well, why not. What do you think, Mom?"

Debbie smiled her consent, adding, "It should be interesting."

We got there a couple of hours ahead of time. Debbie dressed Benji in a red blazer, red, white, and blue plaid pants and matching tie. He had written on a piece of paper what he wanted to say and practiced while we were setting up. First we had dinner, then the camp director, John Ashman, signaled to me and I punched Benji.

Our son strode to the platform, picked up the cord mike and whirled around to face the audience. "Ladies and Gentlemen, may I present to you someone I am proud of—my Dad, Jeff Steinberg."

A real professional, that boy!

Later that evening, after Debbie and I were alone in bed, we talked over the evening and our expanding relationship.

"Debbie, I have a confession to make," I said. "I made the mistake of thinking that when we said 'I do' before Jerry Falwell that our marriage was an accomplished fact. With a lot of help from you, I'm learning that our relationship is very much a part of our relationship with the Lord. I said 'I do,'—and I'd do it again!"

She suddenly raised up and gave me a warm kiss. "You're exactly right, Jeffrey Steinberg. So let's move on with it."

CHAPTER SIXTEEN
· · · · · · · · · · · ·

# A NEW BEGINNING

Debbie accompanied me on my second trip to West
Germany. I was to sing in post chapels, for troops on
maneuvers, and in the big Beer Tent erected on the midway
in Nellingen during the "VolksFest" Celebration. The
"Volksfest" was a goodwill gesture toward U.S.-German
relations.

The afternoon I was to sing in the Beer Tent I noticed
two young men swaggering in and out of the tent, then
circling us and shouting something in German.

"What are they saying?" I asked Jim Farr curiously.

He laughed, "Oh, one of them thinks you're E.T. They're
a little soused."

The tent was jammed with a thousand to twelve hundred
noisy American military and German civilians. I did my
full concert program, opening with Dave Roff's song,
"Talkin' to the Sand" and immediately into "Nothing Less
Than a Miracle." I then talked to the audience on a casual
level and sang Jeff's song, "Making Something Beautiful,"

and shared some humorous stories about kids' reactions to my hook and my size. I then sang, "Bloom Where You're Planted" and walked through the audience, picking on bald generals, making funny faces at kids, and sitting on the laps of the ladies. I went immediately to the introduction to "The Glove" and my personal story. "My name is Jeff Steinberg," I began. "I was born August 18, 1951, with no arms and deformed legs, Phocomelia, congenital birth defects. My dad took one look at me and figured I would die. When I didn't, he put me in the welfare shelter . . ." Nobody now was drinking or yelling. I could whisper and be heard at the back of the tent.

Their eyes were riveted on me now. "I haven't come here to talk about the terrible past. I want you to know that God loves you, not because of the way you look, but because of what he created you to be, "a masterpiece."

John kicked off the sound track for "Masterpiece." When I finished with: ". . . a few more strokes of the brush, and the Master's touch, and I'll be in the image of the Son," the crowd rose to their feet clapping and yelling.

One of the highlights of the tour was when Jim and Sue Farr took us to Dachau. We saw the execution wall where thousands of Jews were shot and fell into the ditch behind them. We inspected the gas ovens where more thousands were burned. We walked by the blown-up, starkly realistic, black-and-white pictures showing piles of naked, emaciated Jewish bodies, male and female, young and old; limbs like matchsticks, heads, torsos, and limbs twisted in grotesque shapes to make human brush piles. Everyone spoke in whispers, awe-stricken and chilled by the horror of it all.

Graphic reminders of the Nazi genocide troubled me more because of a new holocaust in the 1980s, abortion, the one and a half million infants being killed each year in America and infanticide, the hundreds of severely handicapped babies reportedly being denied nourishment and treatment in American hospitals.

At an officers' party, during my first Germany tour the

previous year, I was introduced to a gynecologist who served in the military. He asked me to share a little of my story. One thing led to another and he saw that I felt strongly about abortion.

"How do you handle the question of when life begins?" he asked.

"I have no problem there," I replied. "I learned in seventh grade biology that you never get life from non-life. Either it's a life or it's not a life."

I put him on the defensive. "What do you do with potential life? If it's growing, it must be alive. Have you ever known anyone growing who was not alive?" I asked.

He didn't answer directly. "I see what you're getting at, but if I didn't perform abortions for the military wives and female personnel here, they would go outside and endanger their lives."

"If they knew they had to go outside," I countered, "about one-eighth of the abortions would be performed because of the risk. How much do you think abortions have increased in the United States since the Supreme Court made the procedure legal?"

He downed the remainder of his cocktail. "What do I do about my practice? This is my job."

"Your job is to deliver—not kill life. Wouldn't it be easier to counsel mothers on how to keep the baby or put it up for adoption than to be the executioner? I met a couple recently who have waited five years to adopt and still have not found a child. Doctor, we're throwing away hundreds of thousands of babies a year who could have good homes."

He shifted his weight in the chair uneasily and stared at his empty glass. "What do you do with a woman's right to choose?"

"Doctor, the woman has the right to choose not to fool around. What do you do with moral decisions of responsibility? A woman chooses to have sex and run the risk of conceiving a child. That child shouldn't be killed simply to justify her lack of responsibility."

"What if the mother's life is endangered?"

"Come on, Doctor. How many abortions do you perform just to save a mother's life? One in a hundred? You know that ninety-nine out of a hundred are performed for convenience."

I was coming on strong. People around us were tuning in. The colonel hosting the party glanced uneasily in our direction. "Doctor," I persisted, "the Nazis decided that Jews, the retarded, and certain other people were inconvenient to the New Reich. They didn't have the desired quality of life. If Hitler were alive today, he would love America!

"Doctor, this debate about quality versus sanctity of life touches me. If I were to be born as I am today, they would probably let me starve to death. Thank God, I was born in 1951 when aborting a child for convenience or because of handicaps was unthinkable. Today, I would stack the quality of my life up against any doctor, congressman, or supreme court justice in America."

The doctor sat speechless until the colonel broke up our parlay.

During this tour, we were pleased to learn that the U.S. Army ordered that the military would no longer fund abortions for military personnel or dependents.

The right-to-life movement was then in full bloom in the United States. In Phoenix, Father Shaughnessy, a staunch old Irish priest, arranged for me to sing and speak before a state legislative committee considering legislation on the medical treatment of handicapped infants. I used the famous "Baby Doe" case in Indiana as a springboard.

"Baby Doe," I told them, "had the misfortune of being born with two problems. He was a Down's Syndrome child and would have a less-than-average IQ. That could not be prevented, although many Down's Syndrome children grow up to live productive lives. His other problem was a deformed esophagus which prevented food from reaching

• • • • • • • • • • • • • • • • • • • • • • • • • • • • • • •

his stomach. He could be fed intravenously until that was surgically corrected. Even though scores of people wanted to adopt him the parents said, 'No feeding and no surgery.' His quality of life was not deemed high enough for survival, so he was left to starve to death.

"Who is to determine quality of life. Hitler could say, 'this one shall live,' and 'this one shall die.' Dr. Francis Crick, a Nobel Prize winner, says that 'no newborn infant should be declared human until it has passed tests regarding its genetic endowment and if it fails these tests, it forfeits the right to live.' Now I ask you, who should have the power to set these genetic requirements? Who is smart enough to decide if someone is bright enough or tall enough or strong enough to be allowed to live? Scientists? Politicians? Theologians? White people? Black people? Jews? Gentiles?"

The committee members sat stone still. Later they recommended and the Arizona legislature passed a law making it a crime for any doctor or hospital employee to withhold treatment or nourishment from a handicapped infant.

I feel so strongly that the only experts on the "quality of life" ethic are those of us who have lived to show that one is not bound by his looks. Looks are deceiving. What one sees of another person is only a small part of what that person is. The tragedy in our nation is that on the one hand we applaud the overcomers in our society, while on the other hand we deny future masterpieces their opportunity to shine, convincing ourselves that the struggle for some is too great. It is no harder for Jeff Steinberg to reach the top of the mountain than for anyone else—it simply demands my best effort, no less. The Masterpiece is in all of us. It takes time, diligence and patience for it to come shining through.

Back at home in Memphis, Debbie and I continued to develop closer ties with the Messianic family within the larger family at Central Church. We observed the Passover in remembrance of Israel's deliverance from slavery in

Egypt. We celebrated Rosh Hashana, the Jewish New Year, with celebration and feasting. We solemnized Yom Kippur, the Day of Atonement, by fasting and rejoicing in the once-for-all sacrifice by Messiah for our sins.

Just before my thirty-third birthday, in August 1984, I became aware that something was about to come off in our home. Debbie doesn't plan surprise parties very well. I knew something was up, but I didn't know what until I walked in one evening and saw this strange bunch of characters. One of the ladies came as a dwarf, walking on her knees. Another girl came as a mute. A guy tucked his right arm under his shirt and wore a hook. Debbie got out my old brace, which had been replaced, and wore it on her leg.

"We didn't want you to feel out of place at your party," Debbie announced, "so we all came as handicaps."

Someone brought a bottle of nail polish for my hook. Two people gave me cans of oil for the mechanism in my arm. Another friend handed me a gift-wrapped "Michael Jackson Hook Glove." She had glued sequins all over a sport sock to make it look shiny, then sewed a seam down the middle. The card with it read: "No one wants to be greeted on a cold morning by a cold hook. Wear your hook glove."

The party was hilarious, something to tell my grandchildren about. I loved every minute of it.

The following month our family left on a six-week tour of Pennsylvania and New Jersey, to churches, military chapels, and to the Good Shepherd Home's seventy-sixth anniversary celebration, where I would be a special guest. Debbie packed in Benji's schoolwork so he could do his lessons under her supervision on the road.

This was going to be a real trip down memory lane. Dad Snyder set up a concert at Lehighton Wesleyan Church, where I had attended so many times with the Snyders. Dad Snyder especially wanted me to see his grandson, Steve Pickett, who had lost his right leg in a freak accident.

We would see Quacky, Mrs. Hoffman, my first teacher at Good Shepherd, Dr. Raker, George and Erma Long, and many more dear friends who had helped me make it in and out of the institution.

Then we would stop in Philadelphia, visit Shriners Hospital, and later see my family.

Mom had recently remarried, "a gentleman who lived across the street from me for sixteen months before I met him," she said. I had wanted to come to the wedding, but it was a small private one. None of the family had made the special trip.

"All right then," I said, "after you're settled, I'm coming to see you and we're going to talk about us. Mom, I'm thirty-three years old. It's time, don't you think?"

She didn't answer my question. She made no promises.

Good Shepherd put us up at the Allentown Hilton. We arrived on Wednesday, September 19, got a good night's rest, and drove over the next morning for the big celebration.

Good Shepherd had come a long way since the old farmhouse. The sprawling rehabilitation hospital and therapy center extended a full block along St. John from Sixth to Fifth Street. Behind the hospital was the new Vocational Services Building, where 200 handicapped people were gainfully employed. Across Sixth Street was the remodeled Raker Center, the home for 135 residents of various ages who looked to Good Shepherd for shelter. I shaded my eyes against the blinding sun, squinting to see the familiar verse from Psalm 23, printed across the top of Raker Center. "Well, at least one thing hasn't changed," I remarked to Debbie.

The scores of educational events planned for Good Shepherd Day was mind-boggling. Guests could have their hearing and vision checked, take in a jogger's clinic, hear a lecture on stress management, operate Robbie the Robot, learn how to talk to the deaf, see America's first workshop in micrographics, and so much more.

"Jeff Steinberg in Concert" led the roster of musical programs in the big tent that afternoon.

Three o'clock and the gang's all here. I led off with:

*I'm a Masterpiece in Progress; God is still working on me.*
*I may not look like it yet, But you'd better bet,*
*I'm becoming what he wants me to be.*

The wheelchair brigade along the front kicked off the applause. The crowd clapped, whooped, yelled, screamed. There was nothing more thrilling to me than performing before my old house mates at Good Shepherd.

"It's good to be back home again," I said before a sea of smiles. "I've sung in a lot of places since leaving here thirteen years ago—Canada, Germany, the Caribbean, and in almost every one of the fifty states. People are pretty much the same. They look at me funny when I come up.

"You know, kids are brutally honest. They say just what they're thinking. A little boy in Virginia stared at me and asked, 'Are you a robot?'

"I looked him straight in the eye and said, 'How-do-you-do-my-name-is-Jeff-Steinberg-what-is-your-name?' "

The crowd howled.

"A kid in Arizona walked up to me and pointed to my hook. 'Whatcha got that for?'

"I said, 'Cause I don't have any hands.'

" 'Why don'tcha have any hands?'

" 'Cause I used to bite my fingernails and one day I went too far!' He said, 'Wow!' He hasn't bitten his fingernails since.

"We were in Pittsburgh a few weeks ago. Debbie was getting me ready for bed. The pastor of the church where I was singing called, 'Deb, when you're taking him apart, please don't lose any pieces.'

"I'm here with all my pieces, including my wife and son, the first time they've been to Good Shepherd. Ladies and

Gentlemen, may I present my wife, Debbie, and my son, Benjamin David."

Debbie and Benji took bows to loud cheers and applause. I recognized a number of old friends in the audience, then I took the cordless mike and ambled down in the audience to sing my favorite rib tickler, "Bloom Where You're Planted." I maneuvered among wheel chairs, hugging patients and nurses right and left.

That evening more than 1500 people overflowed the tent for the grand finale. The Allentown Band played, I sang "In All Things We Are More Than Conquerors." Then Dick Vermeil, former coach of the Philadelphia Eagles, spoke on "The Real Heroes—ordinary people who do the very best they can with what they've got." Then Good Shepherd's new president, Dale Sandstrom, presented Presidential Press Secretary Jim Brady the Handicapped Hall of Fame Award, "for the example he has set in his courage, tenacity, and love of life." Tremendous applause greeted this man who had taken a bullet between the eyes, intended for President Reagan, and survived against overwhelming odds.

After the benediction, I stood there in the glare of the TV lights, chatting with Jim Brady, as the Secret Service men courteously but firmly pushed the crowd back. "I really admire you for your courage, Mr. Brady," I said.

"Thank you, and I appreciate your music, Jeff. It's really inspiring."

"We'll be coming to Washington in a few weeks," I noted.

"Let me know when," he said, "and I'll arrange a special tour of the White House for you and your family."

The next morning I climbed up the concrete steps on which Dad had carried me twenty-four years before. Very little had changed in the residence building, now called Raker Center. Dr. Raker, the Administrator Emeritus, came from behind his big desk to greet me warmly. He still stood ramrod straight, dark hair combed straight back and parted in the middle.

For the next hour we reminisced about people and events . . . Ricky, Curtis, Christmas parties, Lawrence Welk, Junior Achievement, and the trouble I caused the staff.

"We couldn't keep you penned up." He laughed. "You were all over town, at the radio station, selling doughnuts, visiting friends. Sometimes I wondered if I had a boy named Jeff Steinberg."

Dr. Raker hugged me when I got up to leave. "People like you make it all worthwhile." He beamed. "Come back real soon."

Quacky came by the hotel and we talked in the coffee shop for three straight hours about her family, mine, and all the sweet memories shared between us. She said she was now teaching developmentally disabled children at the school across the street from her home. "I had to find something to do after you left."

"I took up a lot of your time," I admitted. "Whenever I felt low, I knew I could call you. You never seemed to mind."

She tenderly placed her hand on my shoulder. "It was always a joy, Jeff."

We drove out to see Mrs. Hoffman, retired with her scrapbooks and memories of the hundreds of handicapped children she had taught. She had saved pictures of me, Ricky, Curtis, and others I had never seen before. Every face was a story.

We stopped at William Allen High School and located a couple of teachers who remembered me. John Donmoyer, my algebra teacher, pointed to a desk in his classroom where I had sat behind the door. "We retired that chair after you left," he joked.

On to Lehighton. Because of our tight schedule, we arrived at the Wesleyan church only a few minutes before I was to sing. Dad Snyder, hair now white, but still quite active and full of life, embraced me and my family in the parking lot. "We didn't have a son, so the Lord gave us Jeff," he explained to Debbie.

Mom Snyder, arms extended, shuffled towards me. "Jeff! Jeff!"

"Mom!" I slipped under her protecting arm, as I had so many times as a boy. Mom was not very coherent, she now needed assistance in getting around.

"She's had three strokes and also has diabetes," Dad Snyder confided after he had taken her into the church. "You know how she always wanted to do everything for everybody. Now I must do it all, cooking and cleaning and caring for her like a baby."

I leaned against him, my shoulders shaking, choking back the tears, thinking of the uncountable times she had bathed and dressed me with never a complaint.

Inside the church I looked for familiar faces. Jeff and Joan Rudloff and their two children, Alyssa and Rebecca, were seated in the back. Near them were the Picketts. I saw Steve Pickett, a tall, redheaded boy, standing in the back, balancing on his right leg with a crutch, his left leg amputated at the hip.

I had a few minutes before the service to talk with Jeff and Joan. He was pastoring a small church and working as an insurance agent.

"Behaving yourself, Steinberg?" he asked.

"What do you think?"

"You know what I think. You don't want to hear it."

Joan was holding their little miracle baby. She had been born with a defective heart valve. This was the first time I had seen Becca since her surgery.

Dad Snyder, still the song leader of the church, introduced me. I sang a couple of Jeff Rudloff's songs, then he and Joan joined me for a third. It was like old times. I told stories and the people laughed and applauded.

We went to the pastor's house for a reception. Dad Snyder filled me in with more details about his grandson's accident. "He fell from a tree onto an iron fence post behind our house. I heard him scream and ran out to find the steel post rammed ten to twelve inches up into his thigh. Another two inches and it would have got his kidneys and he would have been dead."

I pulled Steve aside and asked, "Have you ever wondered why?"

"No, my dad told me that the Lord has a good reason for allowing things like this to happen. I just made that my reason, even though I don't understand it at this time. They're making an artificial leg for me at Good Shepherd and I'm planning on going back to Brazil with my parents in January. I want to graduate at the mission high school."

I laid my hook on his shoulder. "Steve, there's going to be a time when you will need to have more dialogue with the Lord than 'Yes, sir,' and 'No, sir.' The Lord will show you things that will explain why and give you an outlook and insight that you never had before. Just as he has shown me."

We went back to the hotel that night and started toward Philadelphia on Route 309 around eleven o'clock the next morning. About twenty-miles out we pulled off a familiar side road for a backyard lunch with George and Erma Long and their daughter Dolores and son-in-law Harley. Erma served thick, juicy steaks hot off the grill, baked potatoes, green beans, and scrumptious apple pie. We laughed, reminisced, and reflected on how far I had come.

As we turned back on 309, I mentioned, "This is the road my folks took when they brought me to Good Shepherd." Farther down the road, I noticed Debbie was sniffling.

"What's wrong?" I asked.

"Jeff, you may think this strange, but I've never felt sorry for you before. You always seemed so strong and independent. As we've been riding along, a picture came in my mind of that frightened little nine-year-old boy being taken to a strange place and left with people he had never seen before. I never thought of you that way before."

"Yeah, I was that boy. I was scared all right."

We rolled into northeast Philadelphia and parked in the back lot at Shriners. I wanted Debbie and Benji to see where I had spent five years of my life.

They gave us the VIP tour. It all started coming back.

• • • • • • • • • • • • • • • • • • • • • • • • • • • • • • • •

The white-coated doctors trooping by on rounds. The
months and months confined to a crib and wearing casts on
both legs. The sickening fear of surgeries.

An operating assistant saw me and about flipped. "You're
not Jeffrey Steinberg?"

"I'm the one."

A cook came rushing out of the dining room. "Jeffrey
Steinberg! Mercy sakes alive, you has changed, Chile. You
lived here for years and years. You was bad! You could cuss!
Mercy, how a little thing like you could cuss!"

"Not any more," I assured her.

"Well, I'm glad, I sho' am glad."

Larry Lange, the youthful director of orthotics and
prosthetics, demonstrated for me an electronic arm and
hand, operated by electrical impulses from muscles. They
called it myo-electronics. I called it bionics. And you thought
it only happened on TV. Larry felt my back muscles. "I
think it would work on you."

"How much? I'm probably too old for Shriners to accept
me as a patient again."

"We'd have to do some checking. Several thousand
dollars at least."

"I guess I'll have to wait awhile." I grinned. "Besides, it
would ruin all my hook jokes. It could ruin my image." I
held my hook up and looked at it with a glint.

I called Mom from Shriners. "We're in town. Will you be
home?"

"We'll be here," she pledged.

My emotions were tumbling as we made the ten-minute
drive from Shriners to her house. We hadn't had much to
say to each other since Dad's funeral. She knew I wanted to
get down to brass tacks about our relationship. Would she
open up, really open up? "Lord, bridge the distance between
us," I prayed.

Mom invited us in and was warm and cordial to Debbie
and Benji as she had always been. She was courteous to me,
as she planted the customary kiss on my cheek. A tall,
smiling gentleman came up behind her. "This is Leon

Brownstein, my new husband," she announced. "Leon, my son, Jeff, his wife, Debbie, and my grandson, Benji." I liked the ring of that word "son."

"Mom, you look great," I said. "I can understand why Leon would want to marry you. How was your honeymoon?"

They described their trip to Acapulco and how they had bought themselves a new Cadillac for a wedding present.

Leon laughed. "She smashed it up yesterday."

"Yeah, a man pulled right out in front of me. I smacked him good."

I couldn't resist it. "And you always worried about my driving."

The laughter lightened the tension. We all got comfortable in the living room. I decided to go for broke.

"Mom, didn't you want to keep me?"

"Jeffrey, I don't know what I wanted or how I felt. I could flower it up and it wouldn't be true. You do something and you think it's the right decision, then you look back and think, 'Maybe I should have done it a different way.' A woman has a miscarriage and she cries for a few weeks and gets over it. But with you, when you see that everybody else has a nice, normal child, and you see what's in front of you, you cry your whole life. Jeffrey, I couldn't cry my whole life. Your father knew that and arranged for them to take you into Good Shepherd."

Her face revealed how painful this conversation was for her, yet I had to press on. "Mom, you told me once, long after I was grown up, 'You're not my child. I don't consider you like one of my other children.' "

"I guess I did say that. A mother takes a child and raises it. I was never able to do that for you and I wasn't your mother. Jeffrey, I didn't raise you. Shriners and Good Shepherd and the Snyders did. I didn't have a son."

I was thirty-three years old and my heart was pounding. "Mom do you care for me at all?"

She drew a long breath and looked straight at me.

"Jeffrey, of course I care. And I hurt. After thirty years I still hurt. There are some days when I wish I could have kept you here and some days I don't.

"Jeffrey, it's very easy for people to sit in judgment on others. You don't know what you would do until you're faced with the problem. I realize that I feel guilty. But I can't do anything about it. When I pick up the telephone and hear your voice, the hair on the back of my neck stands up and I get very nervous. When I see you I get nervous."

I shifted the subject slightly, "Look at it this way, Mom. I made it. My way. I left the institution and survived. I hope you're proud of what I've become."

"Jeffrey, the first time I saw you on TV, I was proud. I'm still proud. You're capable of doing things I never thought possible."

"You saw me on TV?"

"Yes, a neighbor called me and said, 'Jeffrey's on television.' She gave the channel. I turned on and there you were."

"I never knew that, Mom. I remember telling you to watch when Jerry Falwell's program was put on in Philadelphia."

"Well, I saw you, and I was proud. I saw you again when you were on with Pat Boone."

I looked at her with fresh hope. "Where do we go from here?"

She bit her lip. "Where's to go? You have your life and I have mine."

"I'm sorry, Mom, but it just doesn't work that way. I have your grandson. You hardly know him and he hardly knows you. He needs to know his grandmom."

"I know that, but Jeffrey, we come from such different backgrounds. You're Jewish only when you come into my home for my husband's funeral and you play your album."

"Wait, Mom. I've never played any of my albums or imposed my beliefs on you. I've given you albums, but I never said you had to play them. At the funeral, a cousin put that album on. I wouldn't do anything like that—ever. I'm probably the most unevangelical evangelical who ever lived because I made a commitment never to push you into something you didn't want. Dad was always the one who tried to get me into arguments on some of his visits to Good Shepherd, or when I came to visit you. I always said, 'Sorry, Dad, I'm not going to argue with you.'

"That was because I didn't think I knew enough about the Bible or my Judaism then. Dad tried to take advantage of my own immaturity—he had been to rabbinical school, and I wouldn't let him.

"Mom, have I ever come into your home and preached? Have I ever tried to push you into something you didn't want to do?"

"No, Jeffrey. You've never done that."

"All I want, Mom, is for us to be friends. I want us to get to know one another better. Linda said at Harriet's wedding, in tears, 'We're a family. We're all together.' But we weren't, then. We were just in the same place together. Mom, I want all of us, me included, to be a family."

I felt she was reaching out too. She had been caught in circumstances that were not her fault. I kept pressing.

"Mom, what's happened has happened. You're a different person. I'm a different person. But I want to come closer to you."

I stood up and walked to where she was sitting. I reached out with my hook. For an instant, I thought she was going to reach. She didn't.

I had one more thing to say. "Mom, we can't change the past. What's done is done. We can only affect the future. But we can start now."

I looked at the woman who bore me. "Mom, will you try with me?"

She lifted her eyes. "I'll try, but I'm not making any promises."

"OK, Mom, it's a deal. We'll go from here."

"What do you say, we all go out to eat," Leon proposed. "There's a nice diner, the Red Lion, just a couple of blocks over."

• • • • • • • • • • • • • • • • • • • • • • • • • • • • • •

"Yeah, let's go," I agreed. "Come on, Mom, let's go enjoy ourselves."

I sat in the front seat of Leon's car, beside Mom, Debbie and Benji in the back. The spaghetti was delicious, the conversation light and happy. When we finished, I nudged Mom and said, "This is the best time I can ever remember us having. Except for that time when we went to New York for the Passover Seder with Bubbeh and Zayde. Remember, Mom?"

"I remember."

After dessert, we all piled back in the car and went over to the Jewish Federation high-rise for the elderly where Grandmom lives. We took the elevator to the eighth floor and walked down the long hall to her tiny one-room apartment.

We had already called to tell her we were coming. At the sound of our voices this dear eighty-seven-year-old matriarch of our family hobbled quickly to the front door and opened it. We were a while getting in, for she had to hug each one of us.

"My arthritis is very bad, very bad," she apologized as she motioned us to chairs. "But I not gonna give up, no."

Grandmom did most of the talking—about coming to America from Lithuania over fifty years ago. About Grandpa and Mom and Uncle Morty. About my birth and her disagreement with Dad about whether Mom should be told about me. The more she talked the more animated she became.

She got up and led me to a corner of the room. "I want to show you something, Jeffrey." She pointed a gnarled finger at Grandpa's certificate of American citizenship in a glass frame that hung on the wall.

"Your grandfather—you never saw him. He was very sick when you were born." She touched the glass lovingly. "That was a proud day for him, when he got that. He was proud to be an American."

When time came to go, Grandmom kissed me, hugged

me, pinched my cheeks, and gave me a good shaking. She insisted on accompanying us down to the lobby, where she kissed and hugged each of us again.

"I see you on television, Jeffrey. I see you again, yes?"

"Yes, Grandmom, we'll see you again. You'll have lots more to say then."

We went out, Grandmom waving good bye from the lobby. We were expected at my little sister Harriet's house—Mom, Leon, all of us.

Leon went ahead to get the car. Mom walked between Debbie and me, Benji skipping ahead.

It was a new beginning. For the first time, I felt that in Mom's eyes, I was no longer that terrible thing that happened to the Steinbergs.

# AFTERWORD

When I told my good friend Joni Eareckson-Tada that I was thinking of writing a book about my life, she warned that reliving old memories would be very painful. "How painful," she said, "will depend on how you viewed those distressful events that shaped your life when you were going through them."

I have felt pain in recognizing that some characteristics in my life, which I viewed as determination to succeed, were seen by some as pushy, obnoxious, and even intolerable.

But I have felt joy in reliving times when faithful friends stood by me. The remembrances explored in preparing this book have made these friends even more personal and precious.

I could never list all who contributed to the book. Some passed in and out of my life like fleeting comets. Some stayed longer and exited through death or another means of separation. Some remain close to me to this day.

I must name certain persons who contributed

significantly to a better understanding of my life and the book: My wife, Debbie; my son, Benji; my Mom, in Philadelphia; my sisters, Linda, Sheryl, and Harriet; my Grandmom Vedatsky; my long-time personal friend and songwriter, Jeff Rudloff; my assistant, John Bugay; my Allentown confidante, Wanda "Quacky" Gensemer; George and Erma Long; "Mom" and "Dad" Snyder; friends at Shriners Hospital in Philadelphia; friends at Good Shepherd Home in Allentown, Pennsylvania, especially Dr. Conrad Raker, Administrator Emeritus and Mrs. Lona Farr, Director of Development; and Mrs. Martha Hoffman, my former teacher at Good Shepherd.

I thank these and the many others who helped make this book possible. For whatever merit there is in my story, they should receive much credit; for whatever faults and unintentional errors, they should receive none of the blame.

The writing ran through several drafts and computer printouts. I worked with my writer friend, Jim Hefley, in preparing the outline. He wrote the first drafts and we went from there.

We worked from transcripts of many hours of taped interviews, more than five years of medical records from Shriners, eleven years of records from Good Shepherd Home, and many other documents. The index to the research materials ran to well over 100 single-spaced pages.

We took special caution to be scientifically exact in describing my numerous surgeries, treatments, and therapies, while also seeking simplification for lay readers.

No one can remember every word spoken in dialogues of years past. I have sought, however, in every instance to be faithful in presenting events as they happened and describing people as they were. The remembrances are from my perspective and others may recall some details differently.

Some readers may be shocked at my frankness. To you, I say with apologies to a defeated well-known political candidate: What you see is what you get.

# POST-SCRIPT - MAY 1990

It would be nice if all of life's "happy endings" stayed intact. But as long as life goes on, there are no "endings," only rest stops along the way.

I wish I could write today that my marriage is just as wonderful as it was after the reconciliation described in the last chapter of this book. Unfortunately, after every possible effort, Debbie and I separated in May of 1986. I tried everything I knew to keep us together, even to the point of almost losing my Ministry, but the divorce eventually became final July 15, 1987.

In the months that have followed that extremely difficult time, I have viewed and reviewed my entire life more times than I care to remember. I have questioned my motives for every decision and looked for reasons why things turned out the way they did. I even looked for a good reason to quit. I went through a time of real depression, wondering if I would ever be able to sing again.

I decided to call this book, *Masterpiece In Progress* because I saw my life as a series of struggles and circumstances that were teaching me how to become the person God intended for me to be. I have had to re-learn that principle all over again. The struggles have not ended for me, because I am still "in progress." I have, however, survived many battles, though I know that more lie ahead.

Learning this (again!) has been frightening at times; none of us likes to admit that life will bring us reverses. But if, like the optimist, I choose to see the glass as half full rather than half empty, I recognize that this brings me opportunities again and again to be an overcomer.

I am not happy that my marriage has ended. But I have learned (and am still learning) from the experience. Not a complete masterpiece yet, but I am becoming - one color at a time, and that's what's important.

> *"And I am convinced and sure of this very thing, that He who began a good work in you will continue until the day of Jesus (The) Christ - right up to the time of His return - Developing that good work and perfecting and bringing it to full completion."*
> *(Phillipians 1:6, Amplified)*